THE WORKER AND THE JOB

 The American Assembly, *Columbia University*

THE WORKER
AND THE JOB:
COPING WITH CHANGE

Prentice-Hall, Inc., *Englewood Cliffs, N.J.*

Library of Congress Cataloging in Publication Data
Main entry under title:

The worker and the job.

(A Spectrum Book)
At head of title: The American Assembly, Columbia
University.
Background papers for the 43d American Assembly,
Arden House, Harriman, N. Y., Nov. 1973.
Includes bibliographical references.
1. Labor and laboring classes—United States—
Congresses. 2. Job satisfaction—Congresses.
I. Rosow, Jerome M., ed. II. American Assembly.
HD8072.W818   331.2   74–765
ISBN   0–13–965369–6
ISBN   0–13–965350–3 (pbk.)

10 9 8 7 6 5 4 3 2 1

PRENTICE-HALL INTERNATIONAL, INC. (*London*)
PRENTICE-HALL OF AUSTRALIA PTY., LTD. (*Sydney*)
PRENTICE-HALL OF CANADA, LTD. (*Toronto*)
PRENTICE-HALL OF INDIA PRIVATE LIMITED (*New Delhi*)
PRENTICE-HALL OF JAPAN, INC. (*Tokyo*)

Table of Contents

Preface   vii

Jerome M. Rosow, Editor
Introduction   1

PART ONE: AN OVERVIEW

Daniel Yankelovich
1   The Meaning of Work   19

Eli Ginzberg
2   The Changing American Economy
and Labor Force   49

PART TWO: CONTEMPORARY ISSUES

George Strauss
3   Workers: 73
Attitudes and Adjustments

Agis Salpukas
4   Unions: 99
A New Role?

Peter Henle
5   Economic Effects: 119
Reviewing the Evidence

PART THREE: NEW HORIZONS

Richard E. Walton
6   Innovative Restructuring of Work   145

7   *Sam Zagoria*
    Policy Implications and
    Future Agenda   177

    Index   203

    The American Assembly   209

Preface

The premise of this book, edited by Jerome M. Rosow of Exxon Corporation, is that the American world of work is caught up in the cross currents of rapid change and that our society therefore ought to take a new and larger view of this world and a look at the quality of life it reflects.

As the participants of the Forty-third American Assembly (*The Changing World of Work*) at Arden House, November 1973, concluded in their final report, "improving the place, the organization, and the nature of work can lead to better work performance and a better quality of life in the society." The essays which follow discuss the pros and cons of that assertion; and no matter where the authors come out, they agree that the questions posed are vital to the enlargement of public understanding—for the lives of all of us are organized around our jobs and the work ethic embedded in our cultural values.

The American Assembly is a national public affairs forum and remains neutral in its attitude toward the subjects presented. The Assembly should be held accountable for the conduct of the forum but not for the opinions therein, or herein, which belong to the participants themselves. Similarly, no one should assume that the financial supporter of this American Assembly program—The Ford Foundation—endorses the opinions on these pages.

Clifford C. Nelson
President
The American Assembly

The Energy Crisis
and the World of Work:
A Note

The energy crisis has created a new urgency for change at the work place. Today the human side of the enterprise looms as a critical factor in the accommodation of industry to a period of scarcity. Shortages of energy, of materials, and of equipment are evident. The major hidden resource is the untapped human potential of the work force within each organization in our society.

At this time of rising unit labor costs, general inflationary pressures, and the need to remain competitive, companies must turn to their workers to achieve the adjustment effectively. Greater humanization of working life can be advanced in concert with measures to increase productivity, reduce waste, and increase the conservation of energy and materials. The key element involves the active participation of workers at all levels in these mutual goals. The threat of a new era of scarcity presents new motivations for management to take a fresh look at old values, rigid practices, and extravagant programs which have placed a low value upon the human factor.

Irrespective of the degree of automation, mechanization, or computerization, every system depends upon people. These employees have a real desire to do more, to carry meaningful responsibility, and to have personal involvement in decisions and actions affecting their jobs and their products. This applies to almost every occupation and every organization. Employees also have a strong sense of survival and an anxiety to preserve their jobs at a time of major economic readjustment. The first and most logical place for productive involvement is at the work place. Now is the time for experimentation and change to bring the talents of employees to bear on the era of scarcity.

REDESIGN OF WORKING HOURS

There are two interesting options which present themselves:

The Four-Day Week—Longer hours each day in exchange for a full day off is an energy-saving option. It would save energy for everyone—the worker, the company, and the community facilities. Although the four-day week applies to a very small fraction of American business at this time, the rapid shift in economic conditions pushes this option to the forefront. Maximum savings would be achieved if the entire operation shifts to four days; however, the office or plant could remain operational five or even six days a week. The employees would only be required to work four days by alternating their schedules (e.g., Monday-Thursday, Tuesday-Friday, and Wednesday-Saturday). Where the operation could close for three days every week, this could be promoted through communitywide action and possibly linked with the four-day school week. The energy savings here would be substantial. The morale, efficiency, and job satisfaction gains would also be substantial.

Over two-thirds of the companies which have adopted the four-day week attest to significant productivity gains. In recent surveys three-fourths of the workers have indicated improvements in family life, recreation, and job satisfaction and interest in their work.

Flexitime—This is a new trend in Western Europe. It gives workers greater freedom and individuality of life-styles without any adverse effects on productivity. The worker owes a fixed number of hours each week or each month. Within certain limits (such as a maximum and minimum number of hours each day or certain fixed periods when attendance is compulsory, i.e., 10 A.M. to 3 P.M.), the worker may come to work and leave work at times of his own choosing. The worker may select longer hours one day than another, vary the pattern to meet personal needs, and even accumulate enough extra hours to take a half-day or even a whole day off.

Flexitime is a natural for the energy crisis. It would disperse people in large urban areas and break down the peaking of travel every morning and every evening. It would facilitate car pools, ease pressures on urban transportation, and give workers a greater personal freedom, which they desire. Workers could organize their working life schedules to suit personal needs and tastes rather than be forced to conform to rigid and inflexible work schedules. It gives workers more responsibility and a sense of trust. Women could adjust their hours to their child-care needs. All workers would reduce tension and increase both their loyalty and their independence.

J.M.R.

Jerome M. Rosow

Introduction

The Public Debate

Recently Chou En-lai, premier of the People's Republic of China was discussing Maoism with a Western visitor. He noted that only 5 percent of the Chinese people do not support Chairman Mao, or agree with the Chinese way of life. Then the brilliant Chinese philosopher paused, looked thoughtfully at his visitor, and said: "However, 5 percent amounts to 40 million people!"

Apply the same test to America. Only change the question to job satisfaction, instead of political philosophy. In 1973, 77 percent expressed work satisfaction. But 23 percent were either dissatisfied or expressed no opinion. The 11 percent who admitted that they were dissatisfied equals about 11 million people!

Is job satisfaction an issue whose time has come? Certainly the public debate attests to the vitality of the problem. The 1973 auto negotiations attest to the fact that the quality of working life has moved from academic debate to hard talk at the bargaining table and into print in the labor contract.

This Forty-third American Assembly is considering the contemporary issue of job satisfaction. In the changing world of the seventies, are Americans achieving a reasonable degree of social and personal sat-

JEROME M. ROSOW, *assistant secretary of labor in the early Nixon years, is now the Exxon Corporation's manager of public affairs planning. He is chairman of the President's Advisory Committee on Federal Pay and was vice chairman of the National Productivity Commission. Editor Rosow has served as chairman or member of numerous other public and private panels on a variety of work problems during a 30-year career in both government and business. He has written widely on compensation, manpower planning, productivity, and blue-collar problems.*

isfaction in their jobs where they spend over 2,000 hours each year—
and over 40 years in a lifetime?

Somehow the issue has attracted two opposing groups: those who
exalt the American economy and idealize its achievements and conclude American workers never had it so good; and others who are
champions of the worker, idealizing human psychic and social needs,
and decrying the failure of private enterprise to humanize work. In a
sense the heat and vitality of this controversy establishes the validity
of the issue. Otherwise the debate would have died out long ago. The
HEW report *Work in America* is a broad documentation of existing
problems of job satisfaction which has struck a responsive chord. Yet
the issue remains searching for definition and balance, and most important of all, long-term solutions.

The work ethic vs. the welfare ethic has been part of a social and
economic confrontation between two value systems. Thus the work
ethic was politicized so that hard work developed a halo, and the rejection of dirty, dead-end low-paying jobs was associated with laziness
and indolence. The polarization was part of two national political
campaigns in 1968 and 1972 and has contributed to a political split
and some confusion among the national labor leaders themselves.
Somehow the exaltation of work was unrelated to the growing national
concern with the overall quality of life. Yet, more and more the American work force is seeking more from work than money alone.

In recent years the quality of work issue has enjoyed a new vogue of
public attention, despite the fact that it has yet to rank among the top
national priorities. It is an emerging issue which will demand more
attention and better solutions. It is an issue which will not quietly
disappear. The sluggish productivity of the second half of the sixties;
the Nixon attention to blue-collar workers; the formation of a National
Commission on Productivity; the conduct of congressional hearings;
the rash of legislative proposals; the passage of the first Occupational
Health & Safety Act in 1970; the bursting seminars and conferences;
the flood of new books and news magazine cover stories and the re-
surgence of readership interest in such human interest material all confirm that there is a genuine problem. Albeit a problem without simple
solutions.

The Worker and His Job

ATTITUDES

Work is at the core of life. Consider the deeper meanings of work
to the individual and to life values: work means being a good pro-

vider, it means autonomy, it pays off in success, and it establishes self-respect or self-worth. Within this framework, the person who openly confesses active job dissatisfaction is virtually admitting failure as a man, and failure in fulfilling his moral role in society. Since work resides at the very core of life values, self-esteem colors the response to job satisfaction attitude surveys. A negative answer may negate the life style and the very ego of the individual. It may well involve a painful, if not impossible, denial of basic goals in life. It is tantamount to an admission of an inability to achieve and perform an economic, useful, and productive role in society, in the family, in the church, and in the community.

By contrast the "satisfied" response is a confirmation of some measure of success in the real world of work. It reflects a self-image of one's place in the competitive materialistic society of today. It confirms personal adaptability and adjustment to reality and the inner sense of doing as well as can be expected, considering the difficulty of finding and holding a job. The high proportion of satisfied workers in America (77 percent) is a measure of their economic self-esteem. It also reflects on their adaptability and capacity to "fit-in," to adjust themselves and their expectations to the relatively rigid requirements of the workplace. It is a measure of man's capacity to accept the commonplace demands of life, especially the endless demands of the job. It is also a reflection of the low level of expectations of many workers.

EXPECTATIONS

The American worker has a high threshold of tolerance for his occupational world. Frustrations and sacrifices, long hours or unpleasant conditions, nagging supervision, dull, boring work, are all taken in stride. The American adult accepts with equanimity the need to *sacrifice* in order to *succeed* as a full-time, paid employee who exchanges his labor for income to provide for himself and his family. Workers have been inculcated from early childhood, not only with the work ethic, but with the expectations that work is hard, involves sacrifice, and does not equate with pleasure or personal fulfillment. The rising expectations and aspirations of the new entrants into the labor market may change this long-term accommodation as more people expect more from work.

Expectations for satisfaction (plus income) from work are relatively low, except for the younger workers. This has a negative effect upon output, quality, and overall efficiency. The older workers have tempered their expectations by seeking a full release from work through earlier and better pensions. Of course, expectations rise and fall with

the business cycle. In times of full employment turnover rises and workers demand more—usually in pay and benefits. During recessions and
high unemployment workers draw into their shells and lower their expectations.

As long as these expectations remain low and encased in a mold of
self-sacrifice, the workplace will remain immutable. The economic commitment to products and profits exceeds any commitment to human
needs. People continue to accommodate to jobs that are relatively inflexible and locked into a larger total system. The world of work remains unchanged in a changing world. The typical worker seems unable to do anything about it. The typical union is uncertain what it
could do if it tried. Employers are content to perform an effective economic role placing capital and technology ahead of human relations.

ECONOMIC ASPECTS

Wages have advanced at a good clip. The minimum wage initially
fixed at twenty-five cents is moving toward two dollars per hour. Average total private wages are near four dollars per hour. In addition, a
panoply of benefits have evolved since 1947 with the breakthrough of
pension bargaining. Thus the workplace provides varying degrees of:
vacations, holidays, other time off with pay, health insurance, life insurance, severance pay, supplemental unemployment benefits, and pensions. These average about 25 percent of payroll and bring the hourly
labor cost to five dollars per hour.

Employment benefit plans have grown tremendously since 1950. The
number of persons included in hospital insurance, life insurance, and
retirement plans has tripled. Coverage under surgical, regular medical,
and major-medical expense plans has expanded at an even greater
pace. These long-run gains are further accentuated when the number
of workers covered is related to the total labor force. The proportion
of the employed civilian wage and salary force with some type of health
insurance through the place of employment has expanded from 50 to
80 percent. The percent with group life insurance and death benefits
has increased from 40 to almost 70 percent. Private retirement plans
cover nearly 50 percent of the private work force, more than double
the proportion for 1950.

Despite these impressive statistics, under the existing institutional
structure, a sizeable portion of the labor force faces substantial barriers
in obtaining these basic protections through their place of employment. For private retirement and temporary disability plans, the coverage gap remains quite large. Whereas 50 percent are covered by private pension plans—the *other half of the labor force are without any*

private pension plan coverage. These facts assist us in maintaining a sense of proportion.

This growth of money wages and related benefits has taken place within a system of hourly pay without major adoption of incentive systems or profit-sharing programs. The wage earner is controlled by the time clock, not by his product or by the inherent continuity of his effort. The occupational shift to service and government employment and the expansion of white-collar and professional work has spread more security of income by use of payment by the week, month, or year. But the class distinctions in pay systems continue to prevail. Furthermore, work is rarely a process of group participation with a clear relationship between results and rewards. Usually, it is individual hire—pay for the job—without direct linkage to costs, profits, or productivity. Even bonus plans are related to salary levels rather than individual efficiency.

We cannot ignore the fact that millions of Americans are working full-time, full-year and earning less than the poverty level for a family of four. These people labeled as the "working poor" have no economic satisfaction from work. They have no benefits, leisure, or security. In the South about one-fourth of the total labor force earns less than two dollars per hour. Another 4.5 million people are unemployed and unable to find a job.

At the other extreme blue-collar workers are attaining annual incomes between $15,000 and $20,000 and have become part of middle America. Therefore, the economic achievements for American workers are diverse, incomplete, and cannot be exalted without serious qualification.

PSYCHIC NEEDS

Man does not live by bread alone. Even executives and professionals have confessed to serious job dissatisfactions despite salaries in six figures. Every worker wants some dignity in the job he does, some self-respect, a reasonable degree of status and a sense of self-worth.

Since men and women are capable of rational thought, since they are trained, educated and able to learn at all ages, and since they are subject to many pressures to succeed, they aspire for more. Animals may resist physical abuse, but they are not troubled by psychic needs.

Work with dignity has not been defined as a human right. Work without dignity becomes degrading and mean. It imposes serious emotional penalties. Workers are not numbers on the time clock or in the computer. They want to apply their knowledge, they desire to use their physical and mental talents, they want to be treated as people at least

equal to, if not above, the process of production. Fred E. Emery and
Einar Thorsrud have defined an excellent list of the desirable components of jobs:

   (i) The need for the content of a job to be reasonably demanding of the
worker in terms other than sheer endurance, and yet to provide a
minimum of variety (not necessarily novelty);

 (ii) the need to be able to learn on the job and to go on learning—again
it is a question of neither too much nor too little;

(iii) the need for some minimal area of decision-making that the individual
can call his own;

(iv) the need for some minimal degree of social support and recognition
in the workplace;

 (v) the need for the individual to be able to relate what he does and
what he produces to his social life;

(vi) the need to feel that the job leads to some sort of desirable future
(not necessarily promotion).

THE LEISURE MYTH

Leisure for American workers is more myth than reality. Gross average weekly hours in the private sector declined from 40.3 in 1947 to
37.2 in 1972—a drop of three hours per week, or about 8 percent. This
is a very slow decline, and hours have been quite stable during the
late sixties and early seventies. Inflation, taxes, high cost of education
of children, and other economic pressures have intervened to block
any trade-off of income for leisure in terms of the workweek.

Flexitime, increased vacations, more holidays, the four-day week,
voluntary overtime, and other rearrangements in the packaging of the
workweek or the work year are significant developments. But they
should be distinguished from the theory of the leisure class.

The Workplace

Society at large has been more open and responsive to change
than has the workplace. Modifications have occurred in the institutions
of marriage and the family, in sexual mores, and in the legal rights of
youth. Public opinion has induced changes toward abortion, birth control, premarital sex, "open" marriages, rising divorce rates, drug use,
the eighteen-year-old vote, homosexuality, pornography, and the wom-
en's liberation movement.

Contrast this with the workplace. Jobs themselves have hardly
changed. Dr. Robert H. Guest revisited and wrote "The Man on the
Assembly Line—A Generation Later" and drew the overall conclusion
that expressed dissatisfactions and the intensity of these dissatisfactions

are the same today as in 1949. Customs and practices resist change. The organizational hierarchy persists, communication moves through formal channels, participation is limited or nonexistent, opportunity for self-expression is often counterproductive, and conformity by employees is required. Recent concessions to dress and hair styles are surface masks that only convey an aura of permissiveness. They do not reflect the immutable nature of the relationship between a man and his job.

The world of work remains in stark contrast to the world away from work. Particularly today, society is in ferment. Self-fulfillment and a new attitude toward nature and self are emerging—and not only among youth or women. Society itself has become more tolerant and permissive without any apparent shock to its growth or survival. Only the workplace remains unchanged in a changing world.

The emerging confrontation between the worker and his job is more than a psychic demand. It is an issue of major economic significance to the individual firm, to entire industries, and to the economy as a whole. Worker attitudes and adjustments to the workplace have a direct bearing upon productivity, costs, quality of product, profitability, and competitiveness in the world markets.

Serious problems in labor relations and personnel performance can be traced to the quality of working life, as distinguished from direct wages and benefits. Absenteeism, turnover, grievances, and strikes are indicators of the surface abrasiveness of the workplace. Poor product quality, growing customer dissatisfaction, wasted materials, and climbing unit labor costs are other evidences of serious friction between employees and their environment at work.

The employer is not required to establish a *happy* workplace. He is motivated to create and maintain a *productive* workplace. Thus the balance between people and production requires a more sensitive interest in human relations. The notion that people work only for money and seek their real satisfactions away from work is not valid. People have real needs at the workplace and the more these are satisfied, the greater their personal involvement and motivation to participate at their highest levels of achievement.

*   *   *   *   *

This Book: Highlights

AN OVERVIEW

This modest volume is organized in three parts: *An Overview, Contemporary Issues,* and *New Horizons.* Part I, *An Overview,* establishes the cultural, sociological, and economic setting of the American worker. Part I's two chapters relate the past to the present and point toward future developments.

Dr. Daniel Yankelovich's initial chapter is a principal "think piece." He discusses man and his relationship to his family and society at large, with work as the traditional linchpin of these relationships. Through the eyes of a psychologist and leading social thinker we see the continuing transformation of work values and the work ethic. The very meaning of work is traced back to its religious origins which establish the clear and binding moral connotations which prevail to this day.

Four themes describe the contemporary meaning of the work ethic for the majority of the adult population. These serve to sharpen the definition of the work ethic. Against this backdrop the chapter examines new cultural trends which are gradually transforming the work ethic. These include the changing definition of success; reduced fears of economic insecurity; a new division of labor between the sexes; a spreading psychology of entitlement; and a spreading disillusionment with the cult of efficiency. These changes are basic and distinctive since they have cultural impact upon life in general and work in particular.

Against this cultural landscape, Dr. Yankelovich discusses life values and their subtle effects upon work values. Thus, he confronts the controversy which is the eye of the storm in this Forty-third American Assembly—whether or not Americans are *satisfied* with their work! He places the issue in clear focus by defining three critical variables: the age of the worker, the expectations attached to the job, and the distinction between economic and psychological work satisfactions.

Linking the new cultural values to distinct groups in the labor force, the author provides new insights into the future of the work ethic in America. He notes that the five cultural trends are having an uneven effect upon different groups—in particular, upon the young college-educated, the noncollege youth, and women of all ages and levels of education. The impact of these cultural trends is predicted to have uneven effects upon the aspirations and achievements of these members of the labor force of tomorrow.

Finally, Dr. Yankelovich provides a schematic depicting the future impact of cultural trends and contrasting the work ethic of the 1960s with the work ethic of the 1970s.

Chapter 2, titled "The Changing Economy and Labor Force," provides a sweeping review of the employment-related dimensions of the American economy over the past several generations. Dr. Eli Ginzberg, professor of economics and director, Conservation of Human Resources, Columbia University, is one of the nation's leading experts in this subject area. These basic data which delineate the changing character of the American labor force provide a framework for assessing theories of work satisfaction.

First, Dr. Ginzberg delineates the changing contours of the American economy, particularly the structural changes which govern the work in our society. He draws our attention to the extensive, large-scale changes in industrial structure, organizational forms, and occupational distribution. Since these transformations are so complex, the author cautions against simple summaries of their meaning. He especially cautions against the difficulty of relating these changes to the fundamental issue of worker satisfaction.

Examining the changing characteristics of the labor force, Dr. Ginzberg turns from external structure to a study of the individual American worker. He contrasts the worker of the 1920s with the worker of the 1970s, covering a 50-year span of immense differences in family background, education, expectations, and life styles. He then closely analyzes the so-called special groups: blacks, women and youth.

The analysis of *blacks* in the work force reveals striking improvements in formal schooling, definite gains in employment in higher-ranking occupations, and significant improvement in family income. However, Dr. Ginzberg points out that these gains should not obscure the distressing aspects that continue to persist. Among these are lower levels of family income, a small proportion of college entrants, and continuing discrimination in many sectors of American life.

Women are considered in terms of education, occupations, and earnings. Educational trends reveal new breakthroughs in the professions of medicine and law. Occupational findings show persistent differences in long-term concentrations of women in relatively few low-paying fields. Then, the predicament of *youth,* particularly young people with employment handicaps, is reviewed.

Finally, in search of a perspective on the link between the economy's structural changes and changes in work satisfaction, the author draws five inferences. They characterize the transformation of the American labor force. The inferences are: (1) the greater and growing role of women, especially married women, in the world of work; (2) a substantial rise in education of new entrants and a corresponding shift to service and white-collar jobs; (3) little pressure for reduction of the conventional workday or workweek; (4) slow growth of trade unions revealing no new urge to organize; and (5) the dynamism of discontent embedded in work relations in a modern democratic society.

Looking to the future, Dr. Ginzberg foresees some possibility of rising discontent among the better-educated managerial workers. He forecasts a new era of trade-offs between work and leisure and shifts of opportunities from older to younger workers. A larger role for government in resolving collective bargaining within national incomes policies is also hinted without defining structural features. Of course, the issue of discrimination is expected to hold sway in the years ahead. Finally, the combination of more education, reduced fear of unemployment, and higher family income will loosen the tight tie between people and work. Thus, we may anticipate more conflicts in the arena of work. Dr. Ginzberg, the labor economist, joins Dr. Yankelovich, the social thinker.

CONTEMPORARY ISSUES

Part II considers contemporary issues of worker satisfaction under three headings. First, chapter 3 considers the workers themselves—their attitudes toward work, and how they have adjusted. Chapter 4 addresses one of the major dilemmas, namely, the unions' future role in achieving an improved quality in working life. Finally, chapter 5 considers the workplace in relation to the economic effects of worker dissatisfactions. What is revealed by the hard economic data published in national sources?

Chapter 3 considers the central issue—workers, their attitudes, and their adjustments. Dr. George Strauss, professor of business administration, University of California at Berkeley, reviews the growing concern with an alleged erosion of the American work ethic. He addresses basic questions. How dissatisfied are workers with their jobs? Does this dissatisfaction arise chiefly from repetitive, unchallenging work? Or are low pay, inept supervision, or blocked opportunity more important causes? What are the trends for the future? Is dissatisfaction growing?

Dr. Strauss confronts these difficult and often controversial questions in an objective, balanced manner as he weighs the evidence of countless studies and reports to help the reader draw his own conclusions.

The chapter begins with a review of the extent of dissatisfaction, the impact of routine work, and recent changes in work attitudes. Despite divergent trends, the evidence does not support the view that dissatisfaction has increased *substantially*. Neither does it prove that workers are truly satisfied. Rather, it suggests a difficult and continuing process of adjustment between the worker and his job.

Dr. Strauss considers this adjustment process as an accommodation of man to his environment which occurs at some psychic costs. Although these psychic costs may not be very great today, he foresees that they may increase in the future. This leads to a discussion of whether people and organizations clash. The hypothesis of Argyris, Maier and McGregor suggests almost inevitable frustrations for employees, especially in mass-production work, since workers are assumed to aspire for the satisfaction of social belonging, independence, and growth *on the job*. The Maslow theory of self-actualization is considered more limited in application to professors and managers than to workers at large. McClelland's work points to wide individual differences in need fulfillment. Finally, it seems, personality differences are important variables which, in turn, raise questions of cultural and child-rearing practices and their influence on work attitudes.

In a brief, but fascinating section, rural-urban differences are reported to challenge a popular assumption that there is a positive relationship between job challenge and job satisfaction. This section also suggests that rural workers have internalized the Protestant ethic of work for its own sake—a thesis that deserves further consideration, especially in light of America's great urban society.

Dr. Strauss then reviews the job as a primary source of satisfaction. In other words, how important is work in human life? Leisure activities are not effective as escapes from work frustration or as sublimations of the quality of life on the job. In the absence of this trade-off, Strauss finds that apathy is a middle ground for adjustment between the extremes of satisfaction and dissatisfaction.

Discussing the central issue of adjustment, the chapter offers a schematic chart which presents the employee orientation in relation to the type of work. This merits study—testing against occupational and personality data. The analysis continues with a brief look at social life and dreams of advancement as substitutes for job satisfaction. Then it turns to the contemporary issues of health, personality, and political alienation—a subject that caught public attention in the 1968 and 1972 presidential elections. The nature of one's job is seen as an influence on personality and adjustment, both political and personal. However extrinsic, economic factors may equal intrinsic job elements in importance.

Finally, Dr. Strauss concludes with trends for the future. These point to younger, better-educated workers making growing demands based on egoistic and self-actualization needs at the workplace. In conclusion, he agrees with union leaders who argue that economic (extrinsic) factors are a greater cause of dissatisfaction than any intrinsic problems on the job. Yet, remaining open minded and sympathetic to the full breadth of his analysis, he concedes that there is no reason to ignore intrinsic factors since increased productivity is a logical goal, and such increases have been linked to intrinsic factors.

Reporting from the plant levels of American industry, Mr. Agis Salpukas, labor reporter with the Detroit bureau of *The New York Times,* wrote chapter 4—"Unions: A New Role?" Many academics, critics, and journalists have visualized a new role for unions somewhat at odds with the everyday demands upon union leadership. Basically, the author finds the labor leadership cynical, suspicious, and impatient with the issue of job discontent. At the same time, labor leaders do believe major changes are required at the workplace; that workers' expectations are rising; and that there are new frontiers for collective bargaining. Seemingly, humanizing jobs poses a dilemma and a threat to the conventional, economic role of unions.

Reviewing labor history after the turn of the century, the author recounts the origins of Henry Ford's five-dollars-a-day decision announced on January 5, 1914. Sixty years ago workers were quitting the production lines at the startlingly high turnover peak-rate of 380 percent. The five-dollars-a-day almost doubled prevailing rates and provided an economic answer to the inhuman pace of the assembly line. Today, auto wages and benefits equal this *daily rate* on *an hourly basis,* with a surfeit of premium overtime pay to boot. Does this suggest that six generations later accommodation to the assembly line has remained a matter of money and only money? This may be Detroit's answer, but it is not Sweden's.

Mr. Salpukas traces the rise of unions in the 1930s, the sit-down strikes, the fight for recognition, and the legal right to organize and bargain. Despite the great imbalance of power at that time, local strikes did succeed in limiting the work pace. During the post-World War II period, the union movement enjoyed phenomenal growth. Collective bargaining expanded its reach into new areas including pensions, health insurance, job security protection, accommodations to automation, escalation of wages with cost-of-living changes, and productivity issues.

The mythology of the March, 1972, Lordstown strike in which 8,000 workers of UAW Local 112 closed the new Vega plant for 21 days (at a loss to GM of $150 million) is examined by the author. Popular stereotypes and academics' interpretations are set in perspective. Management as well as labor have been disturbed by misinterpretations of both the Lordstown and Norwood strikes, the latter lasting a record-breaking 172 days. "Speedup" emerges as the key issue which Mr. Salpukas traces carefully. This struggle over work standards and manning levels is not resolved. In fact, it is of great significance to the issue of job discontent. The author sees a growing contradiction between the values of a democratic society, with its checks and balances, and the rigid authoritarianism of the workplace.

New challenges are rising from the rank and file in auto and steel, relative to grievances, job discontent, and greater worker rights on the plant level. However, union leadership response continues to lag since wages, hours, fringes, pensions, holidays, and more time off represent immediate pressure and quick payoffs. In a simple and clear explanation of collective bargaining, Salpukas describes the process itself as a bar to consideration of noneconomic issues. Noneconomic issues are not universal, predictable, or subject to cost control. Instead, they are subtle and difficult to relate to workable trade-offs.

Discussing rank-and-file attitudes, the author found that intense dislike for jobs does not translate to pressures for union action for reform. There is an obvious gap. High turnover is a major reason that unions feel little pressure for changing work—the most dissatisfied switch rather than fight. This escape valve is a by-product of free and open labor markets, but it is not a long-term answer to human frustration or to the psychic or economic costs to the individual and his family.

Turning to solutions, Salpukas describes the responses of union leaders such as Reuther, Wurf, Woodcock, and others. Among labor leaders in communications, steel and autos, and especially among the leaders of workers for states, counties and municipalities, Salpukas discerns some shift toward the view that changes in work itself may eventually be needed.

Chapter 5 examines the economic effects of worker dissatisfaction. Mr. Peter Henle, formerly chief economist, Bureau of Labor Statistics, and presently senior labor specialist, Library of Congress, takes a hard, dispassionate look at the available national statistics. Although he finds only limited evidence that work disaffection has impaired the national economy, he does uncover evidence which indicates that disenchantment with work is growing in the United States.

Mr. Henle's discussion is divided into four headings: labor input, performance on the job, productivity, and labor relations. Examining first the issue of any reduction of labor-force activity, Mr. Henle's discussion of participation in the labor force draws a broad conclusion: those who have been working hard would like to quit and those who have not been working regularly would like more work. Men aged 55–64 are pulling out of the labor force (down to 80 percent participation) whereas women have been rushing in (up from 32 to 44 percent). Overall United States labor force participation ranks higher than

Canada, Germany, or Italy; about equals Sweden and the United Kingdom; and is lower than Japan.

Absenteeism data is often cited as a sensitive indicator of employee dissatisfaction. However, national data is sketchy and conceals serious problems within individual companies. Sadly enough, while company attendance records are sufficiently accurate for payroll purposes, they seldom are adequate for an analysis of absenteeism.

Data available since 1967 on part-week and entire-week absences shows a 10 percent increase in the period 1967–72, with the highest rates of part-week absences in manufacturing and government. The sharpest increases in part-week absences appear in service, trade, and finance. The underlying causes, whether contract-approved or work alienation, are not available from the data, but this trend is indicative of both the search for leisure and the desire to avoid work.

Quit rates are also sensitive indicators, and turnover represents significant direct costs to the employer. National quit rates are difficult to interpret because they are highly sensitive to the business cycle and the labor market. Overall, an examination of quit rates reveals no broad-scale changes on a national basis.

Turning to performance on the job, Mr. Henle examines the quantity of output, the quality of output, and the role of alcohol and drugs. Complaints about poor workmanship, poor quality, thievery, or industrial sabotage are also dealt with briefly. On balance, the author finds it probably surprising that pride in workmanship still persists. Meanwhile, the editor notes that individual major corporations in autos, electronics, and consumer goods encounter continuing problems in meeting warranty standards, satisfying customer complaints, and absorbing the costs of poor products. Probably the most significant non-statistical indicator of the decline in product quality is the emerging consumer movement. In fact, in a 1972 survey of national priorities, seven consumer issues ranked among the top ten issues. We can continue to listen for the consumer response—and regard it as the final quality testing of United States products.

Trends over the past 25 years have reflected an annual productivity rate of 3.2 percent for the total private economy. Reflected in this figure is an interplay of technology, economic conditions, employee attitudes, education and training of the work force. The sharp drop below the long-term trend during the 1966–70 period (the average fell to 1.5 percent annually) has caused widespread speculation about a decline in the work ethic. Mr. Henle believes that this drop seems to have been accounted for almost entirely by prevailing economic conditions. Basically, he sees little relation between assembly-line operations or unpleasant working conditions and recent changes in productivity.

Labor relations are reviewed in terms of strikes, contract rejections, grievances and arbitration, changes in union leadership, and decertification elections. The author finds that about 20 percent of strikes are caused by working conditions (up from 15 percent ten years ago), which may reveal an increase of worker discontent. Contract rejections by workers do not indicate any problem since such rejections have declined. Grievances and arbitration present incomplete data, but there has been an increase in arbitrations, the final step in the grievance process. Union leadership reveals higher turnover and shorter tenure. But the reasons are mixed, and the most significant measure of disaffection relates to local union offices where data is lacking. Just as we found a paucity of data for plant-level absenteeism and quits, we have discovered little regarding union elections at the local level. Critical indicators elude us and mask the real facts.

Decertification elections occur when workers feel that the union has not given them adequate representation. To some extent, such a petition to change unions is an indicator of worker dissatisfaction with their union representation and the labor relations system in general. While there has been some increase here among small bargaining units (40–50 workers), the overall number of terminations represents a tiny fraction of total union membership.

Mr. Henle concludes with an optimistic summation of positive factors countering any trend toward job dissatisfaction: occupational shifts; improved work environment; increased education; leisure and retirement trends; the growth of part-time jobs; rising levels of pay; and finally, the great adaptability of the nation's basic labor-relations institutions.

NEW HORIZONS

Part III, *New Horizons,* consists of two chapters which focus upon change and the future. Chapter 6 is an intensive review of case studies of new initiatives to restructure work. Chapter 7 is an extensive consideration of policy implications and an agenda for the seventies.

Richard E. Walton, professor, Harvard Graduate School of Business, has conducted intensive research in the basic restructuring of work to both meet the changing expectations of employees and yield improved performance. He presents his findings in chapter 6, which is an analysis of: (1) the problem of employee alienation; (2) the nature of comprehensive reform in job design; (3) case experiments in innovation, in the United States, Canada and Europe; (4) and problems of survival and growth.

Initially, the author presents employee alienation as a basic, long-term problem deserving of innovative action. He attacks the inadequacy of piecemeal reforms which have been in the parade of changing fashions of personnel programs. Defining a "systemic," or fully integrative reform, Dr. Walton states that this involves the way tasks are packaged into jobs; the way workers relate to each; the way performance is measured and rewarded; the way positions of authority and status symbols are structured; and the way career paths are defined.

This interesting chapter comes to grips with the dynamics of experimental work systems based upon twelve pilots in eleven different companies. The experimental units were manufacturing plants in the private sector, including continuous-process, assembly-line and batch-processing units. Size ranged from one hundred to five hundred employees in over half of the cases. The remainder had fewer than one hundred employees. So, essentially, the experiments were contained within relatively small units. Locations were evenly divided between rural and urban and between union and nonunion (although the United States plants were nonunion).

Three of the experiments (Shell United Kingdom, Norsk, and General Foods) were "grass roots" plants in which management tailored the internal labor force to the new conceptions of work and organization. This preselection of the work force as a hand-picked elite from among a much more heterogeneous group of applicants raises several issues. These experiments contrast with more difficult innovations which must confront old organizations, established institutional and power relationships, older or obsolete equipment and manning levels, and vested management and labor interests. It also raises a more controversial issue which Dr. Walton omits from his evaluation, namely, is prevention of unionism itself one of the basic objectives in such innovation? If such were the case, we could certainly anticipate fear, suspicion, and hostility among unions everywhere. From my own experience in Esso refineries and chemical plants, our grass roots plants have, in fact, innovated new work organizations with few plants remaining nonunion. Labor market institutions play a powerful role in the outcome.

Reviewing the favorable results of these pilot projects Dr. Walton names seven conditions which increase the odds-on chances for success in these high-risk ventures. Results are analyzed critically in terms of manning, quality of work life, and organizational performance. Moving from the short- to the long-term prospects for growth and survival of innovative work systems, the author reveals the underlying, deep obstacles to origination, continuation, and diffusion of organizational changes. This grasp and understanding of the roadblocks to innovation is fundamental to future experimentation and change. New travelers on this high, twisting road to the future can avail themselves of this road map of detours and death-traps. Six threats to innovative work systems are defined and serve to delineate the fragility of human innovation within an existing production plant. The chapter's conclusion summarizes, on an optimistic note, and points to areas for further research and study necessary to advance innovation and improve the quality of working life.

The final chapter discusses "Policy Implications and Future Agenda." Its author is Mr. Sam Zagoria, director, Labor Management Relations Service of National League of Cities, United States Conference of Mayors, and National Association of Counties. Formerly a member of the National Labor Relations Board, Mr. Zagoria speaks directly to the policy issues.

His consideration of the changing work scene in the United States and Europe provides an engaging review which reaches ahead, presenting a realistic agenda. The issue of worker satisfaction is approached from the standpoint of particular interest groups: workers, unions, employers, and finally government. Thus, each special interest and its motives, needs, and responsibilities at the workplace, in the community, and in society are placed in perspective. The author notes that the somewhat inarticulate individual needs for self-fulfillment have yet to be translated into coherent demands for change. Recently, these conflicts between the worker and his job environment have concentrated upon trade-offs for leisure or escapes from the workplace varying from rest periods to the complete escape of early retirement. Union leadership has strong attachments to economic bread, butter, and security issues and considers job satisfaction an issue of lower priority which is elusive and hard to define.

Employers face many constraints in taking new initiatives for job enrichment. Mr. Zagoria lists the critical blockages to change and briefly notes emerging positive trends. Turning to international developments, primarily in Western Europe, the chapter provides a sweeping review of worker participation. This participation concept, which is somewhat foreign to the American lexicon of union-management relations, is placed in the context of the job satisfaction demands from which it emerged. Considering changes over the past few decades, he reviews Yugoslavia, Austria, West Germany, United Kingdom, Norway and Sweden. This review presents a thumbnail sketch of the relationships of management, labor, and government sufficient only to tempt the reader to follow where the scent of sweet success may lead.

Returning to the three special interest groups with power (unions, employers and government), the author confronts the underlying philosophical questions of change in terms of the responsibility of each. Seeking a sense of balance between profits and people, between economic and social roles, Mr. Zagoria introduces tough questions as to the balance between the corporate and the community interest. With a strong pragmatic flavor, he stresses the legitimate special-interest needs opening new high roads to the future. His discussion of policy considerations leads logically to his provocative "Agenda for the Seventies."

This agenda sets goals and objectives for the achievement of a minimum level of job satisfaction for all workers—to improve the standards of living, to protect mental and physical health and welfare, and to advance individual fulfillment. This broad thirteen-point social mandate holds challenges to government, employers and unions, and embraces many of the critical issues that will engage our society for the balance of this decade and probably into the 1980s as well.

Daniel Yankelovich

1
The Meaning of Work

Looking up from the Grindstone

"Americans know more about how to make a living than how to live." Although Thoreau made his astute observation on American life more than a century ago, by and large it remains valid today. We still organize our lives around the struggle to make a living. We place our economic institutions at the center of the society because they create the jobs and produce the growth that keeps the economy rolling. We also organize family life around the job: family responsibilities are parceled out to make it as handy as possible for the male head of the household to be the economic provider, while the wife picks up most of the residual chores. Where we live, how well we live, whom we see socially, how we pattern our daily routines, how we educate our children—all of these facets of our lives are dominated by the work we do to make a living.

Many of these social arrangements are now changing. Under the impact of woman's lib the rigid division of labor in the family is beginning to break down. People are growing balky on the job: they seem less willing than in the past to endure hardships for the sake of making a living. Some unions are now stressing noneconomic issues at the bargaining table. Many people are seeking jobs that may pay less well but offer a more agreeable life style. And even the high value

DANIEL YANKELOVICH *is president of the social research firm bearing his name, a social and marketing research firm. He is also research professor of psychology at New York University and visiting professor of psychology at the New School for Social Research. His latest book is* The Changing Values on Campus.

we place on economic growth as the main goal of our society is cast in doubt. Mr. Nixon, who has spoken out in defense of the traditional work ethic many times, has also, ironically, challenged the premise on which the work ethic rests: "In the next ten years we will increase our wealth by fifty percent. The profound question is: Does this mean that we will be 50 percent richer in any real sense, 50 percent better off, or 50 percent happier?" (*State of the Union Address*, January 1970). In posing this fundamental question, Mr. Nixon has voiced a doubt that is spreading to ever larger segments of the society.

We are living through a period of vast cultural change, the essence of which lies in the transformation of work values and the work ethic. Indeed, so central is the work ethic to American culture that if its meaning shifts, the character of our society will shift along with it. Conversely, if our general cultural outlook undergoes a reorientation, then the changed meanings of work will probably emerge as the salient expression of the country's new social philosophy.

In this chapter, following a brief discussion of the historical sources and present meanings of the American work ethic, we examine five aspects of cultural change in the country that impinge directly on the work ethic. We then look at how these shifts in general life values are affecting specific work-related values, particularly among young people and women—the groups that are most directly influenced. In the final section, we attempt to forecast how the work ethic is likely to change in the foreseeable future.

The American Work Ethic

RELIGIOUS ORIGINS

What do we mean by the American work ethic? To trace its origins, we have to go back to the beginnings of Western civilization, as Adriano Tilgher has effectively done. The early Greeks regarded work as a curse. The word for work derives from the Greek word for sorrow, *ponos,* suggesting drudgery, heavy-heartedness, exhaustion. Work had no inherent value for the ancient Greeks. They felt that work enslaved the worker, chaining him to the will of others, corrupting the soul, and robbing him precisely of that independence so highly valued by ancient Greek civilization.

For the Hebrews, the meaning of work was almost as bleak, but with one saving feature. Work was regarded as atonement and expiation for the original sin of disobeying the word of God.

It was Christian civilization that slowly began to build the accretion of meanings that have evolved into the modern work ethic. The early

Christians followed the Hebrews in their conception of work as a punishment laid on by God for man's original transgressions. Gradually several positive meanings accrued to work. The early Christians saw work as necessary to maintain the health of body and mind and to keep evil thoughts at bay. Contrary to the Greeks, they conceived of work as a defense against despair rather than as the expression of despair itself. Like the Hebrews, they too saw work as an act of expiation. They also looked to work as a way to spread charity and to share with the needy. Eventually, they came to believe that the accumulation of worldly goods need not lead to wickedness and perdition. Since possessions could be shared with others, God's blessings would shine on the giver as well as the receiver.

The integration of work with profit-making and the ownership of property came with St. Thomas Aquinas. Codifying the social practice of his day, Aquinas advanced the concept of the "just price," i.e., the monetary reward for work that enabled a man and his family to scratch out a livelihood. Up to the time of Aquinas, even though the idea of work had begun to accumulate some positive meanings, no inherent virtue attached to work itself. One worked long enough and hard enough to support the immediate needs of self and family. That rare person lucky enough to live without working was not scorned by society. Neither did working longer and harder than the minimum required to meet the practical needs of life earn moral brownie points.

It remained for the advent of Protestantism to invest work with the moral meanings we associate with the American work ethic. Martin Luther took the decisive step when he eliminated the distinction between working and serving God. Luther conceived of work as a way to serve God, indeed as the best way. Luther even condemned the monastic and contemplative life of piety in the monasteries of his day as expressions of egoism: the symbols of the snobbery and conceit of monks who thought themselves superior to the common man. It is Luther, then, who endowed the idea of work with an intense religious and moral character.

Calvinism further strengthened the moral connotations of work. To the strict Calvinist, dislike or rejection of hard work made damnation all but inevitable. Because work is, in effect, "God's work" all men rich or poor must work, and work unceasingly. Moreover, success at work when made tangible in the form of wealth could be taken as a sign that the work was pleasing to God—especially if the profits from it could be reinvested and if the work was carried out in a highly organized, continuous, and rational form. To work hard was not enough: the work must be organized in keeping with strict canons of rationality and efficiency. Although later work was to lose its explicit religious connotations, it has never shaken itself free of the intense moral content with which it was endowed by the founders of Protestantism.

CONTEMPORARY MEANING OF THE WORK ETHIC

The present-day work ethic in America is rooted in this Protestant tradition. A study on basic American life values carried out by Daniel Yankelovich, Inc. in the mid 1960s showed that a majority of the adult population at that time associated four cultural themes with work. These themes link work with peoples' life values and form essential parts of what we mean by the American work ethic:

The "Good Provider" Theme—The breadwinner—the man who provides for his family—is the real man.

Here is the link between making a living and the society's definition of masculinity. Masculinity has little to do with sexual prowess or physical strength or aggressiveness or a virile appearance. For almost 80 percent of the adult population to be a man in our society has meant being a good provider for the family. The concept of masculinity here at issue also conveys overtones of adulthood, responsibility, intensity of loving care for others.

The Independence Theme—To make a living by working is to "stand on one's own two feet" and avoid dependence on others. Work equals autonomy. To work and be paid for it means one has gained —and earned—freedom and independence.

The Success Theme—"Hard work always pays off." Hard work leads to success, its form dependent on one's abilities, background, and level of education. For the majority, the "payoff" comes in the form of a home of one's own, an ever rising standard of living, and a solid position in the community.

The Self-respect Theme—Hard work of any type has dignity whether it be menial or exalted. A man's inherent worth is reflected in the act of working. To work hard at something and to do it well: a person can feel good about himself if he keeps faith with this precept.

Manhood, responsibility, economic security, independence, freedom, self-respect, success in life, self-esteem, dignity—this is the moral stuff from which the daily life of people is shaped. We often underestimate the potency of moral issues in people's lives, giving more attention to the practical and pleasure-seeking sides of life. But most lives are as immersed in a sea of morality as fish are immersed in water: morality surrounds us. It is the element we breathe. It is rarely noticed—except if it is polluted or absent. From this substratum of moral values grows such diverse phenomena as the traditional American resistance to non-punitive welfare legislation (because it suggests that not working is morally acceptable), and the deterioration of morale caused by pro-longed unemployment, apart from its economic consequences (because of the threat to self-respect and self-esteem). Pay for housework has become a demand of great symbolic significance to the women's move-ment, one implication of the work ethic being that work for which one is *not* paid connotes second class citizenship—whether it be that of the housewife or the volunteer.

We begin to see how deeply embedded the work ethic is in general cultural values, and why changes in the culture necessarily color the role and meaning of work.

New Cultural Trends

Let us examine some of the new cultural trends that are grad-ually transforming the work ethic. They are interrelated, each rein-forcing the other. For purposes of analysis they can be identified sepa-rately. Among the most important are: the changing meaning of suc-cess in America; lessening fears of economic insecurity; a weakening of the rigid division of effort between the sexes; a growing "psychology of entitlement" leading to the creation of new social rights; and spread-ing disillusionment with the cult of efficiency.

THE CHANGING MEANING OF SUCCESS

Throughout most of the post World War II era, Americans shaped their ideas of success around money, occupational status, possessions, and the social mobility of their children. To be successful meant "mak-ing it" in the world of business or in high status professions (doctor, lawyer, scientist, government official) or in well-paying white collar or skilled blue collar jobs. Success has also been linked with ownership of one's own home in a "good neighborhood" and with possessions that have status symbol value, such as large cars, fur coats, silver flat-ware, diamond rings, swimming pools, and vacation homes. These have been the tangible signs of success money can buy. If the goods of the world eluded one, a second chance often came along as an op-portunity to encourage one's children to "better themselves" through higher education as a stepping stone to a good job. In contrast to tra-ditional European culture, American children have usually been ex-pected to surpass their parents in social and economic status. The pattern is tritely familiar; however it has been changing for some time now, and in the past few years has taken a significant turn in a new direction.

The old components of success—money, job status, possessions, and mobility for children—still count. Certainly, Americans are drawn to money for its practical uses and also to signify to themselves and others that they have achieved a niche in the world. Yet an increasing number of people are coming to feel that there is such a thing as enough money. And this is new. Few scoff at money or reject the opportunity to enhance their standard of living, but people are no longer as ready to make sacrifices for this kind of success as they were in the past. The crucial question has become: "What do I have to give up for the money?" These days, a "big earner" who has settled for an unpleasant life-style is no longer considered more successful than someone with less money who has created an agreeable life-style for himself. There are, of course, millions of people who adhere to older views of success as defined exclusively in terms of money, but the trend is moving away from them.

Similar considerations hold for the other elements of success. Many studies in the sociological literature show that people find it easy to rank jobs by the degrees of prestige that adhere to types of occupation. Yet the status of doctors, scientists, lawyers, and business executives has begun to lose some of its lustre—especially if achieving occupational success involves sacrifice and unpleasantness. The prestige of the business executive, for example, has plummeted in recent years. A 1973 study carried out by the Opinion Research Company shows the public ranking of the professions in terms of prestige in the following order: Physician (66 percent), Scientist (59 percent), Lawyer (44 percent), Minister (44 percent), Engineer (40 percent), Architect (40 percent), U. S. Congressman (39 percent), Banker (33 percent), Accountant (29 percent), Businessman (20 percent).

Material possessions, too, have begun to lose some of their connotations of success. This is not to say that Americans have lost their taste for material goods. We still surround ourselves with appliances, television sets, charcoal grills, power lawnmowers, snowmobiles, and the other assorted gear associated with American life. And the love affair with the automobile continues unabated. But it has changed its character. The ownership of a huge, gas-guzzling, boat-like car is no longer the crowning symbol of having arrived in the world. Few people these days celebrate each move up the hierarchy of success by the size and make of automobile they own.

Perhaps most significantly, the trend is away from postponing self-gratification in order to insure the upward mobility of one's children. One of the old-time favorite plots of films and books concerns the hard-working, self-denying parent who works day and night as charwoman, laundress or laborer to insure the success of a child. Today, such scenarios are tinged with nostalgia, the campy appeal of a bygone era. The Jewish mother for whom "my-son-the-doctor" is a single word, the auto assembly-line worker who says, "I'll make any sacrifice so that my kids can go to college to better themselves and not end up as I have," the parent who feels that his life will be fulfilled if and only if his children surpass him in socioeconomic status—all are stock figures in a receding past. They exist—but in ever fewer numbers.

It is important to avoid misunderstanding. I am not saying that parents are no longer willing to make sacrifices for their children. They are and they do, perhaps as much as in the past. What I wish to underline is that people tend less to view the success of their *own* lives in terms of their children's lives. They want their children to be successful. They are willing to give them whatever advantages they can afford. But they no longer regard vicarious living through their children as a proper substitute for success in their own lives. They feel they have their own lives to live, and do not need to live through their children.

The era of keeping up with the Joneses—so blatant a part of the American landscape of the 1950s—also appears to be undergoing a gradual transformation. The individual's definition of success has somehow become less firmly anchored in the world of possessions, status, money. In the process it has lost much of its treadmill, rat-race character—that open-ended, never-satisfied compulsion to accumulate more and more money, more and more possessions, more and more status symbols to confirm a higher rank in the hierarchy. The era of the step-up from Chevrolet to Buick; from Buick to Pontiac; from Pontiac to Oldsmobile; from Oldsmobile to Cadillac; and from Cadillac, presumably, to heaven—that era is dead and gone—at least for the majority of Americans today.

What has taken its place? New ideas about success revolve around various forms of self-fulfillment. The emphasis now is on the self and its unrealized "potential," a self that cries out for expression, satisfaction, actualization. If the key motif of the past was "keeping up with the Joneses," today it is "I have my own life to live—let Jones shift for himself." The new consciousness about the self does not destroy the older definition of success as money and occupational status. But it diminishes the relative importance of "goods" to the individual.

They have, as it were, to move over to make way for the newcomer. Money, possessions, a good position—these can and do become instruments of self-expression. But in the process, a subtle but far-reaching transformation takes place. They become means, rather than ends in themselves. And, most significantly, they are not the only means available but must compete with other less materialistic means of self-fulfillment such as being closer to nature, finding new ways to be "creative," spending more time with friends.

The new national preoccupation with self-fulfillment assumes some strange forms which, unfortunately, we must bypass if we are not to be diverted from our main theme. But let me mention in passing several consequences of the growing attachment to self-fulfillment. The emphasis on self modifies the character of the bonds which tie the individual to social institutions—the family, employer, community, church, trade union, political party, nation. No longer can these institutions assume the automatic and "unearned" loyalty of the individual. The willingness of people to subordinate themselves unquestioningly to some larger entity for the sake of an implicit common good is slowly disappearing. Instead, people are asking *why* they should be loyal and what fulfillment for themselves they can derive from being a part of a larger unit.

The sprouting of communes among the young is often cited as a counter-example of the trend toward self-centered individualism. Indeed, many communes with their resemblance to extended families, do express the hunger for belonging to a larger community. Often, however, communes turn out to be loose aggregates of individuals, each one preoccupied with his own personal needs. Without the discipline to subordinate the self to the larger unit, the ties that bind the group become unraveled and the commune disintegrates. This form of change does not characterize all communes, of course, but it does describe a number of them.

The breakdown of certain types of conformity is another consequence of the new ideas about success. Each person is assumed to be unique. Thus tolerance for offbeat and unusual life styles to express one's individuality is spreading. This does not mean that social conformity is now collapsing around our heads. On closer inspection, most "unique" life styles take on a standard look. But conformity in practice is not the same as social pressure to conform, or the feeling that one must conform to get along ("you get along by going along"). People feel it is all right to conform if conformity is one's own free choice. Later in this chapter, I will relate this new attitude toward conformity to the work ethic.

REDUCED FEAR OF ECONOMIC INSECURITY

Less general in its effect on the culture, but equally fraught with significance for the work ethic, is a greatly reduced fear of economic insecurity. Vast segments of the public have grown less fearful that economic catastrophe will strike without warning and render them destitute. Of course, inflation disturbs people and causes them to be distressed about making ends meet. But people today are less afraid of losing their jobs, facing a poverty-stricken old age, or finding themselves in a situation where they are unable to cope economically.

To illustrate the change: in the 1972 presidential election campaign, despite a relatively high rate of unemployment, the unemployment issue proved to be of minor importance. According to the New York *Times*/Yankelovich election survey, the number one issue was Vietnam (51 percent). Inflation was the second most important issue (37 percent). Unemployment was far down the list, in about eighth or ninth position—of concern to fewer than 10 percent of the voters. It was almost as if only the voters who were unemployed concerned themselves with the problem. Several decades ago, politicians would have regarded so negligible a role for unemployment in a presidential campaign as unimaginable.

Economic security has not become less important to people. For most, economic security continues to dominate their lives. But today people take some economic security for granted. If they are working, the future prospect that they might be unable to make a living seems curiously unreal.

For many generations an unspoken consensus prevailed in the country, so widespread and universally accepted that there has been no need to make it explicit: the consensus held that economic security is so important and so difficult to insure that no sacrifice is too great for the sake of preserving it. This silent assumption has dominated our national life. Its unchallenged acceptance has given our society its distinctive character, shaping common goals, and pervading the political and economic life of the nation. For example, if an industrial plant was spewing pollutants into a nearby waterway and the community objected, all the plant manager would have to say was, "That will mean we'll have to lay off a few hundred men," and typically the community would back off from its demands.

In the past few years, the consensus has begun to collapse. A majority of adults (approximately 60 percent) state that they continue to place economic security above all other goals, but a substantial 40 percent minority say that they are now prepared to take certain risks with their own and the nation's economic security for the sake of enhancing the quality of life. We are not surprised to find that the majority still adheres to the old view; what is striking is that so large a minority has adopted this new and far-reaching value-orientation.

One consequence of the lessened fear of economic insecurity is a growing willingness to take unprecedented risks. This confidence pertains both to personal life and to national policy. People are seeking to realize new values relating to the preservation of the environment, to self-enhancement and, as we shall shortly discuss, to the quality of working life.

ECONOMIC DIVISION OF LABOR BETWEEN THE SEXES

Economic factors have played a large role in maintaining the rigid division of labor between the sexes that is so prominent a feature of family life in America. As noted earlier, the prevailing conception of masculinity has turned on economic rather than sexual potency: being a good provider is more highly valued than being good in bed. For a man, especially if he is married, to fail in his economic mission means more than low social status. The standards of the society have been so internalized that failure as a provider suffuses most men with guilt and a sense of inadequacy.

Man is responsible for making a living and this role is all-important and all-consuming. Thus the wife automatically becomes the help-mate and residual legatee of most other family responsibilities, especially care of home and kids. Like the man's role, the woman's, in addition to its practical economic aspects, also takes on emotional overtones edged by fear and anxiety. Divorce has often raised the spectre of destitution for the wife. In the marriage itself, a wide range of rigid moral standards has accumulated around homemaking, child-raising, house beautification, cleaning, cooking, washing, diapering, and comforting the hard-working male. Woe unto the wife who found herself wanting in these roles, however educated and trained she may have been for other missions in life. So deeply internalized have these standards been that women often exaggerated the disapproval of friends and neighbors when they failed to live up to their own expectations. Society has had little need to enforce these standards. The job has been done by the lash and sting of the woman's own guilt. For both men and women any letup in the rigid obligations and willingness to make personal sacrifices in order to preserve economic security has often stimulated fantasies of disaster.

One consequence of the reduced fear of economic insecurity has been a concomitant lessening in the fear and guilt experienced by people when they take a more casual attitude toward their role obligations in marriage. The iron economic discipline that maintained the rigidity of the sex roles in the past has weakened. Under the impact of the women's liberation movement a far greater flexibility has marked the relationship between the sexes.

To say that the role relationships between the sexes are growing more flexible is not to say that they are disappearing altogether. Women, as well as men, almost universally reject the idea that roles and responsibilities for men and women should become interchangeable. The notion that the man should stay home and do the cooking and housekeeping while the woman goes out and earns the living is strongly resisted—more by women than by men. Fewer than one in ten accept the idea that sharply defined roles based on sex should be entirely eliminated. The majority of women continue to feel that homemaking is more satisfying than a job. They also state that they would respect a man less if he permitted his wife to earn a living while he stayed home. Moreover, most women do not feel that their role as homemaker is an inherently unequal role in the family. *Ms.* magazine to the contrary, women generally, especially married women, see men as thoughtful and considerate partners—not as exploitative male chauvinist pigs.

Increasingly, women accept the idea that both husband and wife may work, but the woman's economic role continues to be regarded as supplemental. The responsibility for making the living still falls on the man, although more and more responsibility is coming to be shared.

While most people reject an interchange of roles between men and women, they are very much in favor of an easier, more flexible division of effort. Gradually, year by year, they are accepting a more informal, less fixed separation of obligations, expectations, and responsibilities. A majority of families today feel that it is perfectly all right for men to participate in shopping and in cleaning the home, and more than three out of ten families look with favor on men participating in daily meal preparation. Conversely, the idea of women working for purposes of self-fulfillment rather than economic motives gains wider acceptance all the time. And, in fact, women are pouring into the work force in unprecedented numbers—and at a faster rate than men. (Women now constitute almost 40 percent of the total work force.) These labor participation rates tell us nothing about the psychological reasons for work. It is here that the real change is taking place. Women have always worked for economic reasons, but now, superimposed on the economic motive, is the powerful psychological force of self-realization.

Its effects are changing work values almost as much as they are changing the nature of the family.

THE PSYCHOLOGY OF ENTITLEMENT

A fourth category of cultural change is a spreading psychology of
entitlement, the growth of a broad new agenda of "social rights." This
is the psychological process whereby a person's wants or desires become
converted into a set of presumed rights.

> From, "I would like to have a secure retirement" to "I have the right to
> a secure retirement."
>
> From, "If I could afford it, I would have the best medical care," to "I have
> the right to the best medical care whether I can afford it or not."
>
> From, "My job would mean more to me if I had more to say about how
> things are run," to "I have the right to take part in decisions that
> affect my job."
>
> From, "I'd like to have a job that gives me pleasure and satisfaction, rather
> than just something I do to make a living," to "I have a right to
> work on something that lets me do a good job and gives me pleas-
> ure."
>
> From, "I hope we will be able to afford to send our children to college,"
> to "Our children have as much right to a higher education as any-
> body else."
>
> From, "I hope that this breakfast cereal is fresh," to "I have the right to
> know when it was made and how long it will stay fresh."

This process is not new. Indeed, it is a very old trend, long recognized
by social scientists as part of a worldwide revolution of rising expectations. In recent years it has accelerated, and it has assumed new political and institutional forms. It is the effects of these trends expressed
in various social movements that we have been feeling so acutely in
the past few years.

The concept of social rights has always exerted a strong force in our
society, but in recent years a number of new institutional forms have
sprung up that immensely shorten the time span between the individual's sense of entitlement and political action. In the 1960s a variety
of social movements came into being—the civil rights movement, the
student movement, the ecology movement, the consumer movement,
the women's movement, the gay liberation movement, etc. These movements served to articulate, define, and shape a full agenda of new social rights. The technique of consciousness-raising advanced by wom-
en's lib, for example, institutionalized the process whereby the gen--

eralized discontent of women became transmuted into sharply defined social rights.

Ralph Nader crystallized a vague wave of consumer uneasiness into a powerful pressure for new government legislation. The growing conviction that one has certain rights that are not being met fuels organized efforts to achieve change. These efforts assume the ever more sophisticated form of lobbying, fund-raising, organization of protest, formation of pressure groups, congressional testimony, skillful exploitation of media, drafting of legislation, and other forms of intervening in the national opinion-making and policy-making process. Gradually, each one of the social movements and the new rights they embody come to focus pressure on government—the federal government in particular, but also state and local governments. The logic here is that, by definition, a social right implies that its satisfaction be guaranteed, and in the long run the guarantor is usually the government. As individual desires and privileges become converted into rights, the marketplace—the forum for expressing desires—is gradually being constricted by the political process and by regulative and legislative mechanisms for enforcing rights. It is this process more than any other that accounts for the moving line of demarcation between the public sector and the private sector which, as Daniel Bell has observed working from a different source of data, is one of the hallmarks of an emerging post-industrial society.

THE ADVERSARY CULTURE CHALLENGES THE CULT OF EFFICIENCY

Max Weber, a founder of modern sociology, believed that the master key to the fate of Western industrial societies lay in the implacable unfolding of the process of "rationalization." By rationalization Weber meant a broader version of what a modern plant manager tries to do when he "rationalizes" his production line, i.e., organizes it so that he can produce the most products at the greatest speed for the least amount at the lowest cost, with all the standardization and controls that this process implies. Weber predicted that in modern industrial society the process of rationalization and bureaucratization would not remain confined to the domains of business and government. He foresaw rationalization spreading to areas as diverse as music, religion, economics, law, and politics. All of our large institutions, he observed, tend toward inexorable systematization. In the rationalized society that results, relations among men become ruled by how useful people are in performing their utilitarian function. People, in effect, *become* the roles they play in carrying out the functions of the society. Institutions grow ever more organized in order to contribute more efficiently to the whole. And a false sense of progress, to which we attribute the highest of moral purposes, accompanies the entire process of growth piled upon growth, system on system.

Weber identified the psychological motive for rationalization as the passion for mastering the environment. He predicted that we would pay a high price in human satisfaction with every step we took toward perfecting the process of rationalization. He also noted that one consequence of increasing efficiency would be to strip life of all mystery and charm. Above all, he feared that the process would extend beyond the regulation of man's economic and political activities to stifle his private and personal life.

In the post-World War II culture of the United States, the process of rationalization has reached deeply into the social structure. Our large business corporations, "think tanks," government agencies, and many other institutions model themselves on systems of organization that strive to realize the ideals of cost-effectiveness, division of effort, efficiency, measurement of results, statistical controls, objectification of function, and budget/program/planning systems. Sometimes these ideals are carried beyond the boundaries of practicality, with quantitative methods and "rational" procedures becoming enshrined into rules of operation for their own sake, even when they actually interfere with the task at hand.

In many parts of American culture, the passion for rationalization and efficiency has become, in Gordon Allport's phrase, "functionally autonomous" and exists almost independently of the job to be done. This is a cast of mind, an expression of temperament, a form of relatedness to the world that is peculiarly Western and modern. In Vietnam, for example, the emphasis placed by the United States military command on "kill ratios" and quantitative computer-based methods for comparing village pacification rates became a virulent form of irrationalism rather than the highest expression of the rational mind. There is a quality of evangelical dogmatism and fanaticism in the B. F. Skinners and Dr. Strangeloves of our era, whose approach to every aspect of life betrays a large component of irrationality that lies, like a worm, hidden in the fruits of our technological advances.

This, at any rate, is the view held by the counter-culture, and widely spread among today's best-educated youth. They see the emphasis on efficiency, quantitative methods, and cost-effectiveness as expressions of minds blinded by dogma, if not by evil incarnate. The rejection of the rationalizing mode of thought is implicit in the modern return-to-nature movement and explicit in the works of many of the culture heroes of today's college-bred youth.

In the past few years, a questioning of the values of efficiency has just begun to reach beyond the confines of the counter-culture. The form it assumes in the general population is not nearly as extreme or doctrinaire. But the average American is beginning to wonder whether too great a concern with efficiency and rationalization is not robbing his life, just as Weber suspected it would, of the excitement, adventure, mystery, romance, and pleasure for which he yearns—especially if he is a young American. To be sure, people are annoyed when the telephone does not work or their automobile mechanic does not know what he is doing. Nonetheless, they are beginning to suspect the merits of values centering on efficiency, planning, and organization of time.

Life Values and Their Effect on Work Values

We have been examining five forms of cultural change: emerging new definitions of success; a dwindling fear of economic insecurity; more flexible man-wife role relations; a spreading psychology of entitlement; and the growth in the adversary culture of a serious challenge to the cult of efficiency. These changes, and not others, have been selected out of the vast sweep of social transformations in our society because: (a) they represent cultural as distinct from the kind of *structural* changes that are examined in the next chapter; (b) they are important enough to merit special attention; and, (c) they are either slowly eating away at the work ethic or are likely to do so in the foreseeable future. Let us now examine how these social changes affect work values.

The important question of whether or not Americans are satisfied with their work is presently bogged down in a heated but fruitless controversy. On the one side are those observers of the work scene who cite public opinion polls to prove that the overriding majority of Americans are satisfied with their work. The other side, represented by many sociologists, industrial psychologists, journalists, and other observers, point to a variety of statistics, observations, and studies that show a rising tide of disaffection in the work force.

Which side is correct? Well . . . both are. Each party to the controversy has fastened onto a different facet of a complex, multifaceted problem. The seeming contradiction between them is more apparent than real. It can probably be resolved—and a useful perspective gained —by keeping three variables in mind: the age of the worker, the expectations he (or she) brings to the job, and the difference between the economic and psychological satisfactions people seek from their work.

ECONOMIC SATISFACTIONS

The key economic satisfactions people look for from their jobs are a good salary, the prospects for a secure retirement, and job security. Significantly, most people today who are employed full-time feel that these economic needs are now being met by their jobs, more or less satisfactorily. This feeling, more than any other, creates a climate of social stability that was lacking in the 1930s when the country faced what then appeared to be the insoluble problem of mass unemployment. This is a point of cardinal importance. If we are to retain perspective on changes in the work ethic, we must always bear in mind that most people who work for a living do so mainly for economic reasons and that the large majority of them feel that their economic expectations are met by their current jobs.

This is the picture presented by the public opinion polls (and analyzed in detail by Professor Strauss in chapter 3). Although it is correct as far as it goes, it is a dangerously incomplete basis for judging the present situation. The typical opinion poll question, "All things considered, would you say you are very satisfied, somewhat satisfied or not at all satisfied with your job?" is a poor indicator of underlying work attitudes for a variety of reasons (e.g., expectations are not made explicit, there are ambiguities in what the response means, and an insensitivity to conflict). Yet, even the opinion polls have shown a steady erosion in expressed work satisfaction over the past decade (from an 87 percent high in 1964 to a 77 percent level of satisfaction in 1973, according to the Gallup Poll). If we now take age, expectations, and the psychological benefits sought from work into account, we develop a fuller, more accurate picture. Taking age 35 as a dividing point, we find that most working people over 35 expect and demand little more from their jobs than the economic benefits of income, job security, and secure retirement. Most of those over 35 *want* more from their jobs, but they do not *demand* more as a matter of social right. They are willing to settle for the economic rewards. The psychology of entitlement has not spread to them, but is largely confined to younger people.

The two most disaffected groups of working people in the country are people under 25, both men and women, and blacks of all ages. The reasons for their discontent are sharply different. Typically, blacks are unhappy because their basic economic demands are not being met.

Young white men and women, although they too are concerned with economics, are restive because they are tuned into the psychological benefits of work—and they do not feel they are being fulfilled.

PSYCHOLOGICAL BENEFITS

There are three psychological benefits people would like to gain from their work. One is the opportunity to advance to more interesting, varied, and satisfying work that also pays better and wins more recognition than their current job. This is, of course, a traditional work desire with an economic as well as a psychological component. But the psychological side of the job mobility demand is gradually growing more important.

The desire to do a good job at whatever one is doing—a part of the traditional work ethic—is a second psychological gratification sought by people. This is an even more universal desire than job mobility and is expressed by people of all ages, levels of education, sex, and race. This desire is often misunderstood—and underestimated—by employers. Many employers believe that the desire to do a good job is something they themselves inculcate in employees—either by threatening punishment if people do not do a good job (firing them, withholding recognition, passing them up for promotion, ignoring them in decision making, etc.) or by offering positive incentives in the form of money, praise, and added responsibility. Yet the desire to do a good job is not created by employers by means of their systems of rewards and punishments. It is a deeply rooted need that people bring with them to their work, and as such is one of the country's greatest strengths.

Although employers do not instill the desire to do a good job, they can easily destroy or frustrate it—and often do. Recognizing the fragility of this motive is probably the most persuasive argument advanced by those who criticize the cult of efficiency. Our proliferation of management systems and bureaucratic controls—expressions of the rationalizing mind—often kill off the spontaneous desire to do a good job. People become mere "personnel" caught in a web of rules and contradictory policies that often make it most difficult to enjoy work and get satisfaction from doing it well. There is, of course, nothing new about this psychological need either.

The third category of psychological need is comparatively new, at least in the sense that it is rapidly spreading to more and more people. This is the yearning to find self-fulfillment through "meaningful work." By meaningful work people usually mean: (1) work in which they can become involved, committed, and interested; (2) work that challenges them to the utmost of their capabilities; and (3) participation in decision making. A growing number of young people each year say that they are prepared to trade off salary and other economic benefits in exchange for meaningful, self-fulfilling work, i.e., work that offers them more than money.

It should be stressed that nearly everyone would like to enjoy both types of benefits from their jobs—economic and psychological. Almost all now expect the economic benefits—increasingly as a matter of right. But only the younger people feel they are *entitled* to some of the psychological benefits as a right rather than as a matter of luck or special effort on their part.

Impact of Cultural Trends

This brief sketch indicates that the work population is not uniformly affected by the new cultural trends. Older workers, except for the managerial-professional categories, are least affected. Blacks and other ethnic minorities are too absorbed in trying to catch up to be greatly influenced by what are, to a large extent, tendencies that presuppose affluence. White males in the middle work years, 30 to 50, and in the middle income range, are just beginning to feel the faint stirring of new ideas about quality of working life. There are three distinct groups on whom the new cultural values have left a marked imprint, giving us some clues about where the work ethic may be heading in the future. These are (1) young college-educated people; (2) young people without a college education; and (3) women of all ages and degrees of education. These three groups are the carriers of new attitudes and values about work that will, if present trends continue, spread to the work force as a whole. They must be discussed separately because the new cultural values impact each group in radically different ways.

COLLEGE YOUTH

For the past decade, we have seen many new values incubated on our college campuses and carried by the media to the rest of the country. In our era, the campus is the principal breeding ground for new values. In the mid-sixties some new values appeared on campus in the guise of radical New Left politics. By the beginning of the decade of the seventies, political activism fell off abruptly, no longer stimulated by the draft and the war in Southeast Asia. The true nature of the campus rebellion now stands out more clearly—as a quest for new life styles and life values with work-related values as an important part of this search. Since the nation's campuses are generally regarded as the stronghold of the counter-culture, characterized by alienation and opposition to traditional American values, this is where one might expect to find the most radical departure from the middle-class work ethic and old-fashioned work values. The truth is far more complex. In some ways, today's college students are the least alienated group in the society; in other ways, they are in the forefront of the search for new work values.

Significant findings derive from a series of five research studies conducted among national cross sections of college students by the Yankelovich research organization between 1967 and 1973. The studies were sponsored by the JDR 3rd Fund, the Carnegie Corporation, CBS News, *Fortune* magazine and others.[1] At first, the findings appear contradictory and confusing. They fall into place once we stop thinking about our college youth as rebels and start thinking about them in traditional sociological terms as a privileged upper-middle-class group being trained for positions of authority and influence in the society.

Interest in a practical career-orientation among college students increased steadily between 1967 and 1973. The research shows a slow but constant increase in the number of young people whose main motive in going to college is the practical one of preparing themselves for a successful career in the society. In 1967, 55 percent announced that this was their chief goal in attending college. In 1969, the number had crept up to 57 percent, in 1970 to 60 percent, in 1971 to 61 percent, and in 1973 to 66 percent:

	Total College Students (%)				
	1973	*1971*	*1970*	*1969*	*1967*
"For me, college is mainly a practical matter. With a college education I can earn more money, have a more interesting career and enjoy a better position in the society."	66	61	60	57	55

In response to a question on whether they would welcome less hard work in the future, only three out of ten students said they would, and more students rejected this prospect than embraced it:

[1] The following 1973 data are drawn from a national cross-section study of American youth based on 3,500 personal interviews, conducted by Daniel Yankelovich, Inc. for the JDR 3rd Fund, Carnegie Corporation, Edna McConnell Clark Foundation, Hazen Foundation, and Andrew W. Mellon Foundation.

	Total College Students (%)			
	1973	*1971*	*1970*	*1969*
Would welcome less emphasis on working hard in the future.	31	30	24	31
Reject this idea.	50	44	48	41

In a series of questions exploring the extent of student adherence to traditional American beliefs, the researchers found that in 1973 a large 84 percent majority subscribed to the belief that it was "very important to do any job (one was doing) well."

Thus far, we see a strong endorsement of conventional work values —the pursuit of an education for the sake of a career, a willingness to work hard, and the desire to do a good job. Then we come to some new departures. Among the beliefs probed was the traditional assumption, "Hard work always pays off." Here we find a dramatic pattern of erosion from a 69 percent majority who held this belief in 1967 to a 44 percent minority subscribing to it in 1973:

	Total College Students (%)			
	1973	*1971*	*1969*	*1967*
Believe "Hard work always pays off"	44	39	57	69
Interestingly, this trend may have begun to reverse direction in the 1971 to 1973 period.				

The importance of economic security in relation to self-fulfillment is shown in two findings from the 1973 survey. Asked which comes first in their lives, economic security or self-fulfillment, 43 percent of students answered "economic security" and 56 percent said "self-fulfillment." Also, in ranking personal values in their lives, self-fulfillment turned out to be "very important" to a whopping 87 percent of students (on a par with love and friendship), while work ranked as "very important" to 43 percent.

Exploring the psychology of entitlement among college students in 1973, a 56 percent majority of students said they regarded participation in decision making on the job as a "right to which they were entitled," 26 percent felt that they had a right to expect a minimum income, and 17 percent felt that the society was obligated to provide them with an interesting job:

	Total Students (%)
	1973
Entitled to as a social right:	
The best medical care (whether one can afford it or not)	59
Participation in decisions that affect one's own work	56
Sending children to college (whether one can afford it or not)	52
A secure retirement	37
The right to work	27
A minimum income	26
An interesting job	17

Finally, in ranking the relative importance of various influences on their choice of career, in 1973 as in previous years students placed the challenge of the job, the opportunity to make a meaningful contribution, time to pursue outside interests, and the ability to express oneself *ahead* of money, job security, the opportunity to get ahead, and freedom from pressure:

	Total Students (%)
Major Influences on Choice of Job or Career	*1973*
Challenge of the job	77
Able to make meaningful contribution	72
Free time for outside interests	69
Ability to express yourself	68
Money you can earn	61
Security of the job	58
Chance to get ahead	51
Prestige/status of job	28
Lack of pressure/not too demanding	22
Other	1

The picture that emerges is touched with irony. Just a few years ago, the country was reduced to near panic by what seemed to be the whole-sale alienation of college youth. Now we find an almost classic formula for accommodation and adaptation. The research findings cited earlier in this chapter show that the new definitions of success appeal hugely to college students. This knowledge helps us to interpret the campus-based research. Most college students accept the necessity for hard work as a fact of life. They do not shirk it or shrink from it. At the same time what they regard as a proper "payoff" for hard work has shifted dramatically. Students specifically reject a nose-to-the-grindstone philosophy of life. They do not subscribe to the old credo that if they work hard, stay out of trouble, and put their responsibilities to family and others ahead of their own personal satisfactions, then they will be rewarded with a good living, economic security, enough money to buy possessions, a nice place to live, and a good education for their kids. What we see instead is the active pursuit of a career as a means to self-fulfillment, with money, security and possessions included in the overall scheme, partly taken for granted, partly demanded as a matter of right, but always subordinate to the main goal of finding just the right life style for expressing their psychological potential.

Shifting perspective from a psychological to a sociological point of view, we see a growing majority of college-trained youth readying themselves for careers in the upper reaches of the social order. The professional, managerial, and technical categories are the fastest growing occupational groupings in the country. These prestigious positions will make hard demands on people's trained capabilities, their willingness to respond to challenge, and their ability to adapt to innovation. How convenient it is, therefore, that increasing numbers of young people are heading straight for these upper-level niches, their eyes fixed on the goal marked "successful career." Moreover, they are demanding that these careers be meaningful and rewarding in both the psychological and economic senses. Fortunately for them, it appears that there will be an abundance of such careers available. Today's students are training themselves for positions in an elite group which is peculiarly necessary in a post-industrial society.

From this standpoint, even though these well-educated young adults may be searching for more varied life styles than their parents did, the celebrated generation gap disappears before our eyes in any profound sociological sense. My research shows that in the country today the most satisfied group—those who are most at ease with the society as it exists, the most pleased with their work, gratified with their income, and content with their own personal lives—are the upper-middle-class families that occupy the leading professional, managerial, and technical positions in the society. Looking at the future prospects for this large and growing social class, the "fit" between aspiration and opportunity appears exceptionally good. It is precisely this kind of good fit between values and institutions that makes for institutional legitimacy and stability.

NONCOLLEGE YOUTH

The foregoing optimistic view of the relationship of college-educated youth to their future work dramatizes, by contrast, the plight of the majority of young people who either receive no college education at all, or have one or two years of college before dropping out. This is the situation for seven out of ten young people, since at the present time fewer than 30 percent of all persons age 18 to 25 finish four years of college.

It is astonishing that the work problems of the majority should have been so neglected, for they are grave and threatening. Let me confine my observations here to the cultural aspects of their relationship to work. The noncollege majority recognize full well that, lacking a college education, they are less likely than college-trained people to find interesting work. In the past, this did not matter too much. Most people looked to work for its extrinsic rewards—good pay, a mounting standard of living, economic security. But gradually, the new ideas about success and entitlement are seeping into the consciousness of all young people, not just college youth.

The result is ambivalence and confusion. The idea of meaningful work is attractive to these young high school graduates—but they do not really expect to get it from their jobs. Upward mobility is also important to them, but opportunities for mobility and for job enrichment are often traded away in exchange for economic benefits. (The trade unions tend to be most responsive to the values of older workers.) Opportunities for skilled workers in industrial jobs are shrinking. Low-level service jobs are dead-ends. Information about good jobs open to the person without a college education is difficult to acquire. Good training, apprenticeship, and the acquisition of new skills are sporadic and all too often poorly conceived; and to most young people they do not look as if they will produce results.

Out of this confusion there emerges a split *within* the present youth generation that is far greater—and more dangerous to the society— than the split *between* the generations. The college-educated minority is turning on to work; the majority who lack a college degree are turning off. For their self-fulfillment, these young people search for outlets outside the job—in sports, in family life, in the quest for excitement. Here, once again, we may ask, "What is new?" Are we not seeing the old familiar pattern wherein people make a living from their jobs and look for personal fulfillment outside of the job? Perhaps. But there are some new elements in the present picture. Simply because they lack a college degree does not mean that young people are immune to the vast cultural changes taking place in the country.

Today's young people are less fearful of economic insecurity than in the past. They want interesting and challenging work, but they assume that their employers cannot—or will not—provide it. By their own say-so, they are inclined to take "less crap" than older workers. They are not as automatically loyal to the organization as their fathers, and they are far more cognizant of their own needs and rights. Nor are they as awed by organizational and hierarchical authority. Being less fearful of "discipline" and the threat of losing their jobs, they feel free to express their discontent in myriad ways, from fooling around on the job to sabotage. They are better educated than their parents, even without a college degree. They want more freedom and will bargain hard to keep their options open. A bitter fight over the right to refuse mandatory overtime, for example, does not mean that young workers will not work overtime. It does mean that the freedom to say "no" assumes symbolic significance as an expression of freedom and autonomy. Moreover, if the work itself is not meaningful to them, they will opt for "thirty and out" forms of retirement, shorter work weeks, frequent absenteeism, more leisure, and other methods for cutting back and cutting down on their job commitment.

That the majority of noncollege youth face the threat of alienation at the workplace must be a matter of serious concern to employers. These people, after all, represent the great bulk of the new labor force. The problem they face is compounded by the multiplier effect of higher expectations with lower opportunities: their new values and folkways inevitably clash with the built-in rigidities and limited responses at the workplace. This might be a manageable problem if the numbers were limited or if one could sense an emerging responsiveness of big organizations to the cultural change. The cultural lag, however, is a large one and becomes of increasing concern to the employers in both the private and the public sectors because of the sheer magnitude of the problem.

This future scenario, depicting a disgruntled, discontented work force of high school graduates uninterested in their jobs and searching out every opportunity to cut back on work commitments irrespective of the economic rewards, is far from inevitable. Conversely, the conventional wisdom scenario of a future work force contented because they are making a living and improving their material standard of life is even more unlikely. We are reaching one of those critical turning points in our social history where the options of the future are truly open. The die is not yet cast. The majority of young people continue to bring to their work a deeply rooted desire to do a good job and a hunger for work that will satisfy some of their spiritual cravings—for community, for fellowship, for participation, for challenge, for self-fulfillment, for freedom, and for equality.

This pull toward a new quality of working life carries a heavy burden of responsibility for employers. However, at this juncture the structure of employing organizations is not well equipped to satisfy these needs. Most organizations, especially those in business and industry, are finely honed to win the economic benefits the country has pursued so singlemindedly in the past. The quality of working life has received less attention, though it will inevitably become more important in the future.

Chances are that the methods of industrial organization and rationalization which have prevailed for one hundred years and intensified greatly in the past few decades have become dysfunctional. The cult of efficiency may well be breeding inefficiency. It is quite possible that the gains in productivity achieved annually by technology, by the infusion of capital, and by formal methods of management and organization are more than offset by the tendency to create conditions in the name of efficiency that make it impossible for people to feel they are doing a good job or that what they do on the job counts.

Unfortunately, no one truly knows the relationship between work satisfaction and productivity. The research on this relationship is confusing and contradictory. As psychologist Robert Kahn who summarized the technical literature has observed in *The Human Meaning of Social Change*, "Satisfaction is related to productivity in some circumstances and not in others, and these circumstances have yet to be defined." This fact—that we do not even understand how productivity and human satisfaction on the job are linked together—is symptomatic of the problems that lie ahead. Which turn in the road we take in the future depends largely on how well our institutions come to understand the problem of the growing institutional lag between present methods of work organization and the fundamental human aspirations of people as they respond to the new cultural *Zeitgeist*.

WOMEN

Nowhere is the impact of this *Zeitgeist* greater than on women, especially women who are seeking new work careers. The new cultural values are largely responsible for the influx of women into the work force in recent years. In 1973, the number of women in the work force reached almost 40 percent of all persons employed. While the majority of women seek jobs for the same reason that women have always worked—to help make ends meet—our surveys show that three out of ten women employed in 1973 placed their need for personal self-fulfillment ahead of economic need as their main reason for working. Earlier studies suggest that a negligible proportion of women worked for noneconomic motives in the past. Indeed, for many women whose consciousness has been raised by women's lib, work and careers have almost become a new faith.

Working women are strong advocates of the psychology of entitlement, and the pressures they are putting on employers for equal pay, equal work, and equality of opportunity are proving difficult to resist. Employers are scrambling to eliminate barriers and right old wrongs. The greatest pressure in the future will come at the executive levels of business, government and education, for it is here that women discern, correctly, the sturdiest barriers to equality of opportunity.

These tendencies are already obvious. A more subtle but potentially far-reaching impact concerns the swelling numbers of women in the workplace. Earlier in this chapter we discussed the growing flexibility of the role relations between husbands and wives. Although many women may work for psychological gratification, they insist, and rightly so, on being remunerated on the same basis as men. As a consequence, many women today earn as much or more than their husbands. Even women who earn somewhat less than their husbands often earn enough so that the husband is no longer the sole provider of economic well-being. What effect does this new situation have on the male wage earner? In some cases, the effects greatly improve the family's quality of life. Contrary to stereotypes about male chauvinism, men tend to be more responsive to women's lib concepts than women themselves, especially young men in the 18–24 year age range. Many a man who is over-worked and living under stress has warmly welcomed sharing his economic burden with his wife. In such cases, the result is often an improved family equilibrium, a more satisfying sexual relationship, and a more gratifying partnership overall.

Also, to the approximately one out of five men who say that their work fills their psychological as well as their economic need (primarily in the professional/managerial categories), a working wife is no threat, especially when her economic contribution is not needed. But the working wife who is a good earner can pose a potential threat to the noncollege majority who work hard, manage to make a living, and seek their personal fulfillment through their families. For many of these men "a job is just a job." Their half-hearted satisfaction with their job reflects a precarious social bargain. The attitude of many of them can be summed up this way: "I put up with a lot of crap on the job but it's a living; I do the best I can, and besides I'm willing to make some personal sacrifice to see that my family is well provided for." Many men learn to accept the frustrations of boring work and lack of involvement in the decisions that make work meaningful precisely because they accept the necessity of making sacrifices for their family. As long as the money comes in, and as long as the family provider is not threatened, most men will go along, often cheerfully, with the work routine, however arduous it is. If, however, the man's role as he-who-makes-sacrifices-for-his-kid's-education-and-his-family's-material-well-being grows less vital, the whole fragile bargain threatens to break down.

In other words, the typical American adult man readily accepts the need to make some sacrifices for his family, in particular the sacrifices demanded by the frustrations of the workplace. Accepting these hardships reaffirms his role as the family provider and hence as a true man. Deprived of this role, however, his sacrifice may become meaningless . . . and intolerable. In extreme cases, when such a man is robbed of the role of good provider, he experiences a sense of emasculation because of the close emotional link between being a good provider and the social definition of masculinity which he has internalized.

It may be that a work bargain which calls for a man to endure countless frustrations in the workplace in order to carry out his role as provider for his family is obsolete and should be done away with. Perhaps the bargain is a lousy one. But it would be folly not to recognize that it *is* the prevailing arrangement and it binds the social structure together in important respects. If it threatens to break down, we would be wise to acquire a sound understanding of how to replace it. Unfortunately, one unanticipated and unwanted byproduct of the women's movement may be to intensify men's disaffection with their work. The women's movement with its emphasis on women becoming more economically assertive and independent puts at risk a fragile psychosocial balance which has supported men's job satisfaction for many years.

Summary

To sum up: The present impact of the five cultural trends we have been examining is not evenly distributed. The three groups most directly affected are the college-educated; the young people who lack a college education; and women. For the majority of our college-educated youth, and a growing majority at that, the future effects of these trends seem likely to strengthen the social order. As we have seen, there is a good fit between what these young people want and what the occupational structure of the country requires and is prepared to give in return. For noncollege youth, however, the future is fraught with instability. The work motivations of these young people are being undercut by a myriad of cultural and economic changes. Unless the large employing institutions of the country grasp what is happening and respond intelligently, the negative impact on the economy and on our future social stability may be quite uncomfortable.

The new cultural values are drawing women into the work force in unprecedented numbers and many of them bring a serious career orientation with them. This tendency is, perhaps, the most dramatic cultural trend in the country today. One unanticipated side effect of women's success in the workplace may be to threaten an old social accommodation among men. This, like many other traditions, has some repugnant features but also serves a complex social need that will not be easy to replace if the old values disappear.

Perhaps the best way to summarize these various trends and countertrends is to forecast what changes are likely to occur in the work ethic as defined at the beginning of the chapter. Four principal themes were associated with the work ethic as of the mid 1960s. One is the link between work and psychological independence, especially between *paid* work and autonomy. This link is likely to grow even stronger in the future. In the past, it has been tied mainly to the male adult. In the future, it will be developed increasingly as an entitlement, a social right, appropriate to women as well as men, and to youth as well as the middle-aged.

A second theme, long associated with the work ethic, that of the good provider, will probably change in the future. The change may be slow since there is deep resistance to the idea that traditional sex-linked roles should be abandoned totally. Though gradual, this shift is already in motion: sex-linked roles in marriage are becoming far more flexible, especially among our college-educated young people.

The idea that all jobs possess an inherent dignity, however menial, as long as the work is "honest work" is the third theme. Here, I suspect, we will see rapid change in the future as the psychological satisfactions demanded from work increase in intensity. For better or worse, dignity will adhere to work that the individual can define to himself as "meaningful." Since the definition of meaningfulness is largely subjective, there is no necessary relationship between low status jobs and lack of dignity. The Harvard graduate who chooses to become a farmer or carpenter or forest ranger is still a rarity. But as rigid status stratifications lose some of their iron grip on the society, and as the vagaries of individual self-fulfillment find new forms of expression, we may see the occupational structure lose as much of its hierarchical character as has the General Motors line of cars.

The most far-reaching transformations are likely to occur in the fourth theme, the idea that "hard work always pays off." In the past, the payoff for hard work has come in the form of the extrinsic rewards of money and job security. In the future, as new ideas of success take hold, the definition of what success in work means will also change. There will be far more stress on the quality of working life, with the psychological qualification of work being given as much weight as the economic. The incentives to work hard, if they are to prove effective, will have to include a self-fulfillment payoff as well as a monetary one.

The following schematic summarizes the likely impact of present cultural trends on the work ethic:

FUTURE IMPACT OF CULTURAL TRENDS ON THE WORK ETHIC

Work Ethic in 1960s	Changes in Work Ethic in 1970s
Paid work means autonomy.	Meaning will intensify and spread, especially to women.
The working male is the good provider, the real man.	Slow erosion of this meaning with unknown but far-reaching consequences.
All work has inherent dignity.	Only "meaningful" work has inherent dignity.
Hard work always pays off.	Rapid erosion of this meaning, because of the changing nature of the payoff.

Ours has been a society with its nose held close to the grindstone. Even today most people are preoccupied with making a living and little else. Gradually, and with increasing momentum, Americans are growing restless with the day-to-day routines of dull jobs and drab housekeeping. They are beginning to look up from the grindstone.

The workplace has long been dominated by the rule of the carrot and the stick—as if we were a nation of donkeys. But the carrot—the lure of material well-being as defined by money and possessions—is subtly losing its savor. And the stick—once a brutal club labeled "economic insecurity"—has thinned down to a flaccid bundle of twigs.

We do not know what will happen in the workplace of tomorrow under the influence of the new cultural trends. But one thing is sure: it is not likely to resemble the old grindstone so familiar to those of us who grew up stuck to it.

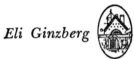

Eli Ginzberg

2

The Changing American Economy and Labor Force

Introduction

This chapter has the task of providing basic data about the employment-related dimensions of the American economy over the past generation or two. The intent is to assist the reader in assessing various theories that are being advanced about the changing role of work in American life. The data, by themselves, will not prove or disprove any theory, but they should provide a framework within which alternative formulations can be tested for congruence with the facts of economic life.

Even prior to looking at the detailed data a cautionary stance is in order when it comes to accepting the hypothesis that the American worker is increasingly discontented with his work. The broad changes in American economic life since the onset of World War II are well known: the hours of work have been reduced; real earnings of workers have advanced significantly; the conditions under which work is carried on have improved; employees have considerably greater job se-

ELI GINZBERG *is A. Barton Hepburn Professor of Economics in the Graduate School of Business and director of the Conservation of Human Resources Project at Columbia University. Professor Ginzberg was earlier director of the National Manpower Council and has been chairman of the National Manpower Advisory Commission since 1962. A frequent consultant to government, he has written dozens of books and articles on behavioral problems, economics, and human resources.*

curity; discrimination against women and minorities has been reduced; workers are less subject to the arbitrary demands of supervisors; a considerably increased proportion of all workers are now in white-collar occupations.

These trends do not prove that the working population in the United States is not more discontented about work than their fathers or grandfathers, but they do suggest that if the thesis of increasing disenchantment is to be supported one had better look carefully at changes originating outside the workplace—in the background, education, expectations, and values of the present generation of workers, and this we intend to do.

The presentation will proceed as follows: it will start by calling attention to some of the principal transformations in the structure of the American economy in terms of industrial composition, entrepreneurial forms, and occupational distributions. Next, the changing characteristics of the labor force will be assessed. Then, the problems of particular subgroups will be reviewed. The concluding section will call attention to a limited number of trends that are likely to condition the near-term future and suggest what, if any, firm conclusions can be drawn from this factual summary.

The Changing Contours of the American Economy

INDUSTRIAL COMPOSITION

In the half century between the end of World War I (1920) and the beginning of the 1970s, the American economy witnessed an approximate doubling in the number of people who work—from forty to eighty million. But our primary interest is to unravel the principal changes in the structure that governs the work that people do. In 1920 more than one out of every four workers was still in agriculture. By 1970 this was true of approximately one in twenty-five. The declining importance of agriculture as a source of employment is the outstanding change in the American economy over the last half century.

Mining also experienced a significant absolute and relative decline, losing about half of its 1920 work force of about 1.2 million. By the beginning of the 1970s, it accounted for less than 1 percent of total employment. Manufacturing and construction, the other two goods-producing sectors, were of the same relative importance at the beginning and end of the period, with manufacturing accounting for about one in four workers and construction for about one in twenty.

The failure of manufacturing and construction to increase their relative share of employment meant that the sizable reduction in agricultural employment (plus the reduction in mining) was absorbed entirely by the service sector, particularly by trade, personal, professional, and business services, and government. The most telling way to summarize the shift that took place is to note that while in 1920 the goods-producing sector—agriculture, mining, manufacturing, and construction—accounted for about three out of every five workers, in 1970 it accounted for only slightly more than one out of three.

Hidden in this sectorial shift from agriculture to the service sector was the escape of a large part of the black population from the South to the urban metropolises—notably those of the North and West—and the relocation of many poor white families in labor market areas with improved opportunities for employment and income.

ENTREPRENEURIAL AND ORGANIZATIONAL STRUCTURES

A second significant change characteristic of the American economy during the first half of the century relates to the entrepreneurial and organizational structures within which work is carried on. If the economy is subdivided into three principal entrepreneurial sectors—private, nonprofit, and government—the present unequivocal finding is the marked shrinkage in the role of the private sector.

Using 1929 and 1960 as our beginning and end points, my colleagues and I estimated in *The Pluralistic Economy* (1965) that during these three decades private sector employment had declined from a high of slightly over 90 percent of the total to less than 80 percent. Correspondingly, government had increased its share from about 7 percent to over 15 percent of total employment, and nonprofit institutions had increased their share from under 3 percent to approximately 5 percent. We carried out calculations for 1963 which showed further declines in the private sector and further increases for the not-for-profit sector (government and nonprofit combined). Professor Hiestand replicated these calculations in the latter 1960s, after the book had been published, and found a continuing upward drift in the employment role of the not-for-profit sector.

The foregoing relates to direct employment. If the analysis is broadened to include the role of government in generating employment among private contractors from whom it buys, i.e., Lockheed et al., then the shift to the not-for-profit sector is even greater. In 1960 the direct and indirect employment of the not-for-profit sector was not less than one in three, and may have been close to two in five—up from one in seven 30 years earlier.

Hidden beneath this sturdy expansion in employment in the not-for-profit sector are a host of challenges that are only slowly being recognized: the difficulties of wage distribution; the implications of unionization of governmental employees; the instability of jobs and careers built on governmental programs, the financing of which is subject to sudden termination; the challenge of establishing work norms aimed at productivity increases and quality control; and the social and political tensions that arise when the more affluent members of the community balk at higher taxes while the less affluent press for more and better services.

Another dimension of the changes that have been occurring is revealed by trends in ownership structure, that is, differences between proprietorships and partnerships on the one hand and corporations on the other. In 1945 there were slightly more than 6.7 million proprietorships and partnerships, with about $80 billion receipts and $12 billion profits, and 420,000 corporations, with $255 billion receipts and $21 billion profits. A quarter century later there were about 10.5 million proprietorships and partnerships, with slightly over $400 billion receipts and $44 billion profits, and about 1.7 million corporations, with about $1.7 trillion receipts and $81 billion profits.

The data emphasize that despite the rapid decline in farms, proprietorship remains an important type of enterprise structure, which enjoyed a fivefold increase in receipts and close to a fourfold increase in profits over the 25-year period.

More detailed data reveal that while corporations currently dominate in manufacturing, mining, transportation and communications, finance and insurance, and wholesale trade, proprietorships are key in agriculture and continue to play an important role in construction, retail trade, and services even though corporations account for the largest part of the total receipts in these sectors.

The latest available figures (1969) show that just over 1 percent of all active corporations account for over 56 percent of total corporate receipts. In manufacturing, the largest two hundred companies have increased their share of total value added in the first two decades after World War II from 30 to 42 percent, that is by two-fifths. Since our primary concern is with employment, it should be noted that in 1971 in manufacturing the five hundred largest concerns employed 14.3 million workers out of a total of 18.6 million—or more than three out of four. In retailing, the 50 largest organizations employed about 2.4 million out of a total of 11.3 million—or slightly over one out of five.

Several points can be deduced from the foregoing data. Despite the substantial shrinkage in the number of persons who make their livelihood in agriculture, individual proprietorships and partnerships have increased substantially in other sectors since the onset of World War

II. At the same time one must recognize that the large corporation has come to dominate in manufacturing and that it has made a significant impact in what has historically been a small enterprise arena, namely retailing. It also looms large in service sectors that are capital intensive, such as transportation and utilities. These data do not confirm the widespread impression that all or most Americans work for large corporate enterprises. Many do, but many others do not.

OCCUPATIONAL DISTRIBUTION

We now come to the changes in the occupational distribution that are linked to the earlier discussion of sectorial, entrepreneurial, and organizational structures but which warrant closer consideration. Initially we will follow a fourfold classification system—white-collar, blue-collar, service, and farm workers; then, after reviewing the broad trends, we will look at some selective details. Using 1920 and 1970 as limits, we find that the white-collar group increased from one in four to one in two. Blue-collar workers declined slightly from 40 to 36 percent. Service workers increased substantially from slightly under 8 to about 13 percent. And, as suggested earlier, farm workers suffered a precipitous drop—from about 27 to 3 percent.

The foregoing categories are gross; hence we must look at the principal subgroupings. In the case of white-collar workers, the following occupational groups are distinguished: professional and technical, managers and administrators, sales workers, and clerical. Blue-collar workers include craftsmen and kindred workers, operatives, nonfarm laborers; service workers include those in private households and others; and the farm workers include farmers, farm managers, farm laborers, and farm foremen.

Between 1930 and 1970 total employment increased from just under fifty million to over seventy-five million or approximately by half. During this period, among white-collar workers, the professional and technical group grew most rapidly (by about three and one-half times); followed closely by clerical (three times); managers and administrators (two times); and, finally, sales workers who experienced the slowest gain—just slightly more than employment as a whole.

Among blue-collar workers the trends were more diverse. Craftsmen and operatives increased at a rate about half again as fast as employment as a whole while nonfarm laborers actually declined by over one-third.

The same mixed pattern is found among service workers. Those in private households declined by about 45 percent while other service workers more than doubled.

In the case of farm workers the decline was precipitous—about 75 percent—and was shared approximately equally by both farmers and farm laborers.

So far the occupational data point to the following: rapidly expanding opportunities for professional and technical workers as well as for managers, clerical workers, and service workers outside of households; marked declines among nonfarm laborers, service workers in private households, and among farmers and farm laborers; above-average increases among craftsmen and operatives.

It may prove illuminating to go down one additional level to catch some of the more extreme changes during this 40-year span (1930–1970). Among professional and technical workers, engineers increased from about 200,000 to 1.2 million; college teachers from 60,000 to 490,000; accountants from under 200,000 to over 700,000; social workers from 30,000 to 215,000—and the 1970 census reported over one-third of a million computer specialists. The number of clergymen, lawyers, physicians—the classic professions—had a rate of increase that more closely paralleled the labor force as a whole rather than the much faster growth of the professional group.

Among clerical workers the number of secretaries, stenographers, and typists almost quadrupled from about one to four million. A very rapid increase also took place among office machine operators, who increased in number under 40,000 to over 550,000.

Within the blue-collar group there was a threefold increase in mechanics and repairmen—from less than one million to almost three million; a similar large increase in foremen—from half a million to a million and a half; but only a modest increase in construction craftsmen, with actual declines in the number of carpenters and painters. Among operatives, the most striking advance was in welders—from under fifty thousand to over half a million.

Among service workers there was more than a fivefold increase in paramedics and more than a threefold increase in food service and cleaning service workers, who together numbered about five million in 1970.

CONCLUSIONS

The present challenge is to determine whether these more detailed figures can be summed up in a few broad generalizations. The first finding points to the influence of technology in creating new occupations such as computer specialists, office machine operators, TV and airplane mechanics, welders. Secondly, the economy absorbed a much larger number of educated persons, including large numbers of college teachers, engineers, accountants, social workers. Thirdly, very large increases occurred among secretaries and typists, workers in commercial services, and hospital workers, reflecting the ever larger flow of paper work, the transfer of services from home to the market, and the growth of the medical care industry.

The foregoing data point to two general conclusions. First, the last half century has seen the American economy undergo large-scale changes in industrial structure, organizational forms, and occupational distribution. Secondly, because of the many different changes that took place, it is exceedingly difficult to summarize the transformations in the labor force and even more difficult to assess their significance from the vantage of workers' satisfaction with their jobs.

Exercising constraint, the following four generalizations can be ventured as to major alterations in the last half century with respect to the occupational distribution of the labor force:

—A striking reduction in the proportion of the labor force engaged in agriculture.
—A sharp decline in the proportion engaged in nonfarm laboring jobs.
—Sharp relative and absolute increases in the numbers employed as professionals and clerical workers.
—More modest increases in the proportions employed as operatives and service workers.

To round out the review of the materials previously presented one must take account also of the following associated changes that occurred in sectorial distribution and organizational forms, both of which operate as parameters of the employment situation:

—The major shift of the economy from goods to service production.
—The declining importance of manufacturing as a source of employment.
—The rapid rise of government as a direct employer of labor, to which must be added its role as indirect employer via its purchases of goods and services.
—The growing importance of the large corporation, particularly in manufacturing, transportation and utilities, and in a sector of trade.
—The continuance of proprietorship as a significant form of business enterprise in agriculture, construction, trade, and services.

No serious effort to understand the changing role of work in American life can fail to deal with the foregoing transformations; but at the same time a cautious investigator must recognize the need to proceed slowly, first because of the range and diversity of the changes that have occurred and, even more important, because the changes per se can be used to support a great number of different inferences. For instance, is the shift out of agriculture to be read as a significant diminution of opportunities for people to be their own boss in the face of the continuing high level of proprietorship in other sectors? Is the rapid growth of professional employment to be interpreted as providing expanded opportunities for many to shape and direct their own work when we know that most engineers and many accountants, among other professionals, are tightly controlled in the nature and place of their work? Does it make sense to talk about the decline in the proportion of blue-collar workers when a closer look reveals that nonfarm laborers—the source of the decline—are matched by an increase in service workers who do much the same type of work? Would it not be better therefore to treat blue-collar and service workers as a single group and to recognize that its relative size has not changed over the period?

Clearly, caution in drawing inferences from these gross data is in order. But there is further reason to avoid broad generalizations. How workers view their work depends not only upon their jobs but also upon what they bring to their jobs—their background, education, expectations, values—in short, what they are looking for in work and what they find. Hence we must look more closely at changes within the working population.

The Changing Characteristics of the Labor Force

1920

If the American economy has undergone a great many changes since the end of World War I, the same is true of the American worker. Here are some of the gross differences between the typical wage earner in 1920 and 1970. To begin with, in 1920 the worker was more likely to have been born abroad or, if born in the United States, to have been of foreign or at least mixed parentage. If he or his parents had come from abroad it is likely that he grew up having impressed upon him the good fortune of being in the United States where even under adverse conditions the prospects for a poor man were better than in the often less developed and more class structured society of the Old World. Even men who had the least desirable jobs, who earned barely enough to keep their family in food, who lived in slum areas, many of whom had no knowledge of English, recognized that they were better off than if they had remained in Greece, Sicily, or Poland where life was often insupportable.

Many native-born workers of native stock were themselves brought up on a farm or were but one generation removed and often knew first hand or by indirection what it was to struggle with the vagaries of nature and the fluctuations of the market. Even if industrial employment and city living left much to be desired, it was many times thought to be better than life on the farm.

The typical worker of the 1920s had finished elementary school and presumably had attended high school for a year or so before starting to work. While there were a limited number of professional and managerial occupations that required an extended period of formal education, most jobs made physical rather than intellectual demands on the incumbents. Even a craftsman could develop a high level of skill on a low-level educational foundation.

In 1920 many middle-aged workers had personal recollections of the deep depression of the 1890s that had caused a great deal of economic and social distress. Younger workers had had personal experiences with the adverse conditions that led to widespread unemployment in 1907 and again in the years immediately preceding the outbreak of World War I.

The threat or reality of unemployment was embedded in the experiences and expectations of the American worker. In fact, 1920 saw the end of the war and post-war boom. The collapse of the economy led to widespread unemployment of such severity that the federal government initiated a study of the problem.

The early decades of this century saw most black persons locked into Southern agriculture where they operated small farms as tenants or share-croppers, with many black women supplementing their families' marginal income by domestic work. White women worked, if at all, between the time they left school until marriage or the birth of their first child. In urban communities they provided much of the labor force for meeting the rapidly expanding demands for office, retail, and domestic and commercial service workers. At the professional level, women were a key source for elementary school teachers, but here, too, they tended to leave the job market once they married.

These then were some of the dominant characteristics of American workers at the end of World War I:

—A high proportion of all industrial workers were of recent foreign extraction or had recently migrated from a rural area.

—Most men started work after eight or nine years of schooling, which was adequate for coping with most jobs.

—On the basis of their own experiences and that of their fathers, workers recognized that the economy periodically went into a tailspin during which many lost both jobs and savings.

—Blacks with few exceptions worked only in Southern agriculture.

Only a minority of all women—for the most part from lower-income families—worked, and then only between the time of leaving school and starting their own families.

1970

Against this background, we must now look more closely at the characteristics of the contemporary labor force. As to origin, we know that while some workers were born abroad and others are of foreign parentage, a higher proportion of the total are of native stock. In fact, with the exception of a relatively few urban centers, such as New York, Chicago, and Los Angeles with their large foreign-speaking populations, the typical worker today is not only native born, but is likely to be at least a third generation American.

Among the urban white working population, rural ties are more distant than was the case in 1920. While one can find recent immigrants from rural areas in all large cities, the proportion is much smaller than at the end of World War I.

The educational preparation of the American worker has undergone a major transformation over the past half century, as evidenced by the following data. In 1920 about one in six of the relevant age group graduated from high school. In 1970 the figure was just a shade under four out of five.

In 1920 approximately one out of six high school graduates went on to obtain a college or first professional degree. A half century later the proportion was approaching one out of three.

If the focus is narrowed to the 30 years between 1940 and 1970 this is what the data reveal: In the former year the median years of schooling completed by the entire population 25 years and over was 8.6, just one semester beyond graduation from elementary school. By 1970, the median had increased by about half and was at 12.2, which meant that the average citizen had completed high school and gone just a little beyond.

If attention is directed to the age group 25–29 years—the group that has recently completed its formal education—one finds that at the outbreak of World War II 38 percent had graduated from high school and under 6 percent had a college degree. The comparable figures for 1971 are 77 percent and 17 percent, a doubling in the proportion of high school graduates and about a threefold increase in college graduates.

There is no need to belabor the fact that the past half century has witnessed a radical change in the educational attainment of American workers. Instead of discontinuing formal education after elementary school, the predominant number of young people now joining the labor force have at least acquired a high school diploma, and about half of all high school graduates are going on with post-secondary education with more than one out of five obtaining at least a college degree.

To these differences in family background and education must be added still another difference between the American worker in 1920 and 1970. This can best be subsumed under the heading of expectations about the economy and, more particularly, about employment. The point was made earlier that periodic depressions with attendant large-scale unemployment were part of the experience and expectations of American workers prior to World War II. But in the 33 years from 1940 to 1973 the American economy has been lucky enough to avoid a serious depression—even though it has not been able to free itself from recessions that soften the market for employment while not usually resulting in sharp reductions in disposable income because of multiple transfer payments.

Today, two out of every three workers is under 44 years of age, and the majority of these were born after the onset of World War II. Rough calculations suggest that not more than one out of ten workers currently in the labor force actually held a job or looked for one during the 1930–33 debacle. In short, first-hand experience with the job market in a severe depression has now almost faded from the consciousness of American workers.

Today's workers, if not personally or socially handicapped, assume that they can find a job. They assume that at worst they may be out of work for a relatively short period should their employer run into bad times resulting from a general recession or more specific dislocations. The unemployment rate for white male heads of households has in recent years not exceeded 3 percent and reached that figure only once in 1971. In the late 1960s it moved in the range of 1.4 to 1.7 percent.

This discussion of the changing characteristics of the work force can be summarized thus:

—Most workers are native born, and most are at least third-generation Americans.
—The educational level of young people entering the labor force has increased substantially. Most young workers have at least a high school diploma and about one in six is a college graduate.
—Most workers have no direct experience with large-scale unemployment and assume that they will always be able to find a job.

Special Groups: Blacks, Women, and Youth

The past half century has seen major changes in the role of women and blacks in the world of work, changes that warrant special attention. In the early decades of this century an analysis of the labor force could proceed in terms of white males unless the employment problems of Southern agriculture or the expanding needs for office, sales, and service workers were the focus, at which point one had to consider blacks and women. In the post-World War II era no such concentration on white male workers is possible, for women have come to account for about 40 percent of the civilian labor force, and blacks are no longer concentrated in Southern agriculture—though they remain disproportionately concentrated among blue-collar and service workers. In addition, in recent decades less educated and otherwise handicapped youth have encountered increasing difficulties as they seek to make the transition from school to work. Even an abbreviated comment on the changing role of work in American life must address what is happening to these three groups not only because of their increased importance in the labor force but also because of changes in the political and social climate which have belatedly led the American public to recognize the pervasive discrimination these groups encounter both in their preparation for work and in the labor market.

BLACKS

To look at the blacks first. Several facts stand out. The post-World War II period has seen a marked absolute and relative improvement in the employment, income, and education of blacks relative to whites. At the same time, the most recent data reveal the presence of wide gaps between the average economic position of whites and blacks.

The most striking improvement has occurred in the years of formal schooling. In 1940 the white age-group 25–29 had approximately half again as many years of schooling as did their black counterparts—10.3 years vs. 7 years. By 1970 only a 0.4 year separated the two: the white average was 12.6 years, the black had risen to 12.2. During this 30-year period the white gain amounted to 1.9 years in contrast to 5.2 years for blacks. But even in 1970 wide gaps remained. The proportion of young people graduating from college in 1971 totaled 16.9 percent for whites in contrast to 6.4 for blacks. And the discrepancies are much greater at the doctoral level. To the extent that many of the best jobs in the economy are reserved for those who have completed a long course of general and professional education, the blacks, despite their very considerable gains in recent years, still lag behind the whites and by a considerable distance.

The education a person receives is one determinant of the income he is able to earn. Another determinant is the type of employment he is able to obtain. Blacks have long encountered overt and intensive discrimination in the labor market, not only in the South but throughout the United States. While such discrimination is still present and oppressive, the 1960s witnessed intensified efforts in both the public and private domains to reduce and remove discrimination against blacks, particularly in the area of employment. The extent to which these efforts were successful can be read in the improvements blacks have made in gaining access to higher level occupations, just as the difficulties they continue to face can be deduced from their continual overrepresentation at the lower end of the occupational structure.

In both 1960 and 1970 blacks accounted for 11 percent of all employed persons. During this decade they increased their percentage in the higher ranking occupations as follows: professional and technical, 4 to 7; managers and officials, 3 to 4; clerical, 5 to 8; craftsmen and foremen, 5 to 7. With the exception of managers and officials, the percentage grows more substantial for a ten-year period. But one must quickly note that blacks continue to be seriously underrepresented in each of these groupings while remaining overrepresented at the lower end of the scale. Today blacks still account for 23 percent of all nonfarm laborers, 42 percent of all private household workers, and 19 percent of all other service workers. Only in the case of farm workers have they drawn equal, today accounting for only 11 percent of the much diminished farm labor force.

There are other distressing aspects to the black employment experience. For instance, white males in the prime working ages have a participation rate of between 94 and 97 percent while the black male rate is between 86 and 93. As far as the unemployment rate is concerned, the black rate has been roughly double that of whites throughout the past decade—and this holds true for both men and women.

The single most dramatic index of racial discrimination has been the median income of black families as a percentage of that of white families. In 1950 the family income of Negro and other races was 54 percent of white family income. In 1964, the year when the comprehensive Civil Rights Act was passed, the ratio stood at 56 percent. By 1970 it had risen to 63 percent. It should be added that the national average hides two important facts. First, it obscures the more pronounced extent of the gap in the South compared with other parts of the country where the percentage varies from 71 in the Northeast to 77 in the West. Secondly, it is not sensitive to the experience of the younger age groups who have benefited most from improved educational advantages and lessened discrimination. In 1969, in the North and West in husband-wife families with the head under 35, the black ratio stood at 91, and where both husband and wife worked it was 99.

The significant improvement in the condition of black workers in the 1960s resulted from the intervention of a series of forces including the largest sustained boom in the history of the American economy, a widespread public concern to reduce and remove long-established discriminatory practices, the more favorable geographic distribution of the black population, and the absence of any competing labor source. But the gains that have been made should not be permitted to obscure the serious disadvantages that continue to afflict most blacks because of their lower level of family income, the small proportion going on to higher education, and the continuing discrimination that pervades so many sectors of American life and that places particular hardships in the path of black men and women who seek to improve their position.

WOMEN

The discrimination that confronts women in their preparation for work and in their labor market experiences both parallels and differs from that of blacks. As far as education is concerned, gaps between females and males do not exist at the high school level where, until recently, a higher proportion of women than men received their diploma; the gap at the end of college can be judged by the fact that 7 percent of all males fourteen years of age and over have completed four years of college compared with 5.6 percent of women or a difference of 20 percent. It is only at the masters and doctors level that males have a distinct advantage: 5.4 percent compared with 2.2 percent.

In the case of the younger adult groups, that is, those between 20 and 35, men still have the lead over women in terms of the percentage earning a college degree, and the same is true for those with advanced degrees even though the percentage base for each is about double that shown above for the entire population.

These educational differences do little to explain the gross differences between the occupational distribution of men and women. The most conspicuous of these include the threefold greater percentage of men than women who work as managers and administrators (15 versus 5.5 percent); the five-time greater representation of women in clerical work (32 versus 6.4 percent); the seventeen-time greater representation of men among craftsmen and kindred workers (32.3 versus 1.4 percent); and the three-time greater concentration of women in services (21.3 versus 7 percent). In terms of gross occupational categories the sexes parallel each other only with respect to the proportions employed as professional or sales workers and as operatives—but it must be emphasized that these parallels relate only to gross classifications. For instance, the largest number of women professionals are school teachers and nurses (most of the latter of whom do not have a college degree) while engineers represent the largest male professional group, and males predominate among the highest-earning professionals in medicine and law. In sales, males have almost a monopoly in the lucrative industrial equipment area and high-ticket retail items while women hold the lower paying positions. And there are twice as many women operatives in nondurable manufacturing where pay scales are lower than in durable manufacturing where pay scales are considerably higher.

Probably the most telling difference in the occupational distribution of men and women is the long-term concentration of the latter within a relatively few fields. About one out of every four women is employed as a secretary, retail sales clerk, bookkeeper, elementary school teacher, or household worker. Half of all women workers are found within 21 occupations while men are much more broadly distributed over 65 occupations. Until the recent legislative push to attack discrimination against women in the labor market, the American economy was bifurcated into male and female jobs, in much the same way that it was bifurcated into jobs for whites and different jobs for blacks.

A first indication of the selective changes brought about by the combined public-private efforts to reduce and eliminate discrimination against women in the world of education and work can be found in the 1972 enrollment figures for the entering classes in medical and law schools. In the mid-sixties, women accounted for about 10 percent of those accepted by medical schools and 3 percent by law schools; in 1972 the medical school figure stood at 20 percent and the law school figure at 12 percent.

The concentration of women in low-paying occupations together with the fact that only one-third of them work full-time, full-year (compared with three-fifths of all men) helps to explain why in 1971 men earned on the average just under $7,000 while women earned a shade under $2,500. However, if one controls for differences in time worked by limiting the comparison to those who worked full-time, full-year, the findings are striking: men earned over $9,600, women

$5,700—or less than three-fifths as much as men. Equally striking is the fact that of all persons with money income in 1971, 30 percent of the men earned $10,000 or more compared with less than 4 percent of the women. A still more revealing comparison is that of the earnings of men and women who worked year-round, full-time by educational level. In the case of high school graduates the figures were $10,700 for men, $6,000 for women; for college graduates, $15,600 for men and $8,700 for women; for those with five or more years of college, $18,000 for men and $10,800 for women.

While as individuals women clearly suffer serious disadvantages in the labor market, it must be emphasized that their social and economic status is often determined by the occupations and earnings of their husbands. Moreover, white women, through their fathers, brothers, and husbands, have a way of learning about the levers of power and how they can be manipulated, a form of knowledge that remains beyond the ken of most members of minority groups who are definitely on the outside of the society and economy. One must be careful therefore not to equate racial and sex discrimination. While they have much in common, they also differ in many essentials.

YOUTH

The third special employment problem that warrants attention is the predicament of youth—particularly youth with handicaps growing out of their racial or ethnic background, sex, education, or criminal record, which confront them with serious problems as they seek to establish themselves in the world of work.

The initial source of the difficulty is embedded in the demographic turnabout that occurred after World War II. During most of the 1930s the birth rate had dropped to about 18/19 per 1000, and in 1945 it stood at 20.5. By the end of the 1940s and until late in the 1950s it hovered between 24/25 per 1000 reaching a peak of 25.2 in 1957. What these figures mean is that throughout the early post-World War II period the birth rate was over a third higher than it had been in the prewar decade. This rise in the birth rate led to a substantial increase in the proportion of families with three and four children and a corresponding decline of those with no children or only one child.

The high birth rates of the late 1940s and 1950s were reflected in the very large increases in the teenage population in the 1960s. The sixteen-to-nineteen-year-old group increased by 46 percent within a single decade. While these demographic factors had multiple effects, including in particular effects upon the expansion of secondary and higher education, military manpower policy, the crime rate, drug addiction, etc., our concern is primarily with its employment-related dimensions. The critical finding is that over the two decades 1952–72 there was a striking transformation in the shape of the labor force, reflecting the relative increases of men, women, and teenagers. The number of men increased by only 20 percent; the number of women increased by about 75 percent; and the number of teenagers increased by over 100 percent!

From the beginning of the 1960s to 1972 the postwar baby crop was also adding rapidly to the numbers of workers in the 20-to-24-year age bracket. The increase for males was from about 4.1 to 6.7 million and for females from 2.6 to 5.3 million. Even though the American economy enjoyed a long period of rapid expansion in the 1960s, reinforced by additional needs for manpower by the armed forces, the demographic explosion among teenagers and young people in their early twenties required a high level of new job creation if all who wanted to work were to find employment.

While many young people succeeded in finding the full- or part-time employment they wanted and needed, a significant number failed to make a successful transition from school to work. The story can be read in rising unemployment rates and in the increasing spread between the unemployment rates of youth (16–24) and those of the mature adult labor force. For the late 1960s–early 1970s, a rough rule of thumb is to take the national unemployment rate and double it for youth, and double it again for minority youth. That means that with a national unemployment rate of 5.5 percent, the youth rate will be 11 percent and the rate for minorities over 20 percent. Teenagers among minorities have unemployment rates in the 25-to-35-percent range for males and close to 40 percent for females. It should be added that these rates are conservative, for many young people who have dropped out of school are not counted as unemployed because they are not actively looking for work.

The unemployment rate for youths tends to be somewhat higher than the average in all industrial countries because of the job changes young people make as they try to find a congenial or at least an acceptable job. However, the data suggest that the demographic explosion together with special institutional constraints have resulted in disproportionately high youth unemployment rates for the United States. The 1960s saw a rapid shift to service occupations, which meant that many poorly educated youngsters had trouble securing clerical or other types of office employment. As long as employers were able to meet their expanding needs with adult women they were loath to hire young people in the belief that they were unreliable and careless.

Protective legislation, long on the books, made it difficult for some employers to hire youth even if they wished to. Rising racial consciousness made some better educated minority youth balk at accepting dead-end jobs, such as in domestic service or unskilled manual work. Employer hiring practices that weeded out young people who had not acquired a high school diploma or who had a police record had a particularly adverse effect on the employability of many minority youth from low-income homes. And some preferred to secure income from illicit and illegal activities rather than accept a low paying job that had no future. There are some economists who believe that the high minimum wage was a further obstacle to employers' hiring young people, although the evidence is far from conclusive and the policy implications in favor of a substantial differential are far from obvious.

The years ahead promise some relief as the demographic bulge diminishes. Unfortunately the increase of teenagers among minorities will be about as large in the 1970s as in the 1960s—44 versus 49 percent. The real relief is among the white teenage population where the rates of increase will decline from 46 percent to 9 percent. Even with an easing of the pressure from the side of numbers, the transition of young people from school to work will remain a difficult problem, particularly for those who enter the job market with assorted disabilities.

The foregoing summary consideration of the work and work-related problems of blacks, women, and youth point up the following:

—Discrimination continues to limit seriously the opportunities open to blacks and women in their preparation for and participation in work. This is reflected in their continued concentration in less desirable and lower paying jobs.
—The decade of the 1960s, particularly after 1964, saw substantial gains by blacks and latterly by women, but the gap between these groups and white males remains wide and is not likely to be substantially narrowed, much less closed, quickly.
—Many youth are experiencing major difficulties in getting a toe-hold in the world of work, among other reasons because of the recent rapid increase in their numbers. While the demographic outlook has turned more favorable, many minority youth, especially those who fail to acquire a high school diploma or who lack the skills required for white-collar work will continue to face special difficulties in finding a satisfactory job that holds promise of future advancement.

In Search of Perspective

The caveat put forward early in this essay concerning the great difficulties of drawing inferences about work satisfaction from data about transformations in the American economy and its occupational structure should now be self-evident. Yet inferences that lead to greater understanding are the touchstone of social science research. In the face of formidable difficulties, let us look backward to see whether a limited number of propositions can be ventured, and likewise let us look ahead to see whether any tentative forecasts can be made on the basis of the review of recent developments.

The advantage of looking backward over a half century, or even over 25 years, is the contribution that time makes to perspective. It is easier to distinguish the important developments and changes that have taken place. We will call attention to five that appear to characterize the transformations of the American labor force.

The period since World War II has seen an ever larger proportion of married women enter the labor force to work full- or part-time. One is forced to infer from this development that when faced with the opportunity to work and earn money income a rapidly growing proportion of adult women decided that this was a preferred alternative to continuing to spend their time at home and in voluntary activities. Admittedly many women who work have no option because they are heads of households, responsible for supporting themselves and their dependents. It is also true that many others who work do so out of an urgent need of the family for additional income. Still, the basic proposition holds: more and more married women who work do so because they prefer to have a job and pursue a career. On balance, work out of the home has a powerful attraction for them.

A second major trend characteristic of the post-World War II era is the substantial increase in the years of schooling of the new entrants into the labor force and the corresponding shift in their industry and occupational attachment. A greatly increased proportion, as compared with earlier periods, are employed in the service sector and are white-collar workers. Despite the much larger number who have entered the labor force as high school or college graduates, their wages and salaries have not suffered compression. The returns on education remained high throughout the period although a minority of the better educated were unsuccessful in getting or holding jobs commensurate with their education. While there are many white-collar jobs that are prestigious more in name than in fact, the rapid expansion in professional and managerial employment did provide attractive work and working environments for many new entrants. The world of the office is less demanding and less enervating for most people than the world of the factory, the mine, or the farm. In short, the last quarter century saw a major shift of the economy away from work where men were controlled directly by the machine.

Work always represents an admixture of pluses and minuses in the sense that those who enter an employment relation give up their time, accept direction and supervision in the use of their energies, submit themselves to rules and discipline, and in return receive wages, benefits, opportunities for advancement as well as concomitant satisfactions embedded in their work and social relations. The post-World War II period was conspicious in that there was relatively little pressure by those who worked to reduce their conventional hours of work per day or per week. In fact, overtime, averaging more than 10 percent of standard hours, became the pattern. Such reduction in working time that did occur was reflected in more paid holidays and longer vacations, attesting to a desire of the working population for blocks of time off in which to enjoy their higher real earnings. The absence of broad pressure to reduce the workday and workweek must be interpreted as evidence that most employees did not find their work life particularly oppressive. Otherwise they would have traded additional income for additional time.

Workers organize themselves into trade unions in order to improve their bargaining position vis-a-vis the employer, not solely with an aim of raising their wages and improving their fringe benefits but also in order to broaden their control over their immediate working environment. The post-World War II period saw a slow growth in organized labor, so slow in fact that even after allowance is made for other factors, such as steadfast employer opposition, a less friendly governmental environment, and weakness at the top of the trade union movement, one is forced to conclude that the great mass of unorganized workers were not ready to pay the costs of organizing. Apparently they did not feel that their present conditions were so hard or that the union could bring them so many new benefits as to justify the turmoil of organizing.

Finally, it would be a serious error to read the evidence that all was right in the world of work, or even that conditions were improving so rapidly that an era of contentment was about to be ushered in. Nothing could be further from the truth. The sources of discontent were legion. Workers and employers in every sector of the economy were in conflict, often latent, periodically overt, about wages, conditions of work, productivity, and other critical dimensions of employment relation. Just as quickly as old sources of difficulty were ironed out new ones emerged, growing out of changes in the economy, the society, and the workers themselves. This dynamism of discontent is embedded in work relations in a modern democratic society.

Against this background of recent changes in the world of work, is it possible to identify several areas where the dynamism of discontent is likely to manifest itself in the years ahead? The following appear to be high on the agenda.

It is by no means clear that the past advantages young people secured by entering the labor force with extended education which led most to better jobs will continue. A 1973 report by the Carnegie Commission on Higher Education suggested that over one-quarter of prospective college graduates in the 1970s will probably have to settle for jobs that were formerly held by nongraduates. And wage compression is a distinct possibility, which points probably to rising orders of discontent among the better educated managerial work group.

The experiments with flexible working hours introduced late in the 1960s, which are still expanding, the rising union objection to compulsory overtime, the growth of forced and optional early retirement, all suggest that we may be entering a new era in regard to trade-offs between work and leisure and between opportunities for older and younger workers. It would be strange indeed if increasing family income did not lead sooner or later to a reconsideration of the hours question. The preferences of workers are likely to run afoul of both technological and cost considerations and result in compromised solutions—but not until both parties have learned to appreciate the priority needs and preferences of the other.

The pervasive troubles all modern economies face in reconciling high level employment with reasonable price stability underscore the necessity for modifications in collective bargaining and in the market mechanisms as they influence price and dividend determinations. Workers will not forego their search for equity, but the domain of the struggle has begun to shift into a new arena where government plays a larger role. No one can see clearly the new structures that must be put into place or what will be required to insure that they become functional, but one can prognosticate that this will be an increasingly important arena for conflict and resolution.

The 1960s saw a major thrust to reduce and remove discrimination, especially against minorities and women in their preparation for and utilization in the world of work. The several levels of government have pursued affirmative action programs, quotas, goals, compensatory actions to expand opportunities for groups previously barred outright or severely handicapped in their efforts to gain access to desirable jobs and careers. In the last few years the initial emphasis on assisting black men to improve their employability has been broadened to include women, the Spanish-speaking, and large numbers of smaller groups such as American Indians. While governmental efforts have unquestionably helped to reduce discrimination in the labor market, the rate of progress has been uneven, slowed in many cases by the small number of qualified minority members in the hiring pool, the recalcitrance of various trade union groups on the matter of opening membership to outsiders, the small number of job openings, as in the academic world, and above all, the growing concern that the rights of the majority not be arbitrarily restricted as a result of corrective actions aimed at helping minorities.

These and other difficulties notwithstanding, it is reasonable to expect the issue of discrimination to be at the fore in the years ahead even while there are likely to be continuing conflicts as individuals and groups struggle over the division of employment opportunity.

Finally, the combination of more education, less fear of unemployment, and higher family income is loosening the monolithic relationship that existed for so long between people and work. In an earlier day men had to work in order to eat. That is less true today. At the upper end of the income scale families support their children well into their twenties. At the lower end, many young people also manage to exist without regular jobs. With more and more couples working, one or the other spouse may drop out for a time to return to school, to raise a child, or to pursue an avocational activity. To the extent that people want more degrees of freedom to structure their lives and their time, one must anticipate additional conflicts in the work arena between employees who seek greater options and employers who are locked into production schedules and the market.

At the same time, modern societies can absorb a considerable amount of conflict without being rent asunder. As workers struggle to find a new balance between work and the rest of their life, they modify the existing reality and develop new expectations, thereby setting the stage for further changes.

NOTE: *The author wishes to acknowledge that primary reliance was based on* Statistical Abstract of the United States, 1972. *Use was also made of* Manpower Report of the President, *1973, and several reports developed from the 1970 federal census. The author further makes special acknowledgment to Daniel Bell for "From Goods to Services," chapter 2 of* The Coming of Post-Industrial Society *(New York, Basic Books, 1973); to Sar A. Levitan and Wilbur B. Johnson for "A Summary of Occupational Trends 1900–1970," table 6-2 in their draft manuscript* Work Is Here to Stay, Alas *(Washington, D.C., Center for Manpower Policy Studies); and to Mr. Levitan and Robert Taggart for "The Economics of Youth Unemployment in the United States" (New York, Joint Council on Economic Education, 1973).*

George Strauss

3

Workers:
Attitudes and Adjustments

Recent years have seen much concern with an alleged erosion of the American work ethic. Social critics and representatives of the Establishment alike have warned that discontent is increasing rapidly and that workplace reforms are urgently needed.

Evidence of this rejection of traditional values is cited on all sides. Children brought up in the ghetto find it hard to adjust to the discipline of a regular job. The Lordstown strike—and the high rates of turnover and absenteeism in automobile plants—perhaps indicate profound dissatisfaction with boring, repetitive work, particularly among younger workers. According to an American Management Association study, 52 percent of the managers surveyed "found their work, at best, unsatisfactory." Half of all workers, ranging up to 61 percent of professionals and managers, say they could accomplish more work if they tried. And a significant and highly vocal group of college students (concentrated among those with affluent parents) have been turned off by the prospects of spending a lifetime working for large corporations, preferring to do their own thing in communes, making craft objects, or serving meaningful social causes.

GEORGE STRAUSS *is professor at the School of Business Administration and acting director of the Institute of Industrial Relations of the University of California. He has been associate dean of the School of Business Administration at Berkeley and also managing editor of the journal,* Industrial Relations. *Chairman of the Personnel Board of the City of Berkeley, he is co-author of three books,* The Local Union, Personnel, *and* Human Behavior in Organizations *as well as author of a considerable number of articles in the fields of labor relations and organizational behavior.*

This widespread unrest has been blamed for a variety of ills, especially declining productivity, the worsening of our balance of trade, and our galloping inflation—as well as political and social phenomena such as opposition to school busing and the heavy blue-collar support for Governor Wallace during the elections of 1968 and 1972. The stultifying nature of work has been held responsible for poor mental and physical health and the promotion of dull, passive forms of recreation. And on the industrial relations front it has been cited as contributing to the defeat of incumbent leaders in union elections, to the trend toward rank-and-file rejection of contracts, and to increased strike-incidence generally.

Among the difficult questions I will discuss in this chapter are the following: How dissatisfied are workers with their jobs? Does dissatisfaction arise chiefly from the repetitive, challengeless nature of work, or are factors such as low pay, inept supervision, and blocked mobility more important? What are the trends for the future? Is dissatisfaction growing? Given the trend of recent public interest, my emphasis will be on repetitive work and the blue-collar workers. However, most of what I say will have a wider application.

Attitudes

THE EXTENT OF DISSATISFACTION

Industrial psychologists have been measuring organizational morale for over 40 years, and from all these studies one finding stands out: regardless of the occupational level examined, only a minority of workers ever report being dissatisfied. Since 1949 the Gallup Poll, for example, has been asking: "On the whole, would you say you are satisfied or dissatisfied with the work you do?" Doubts have been expressed as to the meaningfulness of any attempt to measure job satisfaction by a single question. Nevertheless, the findings of the 1973 poll (despite technical inadequacies) prove very typical of many other studies. These figures are shown on page 75. Note that factors such as age, sex, and education all affect the result, yet even among nonwhites less than one-quarter report being dissatisfied. Somewhat similar evidence comes from the 1968 *Manpower Report of the President,* with percentages of those reporting dissatisfaction with work dropping from 21 percent in 1946–47 to 12–13 percent in 1964–65. Other research of the late sixties and early seventies—including a massive government-financed study conducted by the University of Michigan's Survey Research Center—come to roughly the same conclusions.

	(Percent)		
	Satisfied	Dissatisfied	No opinion
Overall	77	11	13
Sex			
Men	78	12	10
Women	76	10	14
Color			
White	80	10	10
Nonwhite	53	22	25
Education			
College	84	10	6
High school	75	13	12
Grade school	71	9	20
Occupation			
Professional and business	85	10	5
Clerical and sales	81	13	6
Manual workers	80	13	9
Age			
Under 30 years	72	20	8
30–49 years	83	9	8
50 and over	74	7	19

Does this somewhat remarkable convergence of findings suggest that workers are in fact truly satisfied with their work? For reasons I explain later, I think this overstates the case. *Reporting* satisfaction and *being* satisfied may be very different things. Nevertheless, with the possible exception of some black workers, there is little reason to expect an immediate revolt against work.

THE IMPACT OF ROUTINE WORK

Nationwide summaries can easily mask important differences. Despite the data cited above, there is overwhelming evidence that many (*but not all*) workers react negatively to work that is routine and without challenge. A whole series of studies from mass production industry shows, for example, that dissatisfaction appears directly related to short job cycles, lack of autonomy and control over workplace, and jobs which require attention but not challenge. Such factors also relate to absenteeism, turnover, strikes, and even poor mental health.

Similarly, those who work as service engineers in the field are more likely to report that their jobs are "very good" than are engineers who work in laboratories—the differences being attributable to extent of freedom available in the field. And, executives, particularly at the lower levels, express dissatisfaction with their opportunities for autonomy and creativity.

A different kind of evidence is provided by studies which compare mass-production/assembly-line workers with craftsmen (such as printers) and workers in automated process technology (such as in oil refineries). These studies agree that by all indices job satisfaction is considerably higher for craftsmen than for assembly-line workers, with the position of automated workers less clear, but certainly above that of assembly-line workers. Roughly equivalent results have been obtained in studies comparing secretaries (craftsmen), key punch operators (mass production), and computer operators and software personnel (process technology). Those clerical workers whose jobs permit the least autonomy are the ones most alienated from their work.

On the other hand, the need for challenging work must be placed in perspective. The 1969 Survey Research Center study ranked job characteristics as follows, in terms of their correlation with overall job satisfaction:

	Correlation
1. Having a "nurturant" supervisor	.37
2. Receiving adequate help, assistance, etc.	.32
3. Having few "labor standards problems" (such as safety hazards, poor hours, or poor transportation)	.32
4. Fair promotional policies	.31
5. Supervisor not supervising too closely	.30
6. Having a technically competent supervisor	.29
7. Autonomy in matters affecting work	.28
8. A job with "enriching" demands	.26

Note that autonomy and enriching jobs came seventh and eighth. In other words, improving managerial practices may improve job satisfaction as much as changing the nature of the job.

According to the 1973 Gallup Poll, "enjoy my work" came first among reasons why workers were satisfied with their job, with "good pay" coming second. However, "poor wages" ranked first as a reason for dissatisfaction with "boring work" second. Similar findings come from many other studies. Extrinsic factors such as low wages, lack of job security, limited promotional opportunities, and arbitrary management (rather than intrinsic factors, such as challenging work) are frequently listed as the primary causes of job dissatisfaction, alienation from work, as well as personal unhappiness off the job. And there is considerable reason to believe that for a wide range of employees—especially those in lower-income categories—these factors may be of greater importance than having jobs which offer challenge, variety, and autonomy. Certainly union membership demands have been concerned chiefly with obtaining higher pay, shorter hours, voluntary overtime, increased job security, and reducing the power of the foreman. At least during the 1973 negotiations, there was far more reported membership interest in enriching the pocketbook than in enriching the job.

To put it another way: having challenging work certainly does make a difference. But for many workers the question is a secondary one, and there are important individual differences in willingness to adjust to routine work.

LARGE CHANGES IN WORK ATTITUDES?

To what extent has there been a change in work values during the early seventies? Is the picture of general satisfaction rapidly changing?

Certainly there is *some* evidence of rising discontent. However, the trend is far from clear. Most of the discussion has been based on specific incidents which have hit the headlines, and there has been little effort to view the issues in perspective. Hard facts are few, and we lack the long-term studies which would permit us to compare employee attitudes today with those of 20 or 40 years ago.

A few examples may illustrate the difficulty of making judgments on the basis of the limited evidence now available.

—The Lordstown strike made good copy because younger workers were involved, but strikes over production standards are common in the automobile industry, particularly when new processes are being introduced. (A similar strike at Norwood, an older plant, received less attention.) Much of the anecdotal evidence of increased dissatisfaction comes from automobile plants, an untypical example of work life in that in few other activities is the worker's autonomy so severely restricted.

—The rate of increase in productivity declined during the late 1960s, but climbed quite sharply in the early 1970s—however most of these fluctuations can be explained in terms of nonmotivational factors such as rates of plant utilization or unemployment.

—Man days idle (as a percent of working time) due to strikes rose from .11 in 1961 to .37 in 1970, dropped to .14 in 1972 and were running at .09 in the first three months of 1973.

—Quit rates in manufacturing (one form of job rotation) went up from 1.1 in the recession year of 1958 to 2.7 in 1969, but dropped to 1.8 in 1971, went up again to 2.2 in 1972, and generally seem to behave inversely to unemployment.

—Absentee rates in automobile plants went from 2–3 percent in 1965 to

5–6 percent in 1970—and then dropped in 1971. Nationwide absenteeism rose from 2.1 in 1967 to 2.5 in 1970 and then dropped to 2.3 in 1972.

—Recent research suggests that college students, over the last decade, have become less achievement-oriented and more prone to reject authority. On the other hand, student alienation may have passed its peak. At Berkeley —once the pacesetter in student movements—undergraduate enrollment in business courses jumped by 50 percent from 1971 to 1973 and demand for admission to these courses increased more rapidly yet.

—According to studies by the University of Michigan's Survey Research Center there were no significant changes in overall job satisfaction between 1970 and 1973 (although there have been some off-setting gains and losses with respect to specific aspects of employment).

Thus the evidence is fragmentary and confusing. A number of factors are at work, depending on the work group under consideration. Oscar Lewis's "Culture of Poverty" and Charles Reich's *The Greening of America,* for example, both deal with alienation from work, but no one who has read the two pieces can imagine that the same process is involved in the ghetto and on campus.

To summarize, the evidence to date does not support the view that dissatisfaction with work has increased *substantially,* but neither does it prove that workers are truly satisfied. Quite the contrary. Though most employees accept (or become resigned to) their lot, the adjustment process is not always easy. To me, it is far more useful to examine this adjustment process—the question of *how* workers come to terms with their jobs—than to become excessively concerned with short-term indices of morale.

Adjustment

In the pages which follow, I will look first at the adjustment process and then at *long-term* trends which may make this adjustment more difficult. None of the data cited so far—those showing overall satisfaction, those indicating a relative dissatisfaction with routine work, and those demonstrating a relative stability in the satisfaction index—are conclusive. Reality is far more complex than this. My basic hypothesis (still over-simple) is as follows: (1) work is central to the life of most Americans (at least most American males); (2) nevertheless, they differ in their desire to obtain challenge and autonomy at work, depending on their personalities and the subcultures in which they live; (3) if they have to, most people can adjust to nonchallenging work, usually by lowering their expectations, changing their need structure, and by making the most of social opportunities on and off the job; (4) this adjustment process occurs at a psychic cost which for most groups in society today may not be very great; (5) however, in the future this cost may increase. To understand this process, we need to examine some of the larger studies of the role of work.

A CLASH BETWEEN PEOPLE AND ORGANIZATIONS?

What is the role of work in the life of a typical worker? How do people adjust to their jobs? As a first step in examining these inter-related questions, let us look at what might be called the "personality vs. organization hypothesis." This hypothesis, which is implicit in the early work of social scientists such as Chris Argyris, Norman Maier, and Douglas McGregor, suggests an almost inevitable frustration of employees' expectations in their jobs, especially in mass production industry.

Oversimplified the argument runs as follows: workers seek social belonging, independence, and personal growth. In other words, they aspire to ascend what Abraham Maslow has called the "needs-hierarchy ladder," from satisfaction of physical, through safety, social, and ego-istic to self-actualization needs. A critical point is that such satisfactions are desired *on the job*. Organizations, on the other hand, fail to recognize these aspirations and follow instead what McGregor called "Theory X" assumptions that workers dislike work and wish to avoid responsibility. In so doing they structure work in such a fashion that the individual is condemned to isolation, passivity, dependence, sub-mission, and the use of minimal abilities. Consequently employees become alienated from their work.

It is not my purpose to test the validity of this hypothesis here. However, it does suggest some important questions, particularly relat-ing to the role of work in life, and it provides a convenient introduc-tion to the discussion which follows.

The Universality of Self-Actualization—Supporters of the personality vs. organization hypothesis often argue in terms of the Maslow scheme, i.e., as individuals mature they seek increasing opportunities for self-actualization, that is, they seek the freedom to be creative, to develop their skills to the maximum, to exercise autonomy, and the like. The Maslow scheme is highly flattering to professors and managers, two occupations which place great value on self-actualization. Nevertheless, in its oversimplified form, it can be criticized on a number of grounds. For example, the scheme is stated in a non-operational manner which makes it very difficult to prove or disprove (especially since most forms of human behavior satisfy more than one need). Further, there may be substantial differences among people in a relative weight they give to the "basic" (physical, safety, and social) needs as against the "higher" level ones, such as esteem and self-actualization. Maslow himself never claimed that all people would wish to climb his ladder, and certainly not in the same way. In fact, as his later writings make clear, his "mature," "normal" individual is a rather special breed.

The work of David McClelland and his disciples suggests that people vary substantially in the relative importance they attach to various needs and further that there is no necessary ladder, i.e., that people do not inevitably emphasize self-actualization after lesser needs are reasonably well-satisfied. McClelland posits three needs (besides physical needs). As he puts it, they are *need achievement, need affiliation,* and *need power.* Persons high in need achievement react well to challenge; those who are low in this dimension are concerned primarily with playing it safe and avoiding failure. Presumably this latter group (particularly those high on need affiliation) prefers direction to autonomy. One further point: McClelland's research suggests that these needs are rather easily malleable; a relatively short training course can substantially increase need achievement (and also managerial success). If so, perhaps training can also induce high-need affiliation; workers can be trained to prefer challengeless work. Shades of Aldous Huxley's "Brave New World" and the corporate state!

Aside from this probably extreme interpretation of McClelland's work, it does seem reasonably clear that because of personality differences people do vary substantially in their needs for challenge and autonomy. (A study by Victor Vroom, for example, suggests that workers who have a high need for independence and weak authoritarian attitudes are likely to respond to consultation with their supervisors by being more satisfied with their work; those with low needs for independence and strong authoritarian values are less likely to respond in this manner.)

Personality differences, in turn, may be caused by variations in culture and family child-rearing practices (and possibly even genetic factors). A question, to be considered later, is whether child-rearing practices may be changing sufficiently to cause substantial differences in attitudes toward work. Right now let us consider a narrower issue: to what extent do cultural differences affect workers' attitudes toward challenging jobs? Let us examine this question in the context of rural-urban differences.

Rural-Urban Differences—A major corollary of the organization vs. person hypothesis is that there is a positive relationship between job challenge and job satisfaction and that job enlargement is an almost sure-fire way to raise morale. The findings of Arthur Turner and Paul Lawrence's *Industrial Jobs and the Worker* seriously challenged this verity. In a study conducted in eleven firms, these researchers sought to measure the relationship between job satisfaction and complexity of work. To their great surprise they found that small-town workers reacted positively to more complex tasks (as expected) but that urban workers reacted less positively to them. This unanticipated finding was further supported by a series of articles by Charles L. Hulin and Milton Blood reporting on research in a wide variety of communities. Where urban and slum characteristics were high, the correlations between blue-collar satisfaction and job skills were low or negative, the reverse was true in more rural areas, while the nature and location of the community seemed to make no difference for white-collar workers. Finally, a study by Gerald I. Susman suggests that rural workers react to job discretion with greater pride in their job accomplishments, while for urban workers greater discretion is related only to involvement and to time seeming "to drag" less often.

This research may be subject to methodological criticism. But assuming it is valid, there are a number of possible alternate (though partly contradictory) explanations for these unexpected findings:

1. One possibility is that rural and small-town workers have internalized the old-fashioned Protestant, middle-class ethic which glorifies work for its own sake and insists on individual achievement. The city worker belongs to a different culture (or is at least alienated from the traditional culture). Why should the urban blue-collar culture be different?

a. In small towns it is difficult for blue-collar and white-collar values to develop in different directions. The big city permits greater diversity.

b. Rural workers are more likely to be Protestant and urban workers Catholic, thus suggesting that the two religions have different values toward work.

c. Alternatively, it is not a matter of religion, but experience. Urban workers (many of whom are black or ethnics) reject the Protestant ethic because their experience has *not* taught them that hard work pays off. Indeed, rural parents may stress need achievement to their children while the urban child learns need affiliation or need power.

d. Or it may relate to the Maslow hierarchy. J. Richard Hackman and Edward E. Lawler report that urban workers are relatively more concerned with satisfying physical and social (as opposed to egoistic) satisfactions than are their country cousins. The explanation for this is unclear; possibly it relates to the higher cost of living and the greater difficulty in developing meaningful social relationships in the city.

2. Everyone's capacity to cope with uncertainty and change is limited. For urban workers, already living in a turbulent environment, the optimum degree of uncertainty desired *on the job* may be far less than for their rural counterparts.

3. Still another explanation is in terms of "equity theory." Challenging jobs usually require more work, certainly more responsibility, but they command higher status and pay. In rural areas taking on more challenging work may lead to greater *relative* social and economic payoff than it does in the big city, where the highest paid blue-collar worker may still be quite low on the overall social and economic totem pole. The city worker may decide that the reward for taking on more responsibility may not be worth the effort.

4. Finally, work and the job may be much more central to workers' lives in rural areas than it is in big cities where there are a wide variety of other areas upon which life interest may be focused.

This last suggestion raises a much broader question to which we now turn: how central is the job in determining satisfaction with life?

THE JOB AS A PRIMARY SOURCE OF SATISFACTION

Must workers satisfy their higher-order needs on the job, or can they satisfy these after work, with their family, through hobbies and recreation, or in social and community activities (such as unions)? Some argue the central focus of many people's lives is not the job (which is merely a way of "getting a living"), but the home or the community. As Robert Dubin put it in 1959 at the Eleventh Annual Meeting of the Industrial Relations Research Association:

> Work, for probably a majority of workers, and even extending into the ranks of management, may represent an institutional setting that is not the central life interest of the participants. The consequence of this is that while participating in work a general attitude of apathy and indifference prevails. . . . Thus, the industrial worker does not feel imposed upon by the tyranny of organizations, company or union.

How important is work in human life? "Gentlemen" in many societies do not work. Classical Greece devalued work, it was at best *instrumental,* a means to an end. In Communist China, on the other hand, strenuous efforts are being made to make all work *expressive,* a valued end in itself. In our society work is more clearly the central life-interest of artists and professionals than of casual laborers. The college professor's career is both his work and recreation. His self-image is tied up in work; his friends are likely to be college professors—and they talk shop. To an equal or lesser extent many managers, professionals, and even skilled craftsmen behave in the same way. But Harold Wilensky suggests:

> Where the technical and social organization of work offer much freedom— e.g., discretion in methods, pace or schedule, and opportunity for frequent interaction with fellow workers . . . then work attachments will be strong, work integrated with the rest of life, and ties to the community and society solid. Conversely, if the task offers little workplace freedom . . . then work attachments will be weak, work sharply split from leisure and ties to community and society uncertain (*Social Problems,* Summer 1961).

How do workers respond to jobs which provide little opportunity for being expressive? A few seem to have adjusted easily enough to viewing their jobs as purely instrumental. In my own interviewing experience in factories, I often ran across women who repeated variants of, "I like this job because it gets me away from all the kids and pressures at home." A significant number of workers object to job rotation because it disrupts their routine and prevents them from day-dreaming. Similarly, I have run into artists who have deliberately taken on high-paying but boring jobs in order to earn enough to support their real interests. (A related phenomenon is the college-educated hippie postman, who has "dropped" out of seeking creative work.) John H. Goldthorpe concludes that English auto workers consciously take on assembly-line jobs because they view them as an instrument for the attainment of economic ends.

Can a trade-off be made between off-the-job and on-the-job satisfaction? Can the worker who desires higher-order satisfactions on the job make up for this loss off the job? Clark Kerr's 1964 study which summarized trends throughout the world predicted that work in the future would become increasingly routine and provide fewer and fewer opportunities for creativity and discretion. On the other hand, as working hours grew shorter, there would be a new "bohemianism" off the job as people sought self-expression away from work. "Leisure will be the happy hunting ground of the independent spirit. . . . The new slavery to technology may bring a new dedication to diversity and individualism off the job." Certainly there is some evidence of "bohemianism" (now called the "counter-culture") among professionals and managers. But is this "bohemianism" likely to counteract the boredom of blue-collar workers? And will it take the form of active recreation, or of passive escapism, such as drugs, alcoholism, or TV?

The limited research to date suggests that the kinds of recreation people engage in are closely similar to the kinds of activities they engage in on their jobs. According to one study people on active jobs which permit substantial discretion tend to engage in similar forms of recreation, such as running organizations, active sports, house-building, and various hobbies. Those whose jobs permit social contact (but little discretion) engage in social forms of recreation, i.e., visiting and receiving visitors, outings, "beer" and talk. Finally, workers with limited discretion or social contact at work tend to participate in "passive" activities, including fishing, religion, going for a drive, shopping, watching TV, and listening to the radio. According to this study, at least, workers do not counteract the effects of dull jobs through active recreation.

Perhaps this should not be surprising. Participant accounts of life in mass production factories stress that the work pace normally leaves one so exhausted that there is energy enough left only to drink a few beers or watch the tube. But there is another, less kindly explanation: it is not dull work which causes dull recreation, but dull people who pick dull recreation and through natural selection drift into dull work. In any case, for most workers the quality of life at home seems closely related to the quality of life on the jobs. The limited evidence does not support the trade-off hypothesis.

APATHY AS A FORM OF ADJUSTMENT

A further clue as to the role of work is provided in the work of Nancy Morse and Robert Weiss (since frequently replicated) which asked a sample of male, white workers, "If by chance you inherited enough money to live comfortably without working, do you think you would work anyway?" The vast majority (80 percent) of all respondents replied positively (see table 1) even though the percentages were slightly higher for middle-class (86 percent) than working-class workers (76 percent). Why would they work? Here a surprising phenomenon occurs. As expected, the main reason middle-class workers would continue working was for "interest or accomplishment," but for the blue-collar worker the main reason for continuing to work is "to keep occupied." This latter group would rather work than not work, even though working involves just filling in time. This may be a depressing commentary on the meaninglessness of life off the job, but at least it suggests that workers do adjust to boring work, though perhaps at a cost. It also suggests the centrality of having a job to the average American male

TABLE I. SELECTED ATTITUDES TOWARD WORK
(PERCENTAGES)

	Middle Class	Working Class
Would continue working, even if inherited enough not to	86	76
Reasons for so doing		
Interest or accomplishment	44	10
To keep occupied	37	71
Would continue working at same job	61	34
Attitude toward job		
Very satisfied	42	27
Satisfied	37	57
Dissatisfied	21	16

Source of Data: Nancy Morse and Robert Weiss, "The Function and Meaning of Work," *American Sociological Review*, Vol. 20, No. 2 (April 1955), pp. 191–198.

—as a source of identity, status, self-respect, and as an opportunity for social interaction.

Note the last two sets of data. Most blue-collar workers would prefer another job, and yet the vast majority report they are satisfied or even very satisfied with their job. The second finding is consistent with the Gallup Poll and with almost all other research in this area.

To return to a question asked before, does all this mean that a high percentage of workers are *really* satisfied with their jobs? If a substantial proportion of workers (1) report being satisfied with their job, but wishing to change it, and also (2) report they would continue working even if they did not have to, but only to fill time, then this can only mean that these workers accept the necessity of work, but expect little fulfillment from their specific job. Or to put it in the terms of Herzberg (to be discussed below) they are not dissatisfied, but neither are they satisfied. They are apathetic.

Let me back up a bit. The simple personality vs. organization hypothesis suggests that organizational restraints cause workers to become frustrated and to react to this frustration either by fighting back (through union activity, sabotage, or output restriction) or by regressing and producing no more than a minimum amount of work. By 1964, however, Argyris had considerably softened his harshly pessimistic original view. He recognized that many workers seem to adjust to a challengeless work environment. Though such individuals may be psychologically "immature," their expectations of what the job will offer them are low, and they suffer few overt pangs of aggression. They do routine jobs in an adequate fashion, though their performance is not innovative and they are resistant to change. These workers may not be overtly dissatisfied but still are not motivated.

Implicit support for the Argyris view has come from the research of Fredrick Herzberg and his colleagues. On the basis of imaginative research, Herzberg concludes that job satisfaction and job dissatisfaction are not opposite points on a continuum but in fact two separate dimensions. "Extrinsic" factors, such as company policy, incompetent supervision, or unsatisfactory working conditions may lead to dissatisfaction. Such dissatisfaction may be reduced by hygienic measures such as fringe benefits, "human relations" training for foremen, or better company policies, but such measures will not make workers satisfied, only apathetic. For true satisfaction to be obtained, "intrinsic" factors must be provided, such as achievement, accomplishment, responsibility, and challenging work. Note that satisfaction is obtained primarily from the *content* of the work itself, dissatisfaction from its *context* or environment. Only satisfaction relates to productivity. The presence of dissatisfaction may lead to low morale or absenteeism, but its elimination will not raise motivation or productivity. Herzberg concludes that it is a mistake to emphasize traditional "hygienic," "extrinsic" measures which serve only to make the work environment more tolerable. Instead management should seek to enrich (not just enlarge) jobs so as to make them seem interesting and important.

Herzberg's work has led to substantial controversy. But whatever the research's limitations, there seems to be a convergence on the view that there can be a middle ground between the overly pessimistic view that workers actively fight routine jobs and the overly optimistic one that these jobs make workers truly happy. This middle ground is illustrated by an interview I once held with a blue-collar worker on a routine job. This worker told me, in a rather off-hand way, "I got a pretty good job." "What makes it such a good job?" I responded. He answered: "Don't get me wrong. I didn't say it is a *good* job. It's an OK job—about as good a job as a guy like me might expect. The foreman leaves me alone and it pays well. But I would never call it a *good* job. It doesn't amount to much, but it's not bad."

This middle ground might be called apathy. The worker's expectations are low, but he accepts the situation. In a sense he has made a bargain with his employer and does not feel badly cheated. (This does not mean that workers never feel cheated. Quite the contrary. Tyrannical actions of individual foremen, efforts to speed up the production line, and the like can often lead to feelings that the basic bargain has been broken. My point is merely that available evidence suggests that a broad spectrum of workers are at least resigned to their lot.)

Attitudes such as this are not likely to lead to revolt. As Judith Herman puts it, "One needs to distinguish between satisfaction, dissatisfaction, and apathy—the latter suggesting not satisfaction, but not such unhappiness as to generate troublesome on-the-job behavior." In *Alienation and Freedom,* Robert Blauner concludes, "The majority of blue collar workers are committed to their roles as producers, and are loyal (although within limits) to their employers."

ADJUSTMENT TO NONCHALLENGING WORK

Perhaps all this may make greater sense if we think in terms of the scheme illustrated by the following chart:

| | | Type of Work | |
		Nonchallenging	Challenging
Employee orientation	Expressive	3	1
	Instrumental	4	2

We can divide work into that which is challenging and that which is not (using the term "challenge" in an oversimplified fashion to cover such factors as autonomy, variety, opportunity to participate, and the like—factors which are far from perfectly correlated with each other). In a similar oversimplified fashion we can distinguish between expectations toward work in terms of expressive and instrumental orientations. Those with expressive orientations, of course, tend to rank high in terms of need achievement and self-actualization on the job; those with instrumental orientations look upon the job merely as a means toward another end.

By middle-class standards, those who fall in cell 1 are the lucky ones. They are the professors, managers, etc. who seek self-fulfillment on the job and are fortunate enough to find jobs on which this is possible.

Those who fall in cell 2 are far less happy. They are faced with greater challenge than they want. I learned about such employees the hard way when I was working for a governmental agency some years ago and was assigned an elderly secretary. Imbued with the principles of what was then called human relations, I explained in detail the background of every letter I dictated, asked for her comments on style, and even suggested that, if she wished, she could draft some of them herself. At last she burst out, "I'm not paid to do that kind of work! That's your job!"

Maslow and Argyris might argue that my secretary objected not to challenge, but the way I thrust it upon her. Had I involved her in the process of accepting more responsibility (and had she gotten more pay for it), then her orientation toward her job might have become more expressive. And McClelland might suggest that with proper training she could be induced to develop greater need achievement. Alternatively, she might have rejected the challenge outright (as she did) or she might have been more subtle and handled it in the most routine, bureaucratic fashion possible. Either way she would eliminate the challenge from the job and restore herself to a safe, cell 4 solution. Or she could quit!

However approached, cell 2 represents an unstable situation. People placed within it will tend either to change their orientation (and move to cell 1) or change the nature of the job (and move to cell 4). The few who can do neither will undoubtedly report themselves dissatisfied.

Cell 3 is also unstable. Cell 3 consists of those who seek self-actualization on the job and are unable to obtain it. Faced with this predicament some people just quit. Others, through sabotage, fantasy, or empire-building transform routine work into something challenging (i.e., move to cell 1). But the most common solution is to withdraw psychologically from the job, to lower one's expectations, and to change one's orientation from expressive to instrumental (and so move to cell 4). Some individuals develop a rich social life on the job; others transfer their attention to family or recreational activities. One might also identify so closely with an organization that the organization's challenges and successes come to be one's own—and thus the boredom of one's own work becomes irrelevant. Such complete organizational indoctrination may be possible in some religious orders and in various forms of altruistic and personal service work. Certainly it is the aim in Maoist China. I suspect it is rather rare in contemporary America. Others may become alienated from society generally (and so presumably suffer from mental illness). The withdrawal process may also be accompanied by an atrophy in need achievement and perhaps some increase in need affiliation and even need power. A few may fight fate and refuse to change their orientation. These will suffer from what the psychologists call "cognitive dissonance." They, along with those condemned to cell 2, are among those likely to report their jobs as "dissatisfying."

Cell 4 is stable. It consists of those who have withdrawn from expressive orientation and those who never developed this. They work to earn a living or even for self-respect, but not for the challenge of the job. These people are apathetic. In Argyris's term they may be immature. They may even suffer from psychological illness—though I will question this below. In Herzberg's terms they are not motivated. However, as long as management provides hygienic conditions (i.e., fair supervision, good working conditions, opportunities for social interaction, and the like), they will not be actively dissatisfied. Being not dissatisfied they may well report being "satisfied" on the Gallup Poll (but probably not "very satisfied"). Unable to see other alternatives to work, they may well respond that they would continue to work in order "to keep occupied" even if they had enough money to do otherwise.

It must be remembered that for some workers, moving into cell 4 may represent a conscious choice. Both United States and British studies describe workers who gave up jobs providing greater intrinsic satisfaction (challenge, autonomy, and the like) in order to accept higher pay earned on the automobile assembly line. Most people want both extrinsic and intrinsic rewards, but when the choice has to be made they often prefer the financial to the psychic payoff.

SUBSTITUTES FOR INTRINSIC JOB SATISFACTION

As mentioned earlier, those in cell 4 adjust to nonchallenging work in a variety of ways and with various degrees of success—through recreation (as we have seen), daydreaming (an elderly lady told me she liked her repetitive job because it gave her chance to "think about God"), union activity, increased consumption, and moonlighting. Two additional escape routes deserve mention, socializing on the job and dreams of advancement. Each of these adjustment processes is easier for some people than for others and in some technologies than in others.

Social Life—For many workers the social life around the job can provide substitute satisfactions for those lacking in the job itself. In a context of humdrum routine, human ingenuity is able to extract surprisingly rich meanings from seemingly trivial events. Horseplay, lunch-time card games, gossip around the watercooler, football pools, and the like do provide satisfaction, particularly for those with strong need affiliation. As the job becomes less rewarding, the social group may become more so.

But this is not always the case. Cohesive work groups do not arise automatically whenever the work is boring. Jobs differ substantially in the opportunities they provide for social interaction. Once again the automobile assembly line—which permits the typical worker to communicate only with the men directly ahead and behind him in the flow of work—provides relatively less opportunity for interaction than do most other types of work.

High turnover, as well as heterogeneity among employees in terms of age, ethnic and educational background or job duties, all inhibit the development of cohesive work groups. Social cohesion is also affected by the opportunity for association off the job. Those who live in isolated small communities, which work odd shifts, or whose jobs frequently take them from home (such as sailors, railroadmen, or traveling construction craftsmen) are more likely to develop strong occupational communities.

The union also helps provide solidarity, at least for a small group of activists. However, participation in union activity is not likely to be high in groups which are not already socially cohesive. Indeed substantial evidence suggests that workers who are dissatisfied with their jobs also tend to be dissatisfied with their union.

To summarize, a rich social life on the job can substitute for boring work to some extent. Unfortunately, however, those occupational work groups which have the greatest need for the kind of social support that a cohesive group might provide frequently are the very ones which find it most difficult to develop such cohesion in the first place. There is considerable evidence that cohesion and job satisfaction are positively correlated. The development of cohesive groups may increase interest in the job; on the other hand, the very factors which make jobs less intrinsically satisfying may also inhibit cohesion.

Dreams of Advancement—Ely Chinoy's *Automobile Workers and the American Dream* explains in vivid terms one aspect of how blue-collar workers adjusted during the fifties to the frustrations of the assembly line. (The past tense is intentional because of the possibility that this form of adjustment is no longer feasible.) Despite the seemingly dead-end nature of their jobs, a high percentage of Chinoy's respondents looked upon their job as only temporary and dreamed of (fantasied) the day when they would be able to quit the factory and set up their small business or engage in some sort of independent occupation. When the passage of time serves to discredit these dreams completely, they project their frustrated ambitions onto their children and plan how they can go to college and thus escape the assembly line. In either case, as Blauner puts it, "their daydreams serve as a safety valve for day-to-day frustrations."

Effects

Most people can adjust to boring work in one way or another, through social activity on or off the job, through daydreams, etc. But what is the cost in doing so? And how about those who can achieve neither ego or social satisfaction on the job or creative leisure off the job? It is argued that unsatisfactory work conditions constitute a major cause of physical and mental illness and that they contribute to alienation from society generally and therefore to political extremism.

HEALTH—PHYSICAL AND MENTAL

It is well established that work stress can lead to *physical* illness, especially heart disease, ulcers, and arthritis—as well as to alcoholism, drug addiction, and a host of psychosomatic and purely mental ailments. But a significant proportion of these conditions can be attributed to what might be called "overload"—too much variety, uncertainty, and responsibility—or to lack of hygienes (such as adequate pay, job security, or fair management)—rather than to routine work or boredom. Those suffering from overload are likely to fit into my cells 1 and 2, and the solution to their problem is more likely to be job simplification than job enrichment.

The impact of objectively routine or subjectively boring work is less clear and somewhat difficult to measure. There are numerous studies which suggest that dissatisfaction with work is generally correlated with dissatisfaction with life. However, the direction of causation is far from certain: does dissatisfaction with the job lead to dissatisfaction with life, or does dissatisfaction with life lead to dissatisfaction with one's job? Some people are perpetual malcontents, happy with nothing; furthermore, people with unsatisfactory lives often report dissatisfaction with their jobs even when their co-workers, with similar but happier lives, report satisfaction. (For example, unmarried workers tend to be less satisfied with their jobs than married workers.) Clearly one's personal life tends to color one's attitude toward one's job.

A high percentage of people on objectively routine work report having happy and uncomplicated home lives, but there are enough who do not that statistical studies indicate a positive correlation between routine work and off-the-job dissatisfaction. Further there are the previously cited mental health studies which suggest that unskilled factory workers suffer from poorer mental health than do those in more skilled work. Assuming these studies are valid, the question remains whether poor mental health and less satisfaction with life are caused by low job challenge, or by other factors. The unskilled or semiskilled worker suffers not just from boring work, but from low pay (at least compared with higher-skilled jobs), and relatively irregular work. These in turn lead to his enjoying a lower standard of living, living in less desirable parts of town, and being less able to afford adequate medical and psychiatric care. Indeed, for those who belong to minority ethnic groups, the effects of their role in the community may swamp the effects of their role on the job.

Job status is also important. Blue-collar work is looked down upon in our society (especially in urban areas), and the blue-collar workers may well suffer from impaired self-worth. In a period when upward mobility is the norm, the man who remains in a low-status job may somehow blame himself for his failure. And, as an increasing percentage of the work force engages in white-collar, professional, and managerial occupations, the relative status of blue-collar work declines further. TV has contributed to this process by spreading middle-class values throughout the culture. With racially derogatory remarks now prohibited, the "dumb" blue-collar worker remains among the few socially acceptable targets of humor. As a destroyer of public image and private self-pride, Archie Bunker plays for blue-collar workers today the role that Amos and Andy played for Negroes during the 1930s.

Thus it is far from clear whether lower mental health is caused primarily by the intrinsic nature of unskilled work or by the fact that work pays poorly and has low status both on and off the job. Insofar as mental disturbances and dissatisfaction with life are caused by economic and social pressures at home, higher wages may be a better solution than improved human relations or job enrichment. And the overall status of blue-collar work is not likely to be raised by changes on specific jobs.

PERSONALITY

To go beyond mental illness, what is the impact of the job on personality? Obviously there is some relationship. Various studies show that people on challenging, complex, varied jobs which permit self-direction tend to show relatively high self-esteem, to be less authoritarian, more intellectually flexible, more willing to accept change, and to have less mechanistic standards of morality. The reverse tendencies hold true when jobs are boring. Patricia Smith's study of garment workers concludes:

The picture which emerges from these studies of the personality of the person who is satisfied with doing repetitive work is one of contentment with the existing state of affairs, passivity, and perhaps rigidity. His satisfaction would seem to be more a matter of close contact with and acceptance of reality than of stupidity or insensitivity. . . . The preference for uniformity in work extends into daily habits outside the work situation, is related to lack of conflict or rebellion in the home, and is correlated with contentment both in the factory and out (*Journal of Applied Psychology*, 1955).

How is this congruence between personality and job achieved? In part, it is a matter of organizational and self-selection: People gravitate toward jobs consistent with their need patterns and, if they are placed on inappropriate jobs, quit these or mold them to fit their personalities. But the reverse occurs: jobs mold people and sometimes induce fundamental changes in attitudes and values. Obviously both factors are at work, but which is more significant? A highly systematic study by Melvin L. Kohn and Carmi Schooler concludes that in 1973 the jobs tend to determine personalities somewhat more than personalities determine jobs. At the very least, we can conclude that jobs can alter personalities, and sometimes (but how often?) the psychic cost is great.

POLITICS

Do jobs also affect attitudes toward politics and the community? Again the evidence is somewhat mixed, but suggests that having a repetitive job—and especially being dissatisfied with one's job and its rewards—is associated with such factors as personal and political fatalism (including lack of faith in others or the system), low tolerance (particularly to minorities), authoritarian attitudes (e.g., support for the death penalty), political extremism, and unwillingness to engage in sustained political activity. (Note how radicalism, fatalism, and unwillingness to engage in sustained political activity are related to a generalized alienation from the system.)

Once more this conclusion needs careful qualification: economic phenomena such as low pay, blocked mobility, and job insecurity may well be more closely related to politically alienated attitudes than is repetitive work.

To summarize the discussion of mental health and associated attitudes: the nature of one's job does seem to affect personality and adjustment, both personal and political. However, extrinsic, primarily economic elements may be as important causal factors as intrinsic job elements. Further, the apparent relationship between jobs and personality is a function of both people selecting (and even changing) the nature of jobs as well as jobs changing people. The process of adjusting to nonchallenging work does involve a cost, but the exact nature of this cost is difficult to decipher.

Trends for the Future

Have underlying conditions changed? Much of the discussion seems to assume that dissatisfaction has intensified in recent years. Although we have little evidence so far indicating that dissatisfaction with work has increased, there are a number of explanations available to explain such change *if* and when it becomes apparent. What factors might be relevant?

Changes in work force composition, in themselves, have led, if anything, to an increase in satisfaction. Unskilled work has declined relatively and the number of professionals, managers, and clericals has gone up. Thus it has been the relatively better-paid, higher-status, and more demanding jobs which have expanded. However, the change has occurred slowly and its short-term impact may be slight.

In addition, there have been some changes in the job environment. Managers, as well as workers, are better educated. Unionism and the human relations movement have had an effect. Although we have little firm evidence, we have every reason to believe that workers today are better treated by their bosses, company policies are more humane, safety hazards have been reduced, and job security improved. Herzberg's "hygienes" are more prevalent, thus making the job more tolerable and reducing dissatisfaction.

The big change, however, has occurred among workers, and this change is quite significant.

YOUTH

Because of demographic shifts, we have seen a substantial reduction in average age in many industries, especially the automotive. This reduction in age may have had an impact on job satisfaction. As long as studies have been run, younger people have registered less satisfaction with their work than did their elders. Not only is youth more restless, but younger employees normally work at less interesting jobs, receive lower salaries and job security—and yet, if they are married with children, may have the greatest needs. During the late sixties, according to the Gallup Poll, morale fell much faster among younger workers than among older ones. Possibly these younger workers were influenced by the generally more permissive youth environment which accompanied the revolts on campus. Certainly among the younger workers of today's generation the personality vs. organization conflict is particularly acute.

This trend toward youth may be reversed, however. The bonanza crop of postwar youth (born 1946–51) which entered either the workplace or college during the hectic years of 1964–69 is now in its midtwenties. By 1974, the 1946 baby was rapidly approaching Mario Savio's untrustworthy age of 30, burdened down, no doubt, by children and mortgages.

EDUCATION

In 1948, the average education of the employed labor force was 10.6 years; in 1972, it was 12.4. Twenty-six percent had some college. The educational level had zoomed much faster than the demands of most jobs. Almost a million people with three years of college are in unskilled and semiskilled occupations. Automobile manufacturing especially has "old, ultrasimplified methods originally designed not only to avoid waste motions but to accommodate unskilled immigrant labor and farm youths." Understandably, there is evidence that where job level is held constant, education is inversely related to satisfaction.

We see cognitive dissonance at work here. The extra investment involved in increased education has given rise to increased expectations which have not been met in practice. For many workers education has not been a route to success. These workers feel that their skills are underutilized on the job, and this is especially so among younger workers who report "some college."

Education may have two other effects. It may increase the worker's opportunities to find meaningful recreation off the job, suggesting that he will more easily make a trade-off between more boring work and interesting leisure. On the other hand, better educated workers may demand higher wages just to counteract their boredom. Indeed, they may compare their wages with those of their age group who have "made it" in white-collar work.

MOVEMENT UP THE MASLOW HIERARCHY

All during the 1940s and 1950s, workers placed *steady work* as the most important thing they wanted from their jobs. Herzberg's comprehensive 1957 study listed job factors influencing satisfaction in roughly this order: job security, opportunities for advancement, company and management, wages, and intrinsic work—with intrinsic work coming fifth. By sharp contrast, a 1969 survey listed *interesting work* first with job security coming seventh; six of the eight top-ranking work aspects related to job content.

These data may be but a statistical artifact, but if confirmed by other evidence they suggest a substantial shift in the value-ordering of American workers, one which is consistent with the Maslow hierarchy. After all, this is the first generation not to grow up in the shadow of the Great Depression. The specter of job insecurity may have been licked, and with low-level needs largely fulfilled, workers may be in a position to demand satisfaction for their egoistic and self-actualization needs. If so, such workers are less likely to settle for apathy or even for a job which offers high income and a rich social life but no intrinsic satisfaction. Possibly for such workers, money alone may no longer motivate—or as economists put it, it may have declining marginal utility. Possibly. But today's luxuries become tomorrow's necessities. Wants grow at least as fast as paychecks, and I doubt if economic motivation will atrophy as fast as some psychologists suggest.

Conclusion

The discussion above is at least as confused as the underlying data. What sense can we make of it?

It seems reasonably clear that not everyone feels oppressed by his organization. Dissatisfaction with work seems to be a function of technology. The most dissatisfaction is reported on jobs with short job cycles, relatively little challenge, etc.—and also in industries in which such characteristics are common, especially the automotive industry (and also in wholesale and retail trade, where reported job challenge is low). But job challenge alone does not determine attitude toward work. Dissatisfaction is also high on jobs which are paid poorly or low in status and which prevent the development of group life or which suffer from tyrannical or incompetent supervision.

Personality and culture enter the picture in a puzzling fashion. Two alternative hypotheses are possible:

1. Challengeless bureaucratic jobs inhibit the normal development of the human personality, thus leading to poor mental health, apathy, and even the delusion that one prefers highly structured work. Workers suffering from such conditions attempt to redirect their limited energies to activities off the job, to social life on the job, or to sheer fantasy—but never with great success and always with considerable emotional cost.

2. Because of genetic or cultural reasons some people have lower levels of aspiration and/or ability to handle challenging work and/or have low need achievement and/or wish to center their lives off the

job. Their primary demands from the job are economic and instrumental. To the extent they can, they pick jobs which pay well or which make few mental or physical demands.

Inconsistent as these two alternate explanations of the evidence may seem, in fact both may be partly true. Whole cultures may adjust to job opportunities which call for little challenge (as did blacks until recently) and so change "personality." Although such adjustment may be unhealthy, it *can* be stable and not lead to revolt unless the underlying conditions change.

To put it another way, there are a variety of forms of adjustment to "objectively" challengeless work (that is, work which most observers —and especially college professors—report as challengeless). Some workers are able to develop rich social lives on the job or are active in their union. Others obtain a large part of the challenges they seek off the job, through recreation or family activities (though the evidence suggests that for many this recreation may be rather passive in nature). A worker may "adjust" by dreaming of better work, whether for himself or his children. Alternatively he may "enlarge" his job through sabotage or output restriction, or he may lower his aspirations and delude himself that he is truly happy—and thus become resigned and apathetic (and even classified as low in mental health). Finally, he may become a chronic griper and even express his feelings through strikes, absenteeism, or by quitting his job. And as Michael Crozier suggests, he can "play a game with the environment" and quickly change forms of reaction, e.g., from apathy to revolt (thus suggesting that excessive weight should not be given any one given measure of unhappiness).

But dissatisfaction can be caused as much by low incomes, job insecurity, inadequate fringe benefits, or tyrannical supervision. Indeed to me the evidence suggests that for workers at all levels—even managers and professionals—lack of challenge is much less oppressive than lack of income. People as a whole are willing to tolerate large doses of boredom if they are paid enough. In so doing they are perhaps selling their soul for a mess of potage. By my elitist standards this may be a raw deal, especially since it may have an adverse impact on personality and mental health. But why should my standards govern? Life without adequate income can also be pretty grim.

Regardless, most employees today claim that they are satisfied and apparently have reached some sort of adjustment to their environment (in the sense that what they expect and obtain from the job is fair balance). Dissatisfaction may have increased recently, but probably not by much. Nevertheless, the fact that over 10 percent of our work force (possibly 10 million people) is dissatisfied is itself significant. And it is also clear that challengeless work has led to countless further millions leading narrower, less creative, and possibly less happy lives.

I tend to agree with those union leaders who argue that economic conditions are a greater cause of dissatisfaction than any intrinsic sterility on the job. But this is no reason for ignoring intrinsic factors —any more than we should ignore arthritis just because cancer kills more people annually. Furthermore, solutions such as job enrichment have the added advantage that under some conditions they actually lead to increased productivity. On the other hand, job enrichment is not the only solution to work problems. Many workers are more concerned with job security than with obtaining challenging work. For others the most pressing demand may be for a safer work place, a fairer supervisor, a more effective grievance procedure, or more flexible work hours.

Agis Salpukas

4

Unions:
A New Role?

"My people don't talk to behaviorists."

"It is a case of middle-class outsiders looking down at the poor workers again."

"A lot of academics are writing about it. Their goal is to create a lot of jobs for professionals who have not done any real work in their lives."

These are some of the milder comments from union leaders discussing the issue of job discontent. With some exceptions the prevalent mood within the labor movement is one of cynicism, suspicion, and impatience.

Leaders do believe that major changes have to be made at the workplace; that workers' expectations are rising; that there are new frontiers for collective bargaining.

But most object to the way the issue of work has been portrayed by the press, by researchers, and by experts. They are skeptical about its depth, and most believe it will not soon result in rank and file pressure on them to make demands at the bargaining table. They are unimpressed by outsiders writing about it. What do they know about what workers really feel and want?

"What do they expect a worker to say if he's asked, 'Would you like to have your job more interesting?'" one leader of the Steelworkers posed.

Agis Salpukas *is a correspondent for* The New York Times. *He has written extensively on the quality of working life and the environment of the workplace.*

Many are also outraged by what they believe is a by-product of the writing and studies—that workers are portrayed as subhuman because they put in eight or ten hours a day on jobs that are stupid and dirty. "Sure work is dull and monotonous," Leonard Woodcock, head of the United Automobile Workers (UAW) union, told delegates at a conference of production workers in Atlanta, in February of 1973. "But if it's useful, the people who do it are entitled to be honored and not degraded, which is what's going on in this day and time."

Such a view seems defensive and a misinterpretation of the motives of researchers and writers who really argue the opposite: that workers are creative, intelligent people who want to think, to have responsibility and challenge in their work, but are frustrated by the way jobs are now set up.

Union leaders often lash out, however, because they are concerned about raising worker expectations when there are few answers on the horizon. Sure it is good to experiment in a highly controlled situation in a small plant, but what will happen when you try to apply the same methods to large industries? What will happen to productivity? Will the changes be lasting? Can American industry undergo these changes and remain competitive with the rest of the world?

Ben Fischer, director of contract administration for the Steelworkers union, said, "These sociologists and behaviorists are out to destroy the economic system and don't have any idea what will take its place."

Many union leaders are also suspicious of experimentation begun by management to change and enrich jobs. Why should management suddenly reverse its long tradition of increasing efficiency by cutting manpower? Some of the experiments give them good cause for alarm —responsibility and work are often added without a change in wages —and begin to look like the old "speedup."

Some of the early efforts to deal with job discontent often reinforced their cynicism. In the late 1960s some auto plants tried to bribe workers to come in on Fridays and Mondays, when absenteeism ran up to 10 percent, by offering green stamps and glasses to those with good attendance records. Some companies, eager to get aboard the humanization of work bandwagon, sometimes passed off as job enrichment innovations that would have been implemented even if they had never heard of the concept. General Motors in announcing the opening of a new line to build motor homes stressed that teams of men would perform the work. What was not mentioned was that most motor home assembly lines use teams of workers since that is the most efficient way to set up jobs due to the slowness of the line. Several months later, when demand went up and line speed had to be increased, the team concept was abandoned since it did not lend itself to the new production schedule.

There is also a threat to the role of unions themselves inherent in management experiments to change work. At the General Foods plant in Topeka, Kansas, where workers rotate into and learn every major job at the plant, several approaches by union organizers have been rebuffed. Since they have easy access to top management, are consulted on major decisions and get pay increases based on the amount they learn, most workers feel that there is no need for a union. Although the experiment is in a plant employing a small, highly select group of 60 workers, the implications for unions cannot be ignored. Humanizing jobs poses a challenge to unions—at the very least it will lead to a redefinition of their role. It is not surprising, therefore, that union leaders are wary.

Thomas R. Brooks, a labor historian, summed up these feelings in an October, 1972, article in the *Federationist,* the official magazine of the AFL-CIO:

> The impetus for time and motion studies is pretty much the same as that behind job enrichment of participatory management. Substituting the sociologist's questionnaire for the stopwatch is likely to be no gain for the workers. While the workers have a stake in productivity, it is not always identical with that of management. Job enrichment programs have cut jobs just as effectively as automation or engineer's stopwatches. And the rewards of productivity are not always equitably shared.

History

TURN OF THE CENTURY

Labor's stance is explained to a large degree by the way the labor movement evolved in the United States. When the theories of scientific management of Frederick Taylor were being widely applied in industry at the turn of the century and when Henry Ford and James Couzens were building the first assembly line in Highland Park from 1912 to 1914 the trade union movement was small. Its organization was built on skilled workers. The American Federation of Labor craft unions often excluded the industrial workers who were multiplying as fast as the new technology and theories of Ford and Taylor were spreading in American industry in the 1920s. Trade union membership numbered about 4 million during that period when wages were rising, jobs plentiful. The only real challenge to the emerging industrial system came from the Wobblies or Industrial Workers of the World who fought many sporadic battles but never developed a unified movement or concerted strategy. Their hope for one big general strike that would bring about fundamental change in the economic system remained a dream.

Most business leaders had the same freedom from union interference as Mr. Ford and his driving, brilliant engineers. Even though the workers were unorganized they resisted Mr. Ford at first. He divided the jobs of mechanics and tradesmen into 37 tasks which were eventually transferred onto a moving line. Some men could turn out seven thousand parts in a nine-hour day. The skilled workers, however, left in droves. Just as Mr. Ford had perfected the assembly line at the end of 1913, he faced a major labor crisis. The turnover of the labor force for that year was 380 percent and to keep a force of 100 men, he had to hire 963.

He solved the crisis through what has often been considered as a humanitarian gesture but was really a desperate attempt to keep the lines going. On January 5, 1914, he announced a five-dollars-a-day pay, almost double the prevailing wage rates. Thousands of new workers flocked to the gates of Highland Park. This new work force traded skills for money and human pace for assembly-line speed. They also submitted their private lives to the paternal discipline of what Keith Sward in *The Legend of Henry Ford* calls the "Ford Sociology Department." The initial resistance of workers to the discipline of the new industrial system was unorganized and easily defeated by management.

UNIONS IN THE 1930S

By the time the trade union movement began to organize industrial workers on a large scale in the 1930s, the system of work fragmentation, time and study methods, and a hierarchical management which left few initiatives to workers had become firmly entrenched. The early drives by the Congress of Industrial Organizations (CIO), which was founded in 1935, did not challenge the existing system—it was difficult enough to gain recognition and to prevent management from destroying the embryo unions. Although the union movement had the friendly administration of Franklin D. Roosevelt in the White House and had legally won the right to organize and bargain collectively through the National Labor Relations Act of 1935, they still had to win recognition largely through their own efforts.

The most important struggle of that era, the sit-down strike by the auto workers in Flint in 1936 and 1937, clearly shows the priorities at that time. Faced with a hostile police force and local government and management, the union had little energy left even to deal with such basic issues as wages and hours. Before the Flint strike average annual earnings of auto workers were $1,200 to $1,300 and there was little job security. Workers were often selected by foremen on the basis of how quickly they jumped to their commands. Even though the fledgling unions had immediate, pressing needs to fill, they nevertheless made important inroads into management's authority in the plants. In the agreement with General Motors, the skeleton of the present grievance procedure was initiated. It gave the workers a means to deal with what they considered arbitrary treatment. Many local strikes also succeeded in putting limits on the work pace. Shortly after the sit-down strike a UAW worker in Fisher Body plant 1 wrote, "The inhuman speed is no more. We now have a choice and have slowed the speed of the line. And are now treated as human beings, and not as part of the machinery" (Sidney Fine, *Sit-down,* 1969).

UNION AND MANAGEMENT PREROGATIVES

By the end of World War II the union movement had grown to 16 million workers. Most major industries had accepted it as a permanent force in the economic system. Collective bargaining had also become the recognized method by which unions and businesses would work out their differences.

There was great concern on the part of management on just how far unions would press. Provisions of the National Labor Relations Act stated merely that employers were required to bargain "in respect to rate of pay, wages, hours of employment, or other conditions of employment." President Harry S. Truman called a conference of top industry and union leaders to see if they could set specific limits on what could be brought to the bargaining table. They could not reach an agreement. The statement of the labor leaders at the end of the conference held in 1945 gives an insight into the role that they had carved out for their movement.

The union leaders showed sympathy for management's concern that

in the past few years efforts have been made by certain unions to extend the scope of collective bargaining to include other matters and operating problems involving the function of management to direct the operation of business. The functions and responsibilities of management must be preserved if business and industry is to be efficient, progressive, and to provide more good jobs.

It was a basic acceptance of the free enterprise system and management's right to run the industries.

At the same time the labor members of the committee refused to spell out areas that would be off limits for bargaining. "It would be extremely unwise to build a fence around the rights and responsibilities of management on the one hand, the unions on the other," they wrote. "The experience of many years shows that with the growth of mutual understanding, the responsibilities of one of the parties today may well become the joint responsibility of both parties tomorrow." Most unions have maintained that position up to the present—there are no areas that are taboo in collective bargaining.

PRIORITIES AFTER THE WAR

Although free to do so in theory, unions have not made any major thrust to gain management's prerogatives either in running the plants or in how to set up the work. After World War II, the trade unions concentrated on forcing industry to recognize new areas that could be bargained on. When the UAW brought pensions to the bargaining table in the 1949 negotiations, there was a bitter attack on the union for entering an area that management considered its own. Since then unions have pushed into many new areas including health insurance, adequate protection against layoffs, and compensation for disability. In other advanced countries protection was often obtained through government programs. In the United States, where unions did not spawn a labor party, protection for workers when they became ill, were laid off, or retired had to be squeezed out of employers. The unions have never been able to let up the pressure to keep up with the costs in these benefit areas. Walter Reuther and Charles E. Wilson, head of General Motors, also worked out a system for wage increases which committed the union to seek to improve productivity and to support rapid technological change. In the 1948 contract, General Motors gave the union cost-of-living protection—pay would be adjusted to keep up with inflation—and wage increases were tied to gains in productivity.

This system became the pattern for many other unions. Their leaders welcomed rapid technological advance since it could produce a bigger pie from which to cut their slice. In 1955, Reuther speaking on behalf of the CIO told the Joint Congressional Committee on the Economic Report:

> First of all, we fully realize that the potential benefits of automation are great, if properly handled. If only a fraction of what technologists promise for the future is true, within a very few years automation can and should make possible a four-day week, longer vacation periods, opportunities for

earlier retirement, as well as vast increases in our material standards of living.

At the same time automation can bring freedom from the monotonous drudgery of many jobs in which a worker today is no more than a servant of the machine. It can free workers from routine, repetitious tasks which the new machines can be taught to do and can give the workers who toil at those tasks the opportunity of developing higher skills.

Most unions remained passive as their industries were transformed through new technology which often had a big effect on the nature of the work. From the cornucopia of automation came many of the things Reuther spoke about. In the General Motors plant in Lordstown, Ohio, for example, 104 cars an hour roll off the line compared to 55 cars an hour at the average plant. Many of the jobs have been made physically easier. But it has retained the drudgery and has even reduced the skills further. Higher production and speed have been obtained by breaking the jobs down further in the classical Taylor method.

There were also immediate pressures which kept the unions out of dealing with the effects of what Reuther aptly called the "silent revolution" of technology. During the 1950s the intense competition between the free world and the Communist countries made many leaders in the trade union movement concerned that the predominance of the United States was threatened.

Resistance to demands from management for greater efficiency was also difficult considering the inroads that foreign producers had made into the American economy. Trips to Japan have often had a sobering effect on union leaders. Douglas Fraser, the head of UAW's Chrysler Department, on a tour of the Japanese auto industry in 1972 found absenteeism unheard of in many plants and rates of work speed that would not be tolerated in the United States.

STRUGGLES OVER EFFICIENCY

Throughout this period many industries put the pressure on the unions to change work rules and standards which management felt impeded productivity. Perhaps the longest and most bitter of these struggles has been the battle between UAW's General Motors Department and General Motors Assembly Division. The division has been on a continuous drive to improve efficiency and has been willing to go through strikes to achieve its goals. In 1972, there were bitter strikes at the Lordstown plant in which the company lost $150 million in sales. The longest strike in General Motors history, lasting 172 days, was in its Norwood, Ohio, plant and cost the company about $100 million.

The strike at Lordstown in which 8,000 workers from UAW local 1112 closed the plant from March 3 to March 24 in 1972 received nationwide coverage. A mythology has since grown around the strike which in its most radical form contains the following misconceptions: that the strike was caused by a new, "freaked out" generation of workers who because of boredom and stupidity in the jobs revolted against their own union leadership. Talk of the "Lordstown syndrome" symbolizing a worker revolt against present jobs has become common at conferences and seminars.

Such mythology has only driven a further wedge between academics and union leaders who must patiently explain the complex set of issues that caused the Lordstown strike. Both the union and management, disturbed by widespread misinterpretation of the strike, have issued position papers explaining the causes.

Reduced to its simplest terms the struggle was over an old issue—speedup. Ever since the first production line came into existence, there has been continual strife over work rate—unions seeking to set clear standards that would define what is expected of a worker in a job; management seeking to keep a free enough hand so that the standards do not become blocks to new technology and efficiency.

GM Approach—Under General Motors the struggle has assumed a new dimension and sophistication. A whole separate management division made up of tough specialists in assembly-line operations, called General Motors Assembly Division, has been given the task of making plants more efficient. Since 1965, General Motors Assembly Division has undergone rapid expansion, and in 1973 it supervised eighteen plants employing 91,000 workers or about 75 percent of General Motors production.

Each plant that General Motors Assembly Division has taken over underwent the following pattern of consolidation. The separate Fisher Body plant and assembly plant were merged into one unit. This led to duplicate jobs and the new management team cut manpower. Also, most jobs in the plant were reevaluated and cuts made in every department. The result was that workers often were made to take on additional tasks to make up for cuts. Workers resisted, arguing that this violated existing work standards and they often refused to perform the new tasks. The company then invoked its right to discipline workers by barring them from the plant for days or weeks without pay.

The bitterness increased and workers often resorted to acts of sabotage such as breaking windshields, breaking off rear view mirrors, and slashing upholstery.

Management's explanation for the resistance was that it was caused by the political struggle within locals. Since one full union shop committee was eliminated in the consolidations, union leaders vying to be elected to the new committee fed the unrest to establish a reputation of militancy among the workers. During the struggle at Lordstown, management conceded however that cuts were made beyond mere duplication of jobs and that internal union politics, while a factor, was not the main cause of the strike. The intent in each of the consolidations, eight of which resulted in strikes, was to push each local union as far as possible to see how much manpower reduction would be tolerated. At the end of each strike, most locals claimed they had preserved their former manpower levels and the best terms of their old agreements.

The struggle with General Motors Assembly Division over work standards does not end with the settlement of the strikes. For the division has combined the principles of scientific management with the computer and can get an instant reading of the efficiency of each plant down to individual departments. The plants are also ranked according to the productivity. The ranking results in constant pressure on the bottom half of the plants to improve efficiency. Since ranking is never-ending there is no final goal and the pressure is never-ending. To Mr. Joseph E. Godfrey, the general manager of General Motors Assembly Division, the constant pressure is not a disturbing fact but a construction to be proud of—the ultimate competitive system. The position of General Motors Assembly Division, he said, is that it has the right to reorganize jobs any way it wants in order to make them more efficient. "If within reason and without endangering their health," he explained, "we can occupy a man for 60 minutes, we've got that right."

The thrust and philosophy of General Motors Assembly Division is of great significance to the issue of job discontent. The division represents one of the most far-reaching and concerted efforts to apply the methods evolved under Frederick Taylor in our economy. Its goal is to find the best and most efficient way through "scientific analysis" and then have the worker comply. Local contracts, customs, workers' attitudes cannot stand in the way; they must be made to conform.

General Motors Assembly Division has achieved a good part of its goals in the plants it has taken over. After bitter strikes, production returned to normal and years later some plants have developed good relations between management and the local union. But what about worker attitude?

Workers' Response—Charles Tyler, the president of UAW Local 93, recalled that when General Motors Assembly Division took over his plant in 1968 about 1,200 people out of a work force of 4,000 were eliminated. The union members decided not to strike because of the high unemployment at that time. "The people were left bitter," he said. "Frankly it doesn't bother me when I can put something over on management. They hurt so many people it doesn't bother my conscience. That's the view of most workers here."

At Lordstown many workers said in interviews that the atmosphere in the plant had been changed after General Motors Assembly Division took over. "Just a year ago they gave out these awards for quality work," one worker said pointing to a set of newly minted coins on the mantelpiece. "Then this new outfit comes in and says we're not working hard enough. They cut manpower so that you can't do the job right. How can they talk about quality when that's their attitude?"

As Leonard Woodcock put it in a speech before the UAW collective bargaining convention held in Detroit in spring, 1973: "The first big step in humanizing the workplace is for the employers and their representatives to accept their employees, our members, as human beings."

Underneath the immediate issues in the struggle between the UAW and General Motors Assembly Division is a larger one—that the authority that management has in the plants is increasingly being challenged by workers. That greater efficiency is not a sacred principle that should sweep over the personalities and aspirations of workers. That the contradiction between values of a democratic society where the leaders and laws are subject to the check of citizens and the authoritarianism of the workplace is becoming less tolerable to workers. As UAW Vice President Irving Bluestone has frequently pointed out:

> The workplace is probably the most authoritarian environment in which the adult finds himself. Its rigidity and denial of freedom lead people to live a double life; at home they enjoy substantially the autonomy and self-fulfillment of free citizens; at work they are subject to constant regimentation, supervision and control by others.

Challenge by Rank and File

Workers are increasingly raising issues that challenge this dichotomy; there are demands that the present method of discipline in which workers can be punished and then can appeal the action through a long drawn-out grievance procedure should be changed. This system contradicts the basic concept that a man is innocent until proven guilty; that workers have a say about working overtime and should not be disciplined if they refuse because of some prior personal commitment; and that they should have some means of immediate appeal to an impartial official in matters of health and safety.

These aspirations came dramatically to the fore at a meeting called by the leadership of the Steelworkers union in 1970 which brought together a small group of young steelworkers and local union leaders from all over the country. Meeting with I. W. Abel, the president of the union, and other top leaders in small informal groups they were asked: Why the wildcats? Why don't you go to the shop stewards with complaints? Why the conflict with foremen? Why are so many young workers leaving only after a short time in the mills? The young workers were shown a slick, multiple-image film which quickly took them through the history of their union—a proud story of continuous betterment of wages, fringes, and time off.

What the young workers stressed at the end of the meeting, however, was that while they were grateful for the economic gains they felt largely powerless in their daily dealings with management in the plants. When it was too hot or there were fumes, complaints usually brought promises but little action. If there were unsafe conditions why were they not corrected immediately? What's the use of filing a grievance if you have to wait up to a year for a decision? they asked.

Since the meeting, the union and the companies have worked out an agreement where the grievance procedure has been speeded up and made more responsive. First-line supervisors and foremen must now make a greater effort at resolving complaints at the plant-floor level. The basic change has been in the attitude of the foremen who can no longer dismiss a worker's gripe by saying, "If you don't like it, file a grievance."

COLLECTIVE BARGAINING AND NONECONOMIC ISSUES

Often, however, the response by the union leadership is not so immediate. There are a number of reasons why issues related to job discontent and greater worker rights on the plant level have not become primary demands pressed by top union leaders at the major nationwide negotiations. Nat Goldfinger, the head of the AFL-CIO research department, gave a succinct summary of what has motivated unions in the past 25 to 30 years. "Unions," he said, "have been aiming their major guns on the big issues where there is an immediate payoff and immediate pressure from the rank and file. That means wages, hours, fringes, pensions, holidays, more time off."

Recurring major and minor recessions in the economy have not enabled unions to get too far away from bread and butter issues. In such times it is difficult to consider how machines and plants are affecting workers—the priority is to get the factories to produce again. The inflation following these periods again makes economic issues predominate as unions seek to catch up with the rising cost of living in their contracts.

The process by which unions arrive at their bargaining goals and the nature of collective bargaining itself makes it difficult for noneconomic issues to reach top-level negotiations. Every union's bargaining demands are formulated basically through a process which takes thousands of resolutions from union locals and eventually boils them down to a smaller, more manageable list of demands. The thrust of this process is to find those demands that have the most widespread support and to eliminate those that may be unique to a particular plant or area. Obviously, economic matters—higher wages, better pensions, better health insurance—have the most universal appeal. They are also easily translated into specific demands since the costs can be figured and the company can determine how much it is willing to give up. The costs of the agreement can also be planned ahead, a crucial factor for management.

Noneconomic goals do not have the same universality or predictability. Even such a basic issue as voluntary overtime, which has emerged within the UAW, can cause division among workers at a plant—some favoring the idea, others concerned that if enough workers decide not to work they would deprive those who do want to put in overtime. Management also cannot predict the cost: How many workers will volunteer? How much extra plant capacity will be needed to make up the lack of volunteers? What will the cost be of losing the flexibility to meet short, peak demand without overtime? Can the issue be turned against management by workers refusing to work overtime to cut off production and to put on pressure to achieve some other demand?

Due to these factors, management has traditionally been much tougher on noneconomic issues. Management argues that such demands impinge on the sacred area of management prerogatives and are therefore not negotiable.

A candid explanation of this process was given by George Morris, Jr., director of labor relations at General Motors, in a speech before

the Conference Board in June, 1971. He argued that the Nixon administration's wage and price controls had put management at a serious disadvantage in collective bargaining. The effect of controls, he
said, was to encourage unions to seek demands in noneconomic areas
while taking away management's main weapon in dealing with these
issues—its hold over the purse strings. What Mr. Morris was describing was the very essence of collective bargaining—that to get one item
you may have to trade off another. Management's strategy was to make
concessions on money items to prevent gains in noneconomic areas.
In the 1970 negotiations he brought out that through this trade-off
strategy,

> without controls and through tough collective bargaining, we prevented
> any erosion of the right to subcontract work which is so necessary to our
> business, to introduce new technology, to schedule overtime and to main-
> tain efficiency and discipline, all of which matters, among many others,
> were the subject of serious union demands.

The evolution of nationwide industry bargaining, where union and
management meet once every three years to work out a new contract,
has tended to defer dealing with the everyday frustration that workers
experience in the plants. Local bargaining units do not have the power,
even with strike action, to make a breakthrough on such a major issue
as voluntary overtime on the local level. Nevertheless, certain issues
such as health and safety, which in the past were dealt with mostly
on the local plant level, pushed their way into the national bargaining table in the early 1970s. Even before the passage of the Occupational Health and Safety Act in 1970 many workers in heavy industry
had become concerned about noise and pollution in their work environment. They often resorted to wildcat strikes to correct conditions.

Since the passage of the act, federal, management, and union educational campaigns have further increased worker awareness. Within the
UAW, for example, some workers regard the right to strike over health
and safety and the setting up of an independent plant official to deal
immediately with unsafe conditions as a more important demand than
an increase in wages. The ability to trade off noneconomic issues with
a good economic package has therefore become more limited.

RANK AND FILE ATTITUDES AND JOB DISCONTENT

So far, however, discontent with the work itself has not emerged as
an issue that brings such immediate pressure from the rank and file.
In interviews during the early seventies with many workers who had
an intense dislike for their jobs and working conditions, I found few

who thought of working through their unions to bring about changes. Usually they saw the solution up to themselves. They hoped to escape from the plant through more education or by saving up to start their own business, or by piling up seniority to land one of the more desirable jobs.

Thousands do leave every year as shown by the high turnover in many industries. The high turnover is a major reason unions feel little pressure for changing the work—the most dissatisfied leave rather than fight.

Those who do stay and fight often find themselves isolated from their fellow workers and the union. A 24-year-old worker who helps assemble gasoline tanks in a plant in Buffalo explained: "The guys will fight on wage issues, but when it comes to taking on a foreman for the way he treats you—in that kind of thing nobody sticks together. I'm not crying. You can make your own fight."

When one does make his own fight he is often disciplined and becomes involved with the grievance procedure. This procedure has emerged as an important alternative for a worker who wants to redress a wrong in the plant. But he often approaches a shop steward who has many other immediate problems to deal with and may discourage a worker from going through the process which may take up to a year to resolve if the complaint is serious. Also, while the grievance procedure is beneficial in keeping off the bargaining table many problems unique to an individual worker, it can also serve as a safety valve and keep problems out of negotiations that should become part of collective bargaining.

Rank and file attitudes are also a factor. Some workers are suspicious of change—a feeling that the plant may not be the best place but at least the rules are known. Lee Jones, a committee man at the Ford Stamping plant in Buffalo represented by Local 897, recalled that when he worked in the plant in the 1950s he had tried to get his department to rotate jobs.

> I got the guys to go along with me and we approached the foreman. We want to rotate, we told him. Most of the time we were told no. We'd pretend we were using our tools, goof around, slow down. Then we'd come back and say, "It's monotonous. Why don't you let us rotate, change off during the day? We'll feel better, be more awake, and we'll go beyond our quota." So some times for a while he'd let us rotate. But I tell you, guys with my attitude were definitely in the minority. Most guys want to get that better job and hold on. If you try to impose something on the guys they didn't ask for, often you'll just have chaos.

He said that even making a simple change without getting a good idea of the sentiment of the members can leave union leaders out on a limb. His local, he recalled, had won an agreement from management to have vacations split so some of the younger men with less seniority could get a week off in the summer to be with their children who were out of school. "The older guys just raised hell, and the clause was dropped from the agreement," he said.

Differences between older workers, who usually have the seniority and better jobs, and the younger workers can be a major obstacle to change.

During a tour of a Chrysler plant which had a program to enrich jobs, I asked an older worker whether he wanted his job changed. He had been in the plant since 1935, had one of the more skilled jobs, and was due to retire in several years. He was responsible for adjusting and balancing the front wheels. "I've got it down. I really wouldn't want anyone fooling with it," he answered.

The issue of job discontent also has surfaced only rarely at the conventions and meetings held by unions to form their bargaining goals. An exception was the February 1973 conference of production workers of the UAW in Atlanta where union leaders asked the delegates to focus on noneconomic issues. Numerous speakers advocated improvements in health and safety in the plants, the right to refuse overtime, and the reform of the way discipline was meted out. Many examples were given of workers bringing up these issues right on the plant floor.

Only one speaker brought up the issue of the work itself. Charles Gifford, president of Local 999, addressed the conference near the end and asked Mr. Woodcock: "You can't build a union based on economics only. We have to deal with the boring, repetitive jobs in production. How can you continue to restore the dignity of work if you just talk about economics?"

Solutions

Up to 1973 most union leaders sought the solution in more free time, a shorter work week, more break time and holidays, and earlier retirement. In an interview with Mike Wallace in 1960, Mr. Reuther said that the way to satisfy a worker's inner needs was through greater leisure where he could find satisfaction for his creative urges. The Steelworkers union won a major breakthrough in 1963 in this direction when 250,000 of their production workers became eligible for a

13 week vacation every five years. The UAW, when the issue of working conditions became pressing in the early 1960s won 24 minutes relief time from General Motors in 1961 and in the next contract the time was increased to 46 minutes per shift.

1973 UAW NEGOTIATIONS

A significant breakthrough came in the 1973 UAW negotiations where noneconomic issues dominated the bargaining. That was the first nationwide bargaining where working conditions overshadowed wage demands. For a decade rank and file and local union leaders had been unhappy over mandatory overtime, health and safety, and the slow grievance procedure in the plants.

During the negotiations, at the height of the heat wave in July and August, three inner-city plants with a mostly black work force staged wildcat strikes. The walkouts were sparked by small radical groups of workers who succeeded in getting the support of many workers who walked off job areas where temperatures were above 100 degrees. The UAW revived the "flying squads" of the 1930s to isolate the radical leaders and persuade the rank and file to return to work. During the 1930s these squads had been used to protect UAW pickets from goon squads hired by the auto companies to break strikes.

Also, in an unprecedented step the UAW suspended national bargaining so top union leaders could tour the Chrysler plants. They found conditions in some of the older plants deplorable. Throughout the rest of the bargaining UAW leaders resisted Chrysler efforts to turn them away from the noneconomic issues. In the past, company negotiators had often succeeded in getting the union to retreat from such demands by sweetening the wage and benefit package.

None of the gains in the new contract matched what local leaders and workers had expected, but they were important chinks through which the UAW can win further concessions. On overtime, the UAW failed to achieve its goal of making it totally voluntary but a worker can be asked to work only one extra hour a day. Workers can also insist on taking every third Saturday off with no forced overtime on Sunday. However, to qualify for such limited overtime a worker must have a perfect attendance record for the previous week—an important gain for Chrysler management which in the 1970 negotiations reported to the UAW leaders that increasing absenteeism was seriously disrupting production. Chrysler also won the concession to schedule mandatory overtime during model start-time and guarantees that its key plants would also get special consideration.

On health and safety local union leaders had sought the right to strike over uncorrected safety violations and to keep a full-time representative on duty who could shut down a work area that he found to be hazardous. This they failed to win. The agreement provides, however, for weekly inspections of plants for safety and cleanliness and allows the UAW's International Safety Committee to respond immediately to disputes that reach an impasse.

The union did not win the principle that a worker cannot be disciplined until he has gone through the grievance procedure. This has been an emotional issue in which workers want to gain a right similar to that recognized in procedures before the courts—that a person is innocent until proven guilty.

Chrysler also gave the union a letter in which it pledged to include the UAW in the company's attempts to improve jobs. The UAW can bring in outside consultants or have the company look into experiments in the field of humanizing jobs if union leaders believe that promising attempts are being overlooked. The letter of intent is unique to collective bargaining and could lead the UAW into greater efforts to change assembly-line work.

There has been some shift, however, within the union movement toward the view that changes may eventually be needed in the work itself. The UAW meeting for the production workers in the 1973 negotiations was the first of its kind in the union's history, and the leaders called the conference solely to get a sense of what was bothering the workers in the noneconomic areas.

Increasing turnover and absenteeism are not only beginning to worry management but union leaders as well. It affects their bargaining and union strength. In return for the gains they make in the contract, they have the responsibility of guaranteeing to the company that the members will live up to the agreement. When a union's ability to maintain the discipline of its own workers is jeopardized, its power is weakened in the eyes of management.

BEGINNINGS OF UNION INVOLVEMENT

The Communication Workers Union, for example, has kept an eye on the efforts of Robert N. Ford at American Telegraph and Telephone to enrich jobs, but has not become a part of the effort itself. John Morgan, assistant to the union president, has kept close watch on the efforts to see what effects they have on the existing contracts. But the union has no plans to become involved. "Our people," Mr. Morgan explained, "tend to feel that our primary job is to look after wages and hours which are tangible. When you get into job enrichment it is hard to define and to get agreement as to what it means."

The American Federation of State, County and Municipal Employees of the AFL-CIO, one of the fastest-growing unions in the country, has gone further. Aided by federal funds, the union has embarked on a career development program. Workers doing the lowest jobs in hospitals, such as mopping floors, changing sheets and emptying bedpans, have been upgraded and given some of the responsibilities of practical nurses. "We got them involved in delivering health care," Jerry Wurf, the president of the union, said. "Instead of being people who felt they were always in the way, they now feel needed. There's been a big jump in morale." He continued:

> The trouble with unions, is that they are still trying for that five or ten cents an hour. That's a carryover from the Depression. We've got to concentrate more on a worker's overall satisfaction, with what he does in the world. American labor leadership doesn't have an understanding for that yet and they don't have the guts to quarrel with the old goals. They often wait for the hysteria of the workers to think of wider horizons.

Yet most union leaders hold the view as expressed by William Winpisinger, a vice president of the Machinists union, who in an article in the *Federationist* in 1972 wrote: "If you want to enrich the job, enrich the paycheck. The better the wage, the greater the job satisfaction. There is no better cure for the Blue Collar Blues."

This simple maxim has been contradicted daily by the behavior of the rank and file. Increasing absenteeism, turnover, local strikes, limits on overtime, challenges to foremen, demand for early retirement, all indicate that workers have been willing to risk economic gains to improve their lot.

There is a story told around Detroit in which a union leader asked a worker on the line why he was absent on Fridays and only worked four days a week. "Because I can't make enough money by working only three days," he shot back.

The satisfaction of a big paycheck, while still important, no longer makes up for unsatisfying work under bad conditions. With a work force that spends more time in school and enters jobs with more education and higher expectations, the demands for improvements in the noneconomic areas should continue to grow.

The present system arriving at bargaining goals and the process of collective bargaining itself, however, have not adequately responded to these trends. Unions and management have not evolved adequate methods to deal with these issues. The meeting of young steelworkers in 1970 was held in secret and its results not publicized. Just the fact that there was a need for the meeting, brought out that the regular union machinery, such as union conventions, were not adequate in getting a sense of what was agitating rank and file members.

It is not so much a matter of reforming the procedure as a change in attitude of union leaders that is important. The danger in being cynical and suspicious is that unions may be left standing by the wayside while management begins to experiment with changing jobs and searching for new incentives. It would be unfortunate if the trade union movement did not have influence over the attempts. A good hard-nosed interest by unions into the research would serve as a check on manipulative and phony solutions, such as giving green stamps or free glasses to workers who have a good attendance record.

It is also doubtful that extensive, meaningful changes can take place without unions being willing to use their main weapon—the strike threat. Leonard Woodcock told the bargaining convention in 1973 that you can only have confrontation in collective bargaining, "if you have in sight a solution to the problem which has produced the confrontation. And as matters stand, we do not have, no one has, the ready answers to the question of how best the work can be done in a humane way."

Yet given the thrust of management, which is still toward greater work fragmentation and adaptation of the worker to the plant, one must ask how seriously management will pursue the solutions without prodding from the labor movement. Also, the long-range answers to increased job satisfaction may mean no improvement or even a decline in productivity. Clearly those solutions will only be applied if union leaders begin to think that the overall satisfaction of their members is as worthwhile as enriching the paycheck.

Peter Henle

5

Economic Effects:
Reviewing the Evidence

Change is the hallmark of today, and the working world is no exception. But whether the changes in the world of work contribute to economic efficiency or personal happiness is a matter of some dispute. In fact, there is disagreement over exactly what changes are actually taking place in the world of work. Some changes are easy to measure. One is the continuing influx of young people and women in the labor force. Another is the shift in the nature of jobs as the economy matures —fewer in farming and mining, more in trade, services, and government. Similarly, in terms of occupations, there are relatively fewer blue-collar jobs but more professional and white-collar positions.

Less subject to verification are changes in worker attitudes that many investigators have reported: a growing alienation toward the "system" or the "establishment," increasing dissatisfaction with one's job, greater resentment with authority in the workplace. This chapter is concerned primarily with these attitudinal ones. It does not aim to provide a definitive assessment of the extent and significance of these changes. It explores only one fundamental aspect of such an assessment: to what extent are attitudinal changes reflected in the functioning and performance of the national economy? (The discussion will not be concerned with individual plant or company experiences, many of which have been fully reported in various professional journals.)

PETER HENLE *is senior specialist (labor) in the Congressional Research Service, Library of Congress. He has also been on the research staff of AFL-CIO. In 1966–71 he was chief economist for the U.S. Bureau of Labor Statistics.*

At the start it might be useful to indicate some ways in which changes in worker attitudes might affect economic performance. On such a list would be a reduction in work activity (lower rates of participation in the labor force, increased absenteeism, higher rate of quitting), less efficient operations (lower rates of productivity gains), less interest by the worker in his product (poor quality, industrial sabotage), and more protest against authority (increases in grievances, labor disputes, strikes, and rejections of contract settlements). These are the aspects of the changing world of work that this chapter will attempt to examine. For convenience, the discussion is divided into four headings: *labor input, performance on the job, productivity* and *labor relations.*

Labor Input

The changing work environment might affect the economy's availability of labor in various ways: by changes in the number of individuals who wish to work, in the number of hours worked by those employed, in their attendance on the job, and in the rate at which they leave jobs.

PARTICIPATION IN THE LABOR FORCE

Recent cross-currents in the rate at which the population participates in the employment process seem to point to one conclusion: those who have been working hard would like to quit and those who have not been working regularly would like more work.

This grows out of the divergent trends in recent years among men and women of different age groups (table 1). Among adult men, there has been a slow gradual drop in the labor force participation rate. It is most pronounced in the older group, age 55–64, where today about 80 percent of all men are in the labor force compared to 89 percent 25 years ago. In the younger categories, age 25–54, there has also been some slippage although not nearly to the same extent. Among teenagers, however, there has been some increase during the last five or ten years.

Among older men the figures reflect a trend toward early retirement and the greater availability of private and public income supplements, including Social Security retirement benefits at age 62, the removal of any age limitations for Social Security disability payments, and various forms of early retirement benefits worked out through collective bargaining. The sharpest decline in labor force participation rates has been among men aged 62–64, only about two-thirds of

TABLE I. LABOR FORCE PARTICIPATION RATES FOR PERSONS 16 YEARS AND OVER, BY SEX AND AGE

Sex and Year	Total 16 Years Over	16 and 17 Years	18 and 19 Years	20 to 24 Years	25 to 34 Years	35 to 44 Years	45 to 54 Years	55 to 64 Years
Male								
1947	86.8	52.2	80.5	84.9	95.8	98.0	95.5	89.6
1950	86.8	52.0	79.0	89.1	96.2	97.6	95.8	86.9
1955	86.2	49.5	77.1	90.8	97.7	98.1	96.5	87.9
1960	84.0	46.8	73.6	90.2	97.7	97.7	95.8	86.8
1965	81.5	44.6	70.0	88.0	97.4	97.4	95.6	84.7
1970	80.6	47.5	69.9	86.6	96.6	97.0	94.3	83.0
1971	80.0	47.3	69.3	85.7	96.2	96.6	93.9	82.2
1972	79.7	48.3	72.0	85.9	95.9	96.5	93.3	80.5
Female								
1947	31.8	29.5	52.3	44.9	32.0	36.3	32.7	24.3
1950	33.9	30.1	51.3	46.1	34.0	39.1	38.0	27.0
1955	35.7	28.9	51.0	46.0	34.9	41.6	43.8	32.5
1960	37.8	29.1	51.1	46.2	36.0	43.5	49.8	37.2
1965	39.3	27.7	49.4	50.0	38.6	46.1	50.9	41.1
1970	43.4	39.4	53.7	57.8	45.0	51.1	54.4	43.0
1971	43.4	34.3	53.2	57.8	45.5	51.6	54.3	42.9
1972	43.9	36.6	55.6	59.1	47.6	52.0	53.9	42.1

Source: Bureau of Labor Statistics.

whom are currently in the labor force. The age groups 55–59 and 60–61 have experienced a somewhat slower rate of decline. The magnitude of these declines can be indicated by the fact that an additional 750,000 men would now be in the labor force had the participation rates of the late 1940s been maintained.

Among younger men the continued increase in the proportion of young people attending college and graduate school tends to cut down on labor force participation since a smaller proportion of in-school than out-of-school youth enter the labor market. On the other hand, the rise in labor force participation in the teenage groups reflects the greater inclination of those in school to join the job market in search of part-time employment.

The net effect of these divergent trends has been a slow increase in labor force participation among the population age 16 and above. The slow increase, of course, is the result of combining a steady decline for men (dropping from 87 to 80 percent) and a more rapid rise for women, from 32 to 44 percent. The conclusion seems to be that men in the middle and older age groups who have been working most of their lives have been turning in greater numbers to early retirement. However, the strong continuing interest of women and young people in the labor market seems to belie any assumption that work has lost its popularity for everyone.

In this connection, it is worth noting that despite all the cross-currents affecting the United States, this country compares favorably with others in labor force participation. In a 1971 comparison with six other industrialized countries, United States participation ranks higher than in Canada, Germany, or Italy, about equal to Sweden and the United Kingdom, and lower than in Japan. For men, despite recent slippage, the United States national average is still higher than that of those other countries except Japan. For women, the United States rate is excelled only by Japan and Sweden.

ATTENDANCE AT WORK

Although more people are employed, perhaps changes in the work environment have caused more frequent job absences, particularly for what some have considered petty or trivial reasons. In recent years many management officials, particularly in mass production industries, have complained publicly about an increasing absenteeism rate among their production workers. Special programs, often involving union-management discussions, have been initiated in an effort to reduce unscheduled absences. It has been hard to judge whether these complaints represent a nationwide phenomenon or whether they might reflect only isolated or special circumstances. On this issue factual evidence is sketchy. No historical statistical series has been maintained regarding absences from work. No agreement has ever been reached on the precise definition or classification of such absences. Company attendance records, while accurate enough for payroll purposes, seldom provide sufficient detail for analysis of absenteeism. Moreover, it would be difficult, for example, to distinguish (during a personal interview or even from company records) absences attributed to minor illness or ailments from absences to enjoy the opening of the hunting or baseball season.

Some data on absenteeism are collected in conjunction with the monthly household survey from which the well-publicized employment and unemployment figures are obtained. Information is obtained on a person's activity the previous week; and if he was employed, whether he was at work and if not working, the reason. Because of the recent interest in absenteeism, a more thorough analysis of this data has been made, but the deficiencies in the data quickly become apparent. For example, some of the most critical series date back on a continuous basis only to 1967, and because information is not necessarily obtained from the individual concerned, but only a member of his household, there are almost certain errors in response, particularly with reference to the reason given for not working.

Considering its limitations, what does this analysis show? The result seems to be "a mixed bag." Data are available on two aspects of the absentee question: (1) part-week absences and (2) full-week absences. Information was analyzed for what are called absences "for personal reasons" classified in two groups: (1) illness or injury; and (2) miscellaneous personal reasons, as widely varied as jury duty, funeral leave, family responsibilities, personal business, and "didn't feel like working." Each group includes some proportion of unavoidable absence and some proportion of what is commonly termed absenteeism in the sense of a deliberate, often irresponsible, decision.

The rate for both part- and full-week absences has increased moderately in the 1967–72 period (table 2). Increases due to illness are

TABLE 2. WAGE AND SALARY WORKERS ABSENT FROM WORK
FOR PERSONAL REASONS
(ANNUAL AVERAGE 1967–1972)

Year and Work Schedule	Number Absent (In Thousands)			Percent of Total Workers		
	Total	Illness	Misc.	Total	Illness	Misc.
On Part-Week Absence						
1967	2,015	1,186	829	3.9	2.3	1.6
1968	2,147	1,247	900	4.1	2.4	1.7
1969	2,199	1,260	939	4.1	2.3	1.7
1970	2,275	1,298	977	4.2	2.4	1.8
1971	2,343	1,351	992	4.3	2.5	1.8
1972	2,435	1,431	1,004	4.3	2.5	1.8
On Full-Week Absence						
1967	1,351	939	412	2.1	1.5	.7
1968	1,468	1,040	428	2.3	1.6	.7
1969	1,575	1,086	489	2.4	1.6	.7
1970	1,674	1,153	521	2.5	1.7	.8
1971	1,666	1,120	546	2.4	1.6	.8
1972	1,660	1,162	498	2.3	1.6	.7

Source: Bureau of Labor Statistics.

roughly the same as those for "miscellaneous" reasons. There is a somewhat sharper increase during the period for part-week absences than for full-week absences.

Interpreting these data is not a simple matter. These increases occurred at a time when paid leave arrangements were being liberalized for illness, death in the family, jury duty, and for other personal reasons. Absences of this type are included in the data. Thus, to an undetermined extent, the 1967–72 increases reflect management and labor decisions shifting some of these absences from an unauthorized to an authorized category. It should also be noted there was a slight increase in the frequencies of work injuries in manufacturing, which might have had some effect on the rate.

More specific figures for each year by occupation and industry of the individual concerned and by age and sex indicate that a variety of forces may be at work to produce the overall figures. In terms of occupation, it is interesting to note that the level of absences varies considerably by occupation and that the increase during these years, although widespread, was especially pronounced in the professional, managerial, and clerical occupations. By industry, the highest rates for part-week absences are in manufacturing and government, where either through collective bargaining or legislation, the employee typically is entitled to extensive paid-leave arrangements. Since 1967 the part-week absence rate has grown most sharply in the service, trade, and finance industries. On the other hand, relatively slight increases have taken place in manufacturing, transportation, and utilities.

Within manufacturing, those with the highest rate of absences include such low-wage industries as tobacco, apparel, and textiles and certain high-wage industries such as automobiles and primary metals, where the jobs may be particularly monotonous or burdensome (table 3). With respect to automobiles, it is interesting to note that 1972 rates were not significantly higher than those of 1967. The president of General Motors has observed that the absenteeism rate for his firm recently dropped after more than doubling over a ten-year period.

Younger workers have the highest rate for part-week absences but the lowest for full-week absences. Furthermore, during 1967–72 the full-week absenteeism rate for younger workers held steady or declined slightly while the rate for the middle-aged showed little change, and the sharpest increase occurred among older men. This may reflect the forces previously cited producing similar changes in labor force participation.

In summary, the data do reflect an increase (10 percent over a five-year period) in the rate of absenteeism because of illness or miscellaneous personal reasons. The forces or motivations producing this increase cannot be determined with precision; but they undoubtedly include not only any disaffection with work arrangements

TABLE 3. WAGE AND SALARY WORKERS ABSENT FROM WORK
FOR PERSONAL REASONS
(BY MANUFACTURING INDUSTRY 1967 AND 1972)

	Percent of Total Workers	
Industry	*1967*	*1972*
Total	2.3	2.7
Higher		
Tobacco	3.2	4.1
Automobiles	3.7	3.8
Apparel	2.6	3.6
Primary metals	2.4	3.3
Textiles	2.4	3.2
Paper	2.0	3.0
Medium		
Rubber	3.2	2.9
Furniture	2.1	2.7
Stone, clay and glass	2.1	2.7
Instruments	2.1	2.6
Food	2.1	2.5
Machinery	2.1	2.5
Petroleum	1.6	2.5
Lower		
Electrical equipment	2.2	2.4
Fabricated metal	2.6	2.4
Lumber and wood products	2.4	2.3
Chemical	1.9	2.2
Leather	2.3	2.1
Printing and publishing	2.0	1.8
Transportation equipment, except auto	1.9	1.8

Source: Bureau of Labor Statistics.

but also the continuing accommodation between management and labor granting more frequent approval to absences of this nature.

QUITTING A JOB

Any lessened interest by workers in their jobs could easily lead to more frequent instances of job turnover. The picture is drawn of an individual with limited job satisfaction but with considerable educational and technical knowledge who tries many jobs over a relatively brief period of time in an effort to find one that meets his needs. If this phenomenon became widespread, the result, of course, would be higher rates of job turnover with greatly increased management costs for recruiting, processing, and training new employees.

If these developments have in fact taken place, they should be evident in the basic statistics dealing with the rate of job quits in manufacturing. In the past, a number of different analysts have examined the data on quit rates in an effort to find a long-term trend. Some have found the quit rates to be increasing. Others have found them to be declining and creating what has been called "a new industrial feudalism," where the employee in effect was being trapped to remain on the job by the benefits he would obtain through additional service, including promotions, longer vacation, and large retirement pension.

Part of the difficulty with quit rates is that they are quite sensitive to changes in the business cycle. As might be expected, people are more inclined to leave their job and look for another during times of prosperity, when new jobs are plentiful. Consequently the major difficulty in any statistical analysis of quit rates has been to separate out the fluctuations related to the business cycle from those caused by any longer-term factors.

A more rigorous analysis in 1972 of manufacturing quit rates confirmed the close relation of quits with business cycle conditions and even went further in an effort to find a long-term trend over the past 25 years. The search was unsuccessful, and the study concluded that "on the average, the manufacturing worker is no more or less mobile in seeking new employment than he was in the years immediately following World War II."

The only industrial sectors other than manufacturing where labor turnover data are available over a period of years are mining and communications. Here the evidence is mixed. In both metal mining and coal mining, the quit rate has increased over the postwar period and even though it has dropped back somewhat during the recent recession, the current level is considerably higher than in earlier recession periods. In telephones, however, although there was a slow but steady increase in the quit rate during the 1960s, a sharp drop beginning in 1969 left the 1972 rate at a new record low. According to industry officials, the drop can be attributed to at least two factors: a higher wage schedule for low-skill jobs, and a program of job enrichment initiated by the Bell system.

If data were available to cover other sectors of the labor force, especially those with a larger proportion of young people, perhaps more striking advances in the quit rate would have been noted. But on the basis of the limited evidence there is little indication of widespread job dissatisfaction in the behavior of this key economic indicator.

Performance on the Job

Changes in worker attitudes not only may lead to changes in the amount of labor input but also may affect performance on the job. This is a rather uncertain area for any definitive analysis, but three specific questions present themselves: (1) Is the traditional pace of work and flow of output being maintained under today's conditions? (2) Does management find that it has to devote a larger share of expenses to such items as extent of supervision, control of quality, prevention of theft, and management of materials than has been the practice in the past? (3) Are workers turning to artificial stimulants such as alcohol or drugs which can adversely affect their performance?

Each of these questions has, of course, been the subject of some discussion in management journals and more popular media. There have been complaints that today's worker will not accept the same pace of work as his father or grandfather. There are also complaints that today's worker does not have the same interest in the quality of his output and is less trustworthy in handling materials and finished products. The spread of drugs to the industrial scene has been raised as a management nightmare. Hard evidence on these issues is difficult to find, and the following comments are not offered as definitive analysis.

QUANTITY OF OUTPUT

The pace of work has always been a matter of dispute (in some cases guerilla warfare) between management and organized labor. This issue takes on special meaning if the production process is automated, with the pace of work outside the control of the employee, as on the auto assembly line. The United Auto Workers has always insisted that disputes over the speed of the assembly line remain outside the scope of the no-strike clause of its agreements with the auto manufacturers. It has always preferred to retain the right to strike over such questions, rather than submitting them to final and binding arbitration. In many other industries, as well, unions have fought vigorously to reduce the pace of work and have been at least moderately successful. It seems fair to say that a combination of union pressure and responsive management has reduced the work pace in many mass production industries.

QUALITY OF OUTPUT

Complaints about poor workmanship, lack of interest in quality, petty thievery, or industrial sabotage are even harder to evaluate. It would be difficult to disentangle the extent to which these complaints reflect a higher rate of negligence by employees or simply more complete reporting of negligence cases. Probably some of each is involved.

From time to time, dramatic examples of worker alienation and its effect on quality do come to the surface. In May 1973 the Associated Press reported

> how mechanics practically dismantled a $14,500 car looking for a rattle and finally discovered a ball bearing in a door panel. The bearing was wrapped in a note that read: "Well, you finally found it, didn't you, you rich so-and-so?"

One factor in this complicated picture is the demands placed on the production process by today's complex technology. The greater use of automated equipment, the finer tolerances required, and the use of more expensive equipment and materials all put new strains on work arrangements. It becomes more important to obtain fuller utilization of such equipment, to avoid waste and damage, to assure quality of output. Greater pressure to meet higher standards of quality is placed on the individual. The result is almost bound to be greater expense for such items as quality control, supervision, maintenance of equipment, and the like.

Another factor adding to pressure on quality is the wide variety of consumer standards that have been adopted either as a result of federal and state legislation or voluntarily by manufacturers. These standards, assuring that the product incorporates certain environmental, safety, and health features, add further pressure. Along with them has come a growing awareness by consumers of their rights with respect to such issues as return of defective merchandise and use of product and service guarantees—and thus putting still more emphasis on the quality of the final product.

In some cases changes in technology have reduced the potential damage to output. For example, petty thievery by longshoremen has been a traditional aspect of waterfront work. In more recent years the use of containerized shipments has cut down the amount of easily accessible cargo awaiting shipment and thus improved security. (Occasionally, of course, someone hijacks an entire container.)

From a longer-range viewpoint, is it reasonable to expect the same pace of work and the same interest in workmanship from an individual in today's high-income economy as from his father and grandfather working in quite a different era? If jobs are more plentiful, family savings more substantial, and income support during periods of unemployment more available, it seems only logical to expect today's worker to be somewhat less concerned with the necessity of retaining his job under all circumstances and thus less concerned with the finer points of his work assignment. While there are factors on the other side of the calculus, including the heavy load of debt which most families now carry, what is probably surprising is the extent to which the spirit of workmanship and pride in one's product still persist throughout American industry.

ALCOHOL AND DRUGS

Another threat to quality of output is the widely discussed rate of alcohol consumption and drug usage. These two are often depicted as a menace to work performance and a cause of increased absenteeism, more frequent accidents, and more hazardous working conditions for others.

The only difficulty with this scenario is that it cannot be documented. Evidence of greater consumption of alcohol and increased usage of dangerous drugs among workers is hard to find. Undoubtedly individual workers and firms have been seriously affected, but any indication that the economy as a whole has been seriously damaged is impossible to obtain.

Data are fragmentary at best, and more reliable regarding alcohol than drugs. The accuracy of results obtained from surveys of households or consumers is somewhat suspect since extensive response error may be involved. For alcohol, data on consumption are available through the tax system. These indicate that per capita consumption of alcohol remained virtually unchanged for 110 years, from 1850 to 1960, after which it has been rising slightly. The increase may reflect the spread of deviant drinking in American society, or it may be a statistical artifact. One authority contends that the legalization of alcohol sales in many areas of the country during the past decade has simply resulted in a more accurate recording of the actual amounts of alcohol consumed. Moreover, since there has been a general decline in the per capita amount of alcohol consumed in the form of hard beverages and an increase in the consumption of light beverages, such as beer and wine, the increase in per capita consumption may simply reflect moderate drinking by a greater proportion of the population.

Data on number of alcoholics at work are also "iffy." It has been estimated that approximately nine million Americans are alcoholics and about half of these, or 5 percent of the work force, are currently employed; but there is little evidence to indicate whether this proportion has been increasing or decreasing.

Evidence on the effects of alcoholism is somewhat contradictory.

Surveys by company personnel offices confirm the association of alcoholism with higher rates of absenteeism, but it is interesting to note that no one has yet been able to document the charge that the industrial accident rate among alcoholics is higher than that of other workers. In a study conducted by two industrial physicians in 1955 in a company of 1,800 employees, it was found that for fifteen years only one injury (which was not fatal) could be either directly or indirectly attributable to alcohol. The work histories of members of Alcoholics Anonymous who were exposed to accidents also revealed few on-the-job occurrences. These members attributed their low-accident rate to the routine nature of many of their jobs, their own exceptional caution, protection from accidents by fellow workers, absenteeism when especially vulnerable to accidents, and assignments to less hazardous work.

Nor does the typical alcoholic seem to be a chronic job hopper. One study showed that members of Alcoholics Anonymous reported low rates of turnover; approximately 65 percent of the respondents reported four or fewer job shifts and almost 40 percent reported no changes at all. To some extent, the job stability reflects the mature age of the alcoholic. According to the National Council on Alcoholism, the typical alcoholic is age 35–54 and has been at his job for twelve years. (In some instances, the job stability of the alcoholic may be costly to his employer, if this stability simply reflects his employer's kindness in not dismissing him.)

Drug usage in its present form and infinite variety is much more of a modern phenomenon than alcohol. However, its extent in the working world as opposed to the scholastic world of high school or college is not subject to any accurate determination. Obviously individual firms have had specific problems, but surveys of business concerns generally conclude that it has not been a serious impediment to efficient operations. In a 1970 survey by the Conference Board, less than 20 percent of the 222 cooperating companies reported a significant drug problem in their organizations. Nearly 40 percent reported no drug problem, about one-third reported only "minor instances" of drug use, and 9 percent simply did not know. About half the firms reporting a drug problem identified it as significant among a particular segment of the work force, mostly the young. Among the ways in which drug usage affected company operations were poorer attendance, excessive turnover, higher employee theft, and lower productivity and morale.

Another study conducted about the same time by the New York State Narcotics Addiction Control Commission provides data on drug use by occupational groups. Sales personnel consistently reported the highest rate. This may be related to the high proportion of part-time and seasonal workers in sales jobs. Blue-collar workers reported below average use of most types of drugs while professional, technical, and managerial workers reported average rates of usage in most categories.

Although drug usage is a continuing problem for American society, it does not appear to have made major inroads into the operations of the economy. In essence, it may have greater impact in keeping a small fraction of young people out of constructive employment rather than reducing the effectiveness on the job of any large proportion of the work force.

Productivity

The efficiency of the economy is normally viewed as the relation between its output and the labor, capital, and material resources required to produce that output. As technology, education, and management methods improve, a fixed amount of human and capital resources can generate an increasing quantity of output.

This efficiency is measured by productivity, the relation of output to one or more of the inputs. One specific measure—the most highly developed and perhaps the most useful—is the relation of output to labor input, typically defined as output per manhour. Over the past 25 years this productivity measure has increased at a rate of 3.2 percent annually for the total private economy. Obviously, this measure is influenced by a variety of factors, including technological change, economic conditions, and the education and training of the work force.

Another factor which could conceivably affect productivity is the attitude of employees. In recent years the importance of attitudes toward work and other noneconomic factors influencing productivity change has been sharply debated in the light of the decline in productivity gains experienced during the years 1966–70. For those four years the average productivity gain for the total private economy was only about 1.5 percent annually, about half the average postwar increase. The question raised by this performance was whether the slowdown simply reflected economic events or could be attributed in addition to noneconomic forces. Some slowdown was to be expected since productivity tends to drop as the economy expands close to full capacity, a characteristic of the 1966–68 period. In addition, the downturn in output beginning in late 1969 also helped to retard productivity growth. Another contributing factor seemed to be the attitude of employers who had become so accustomed to operating in a tight labor market that they were slow to reverse their attitude when the labor

market changed to a condition of slack. Thus many relatively un-
needed employees were maintained on the payrolls during 1969 and
1970. Beginning in 1971, the economic picture improved and carried
improved productivity gains with it. In terms of annual data, by 1972
the economy had recovered about one-third of the productivity shortfall in the total private economy and two-thirds in the nonfarm economy. Continuing above average gains in the last half of 1972 and the
first quarter of 1973 further reduced the shortfall, with the result that
the trend of productivity gains came close to the long-term growth
path, although a subsequent fall-off occurred during the remainder of
1973.

Statistically, at least the drop in productivity gains during the 1966–
70 period seems to have been accounted for almost entirely by prevailing economic conditions and, three years later, to have been balanced by the greater-than-average improvement in the previous two
and one-half years. While noneconomic factors, including employee
attitudes, are always present, they do not seem to have had a major
effect on the economy's overall performance.

More detailed examination of data reveals a very mixed picture—
with some industries whose working conditions have been considered
oppressive, such as coal mining and tires and tubes, showing drops in
productivity during the 1968–72 period, while others such as foundries
and motor vehicles have continued to increase at historic or higher
rates. There seems to be no relation between the existence of such factors as assembly-line operations or unpleasant working conditions and
changes in the rate of productivity gain.

Labor Relations

The American system of labor relations had its origins in the
rough and tumble days of an earlier stage of the Industrial Revolution.
The chaos, discipline, and violence of those days were gradually transformed into a more stable system of union-management and personnel
relations.

Today's labor relations system is essentially a mechanism for setting
and implementing the terms and conditions of employment. Where
a labor union represents the employees, the system includes arrangements for bargaining collectively, for embodying the agreed wages and
working conditions in a written agreement, normally for a fixed term
of years, and for agreed-upon procedures to resolve any disputes regarding the meaning or application of the agreement in specific cases.
The system, therefore, provides a machinery for the settlement of com-

plaints, not just when the contract is open for renewal but throughout the life of the agreement.

More recently, questions have been raised whether this system, like other parts of the American system, may have outlived its usefulness. Is it still able to serve the interest of the ordinary worker? Does the system give him a fair deal, or has he become boxed in by twin organizational giants, the corporation and the union?

Chapter 3 is directly concerned with the thinking and attitudes of the average worker. The interest here is not so much with the worker's thoughts as with his actions. Certain options are open to him to demonstrate his dissatisfaction with his job and with the way the labor relations system operates. As an individual he can file grievances under the existing grievance machinery. As a member of an employee group he can go on strike with or without union authorization; he can reject contract settlements recommended by the union leadership; he can elect new union leadership; he can vote to switch unions; and he can petition the National Labor Relations Board for the union representing him to be decertified. Regarding some of these options, sufficient information is available for analysis.

STRIKES

The strike is the ultimate weapon of the worker. It represents his direct action against either his current wage and working conditions or the proposed future conditions as set forth in a management proposal for a new bargaining agreement. Changes in the number of strikes and amount of strike idleness do reflect changes in worker discontent, but they also may reflect economic conditions and the union leadership's evaluation of the strike's chance of success.

Data on strikes have been maintained ever since 1881, including information on the number of strikes, the workers involved, and the total number of man-days idle as a result. Viewed as a whole, the most extensive period during which production was disrupted by strikes occurred directly after World War II, when companies and unions locked horns over wage increases in the light of the postwar inflation and the end of overtime at premium war rates. Nothing has since approached the record of workers involved and the number of man-days idle in 1946. The ten years culminating with 1970 have seen slowly rising levels of strike activity, after which came a drop-off in 1971 and 1972 (table 4). The first nine months of 1973 showed even lower totals than 1972 and, in terms of total idleness, were the lowest in nine years.

Additional insight can be gained from data on the circumstances

TABLE 4. WORK STOPPAGES IN THE UNITED STATES 1947–1972

Year	Number of Work Stoppages	Duration (Days)	Workers Involved Number (Thousands)	Workers Involved Percent of Total Employed	Man-Days Idle Number (Thousands)	Man-Days Idle Percent of Estimated Working Time
1947	3,693	25.6	2,170	4.7	34,600	.30
1950	4,843	19.2	2,410	5.1	38,800	.33
1955	4,320	18.5	2,650	5.2	28,200	.22
1960	3,333	23.4	1,320	2.4	19,100	.14
1965	3,963	25.0	1,550	2.5	23,300	.15
1970	5,716	25.0	3,305	4.7	66,414	.37
1971	5,135	27.0	3,263	4.5	47,417	.26
1972	5,010	24.0	1,714	2.3	27,066	.15

TABLE 5. WORK STOPPAGES DURING TERM OF AGREEMENT

Year	All Work Stoppages Number	All Work Stoppages Workers Involved (Thousands)	Stoppages During Term of Agreement Number	Stoppages During Term of Agreement Percent of Total	Workers Involved Number (Thousands)	Workers Involved Percent of Total
1961	3,367	1,450	1,084	32.2	378	26.0
1962	3,614	1,230	1,078	29.8	349	28.3
1963	3,362	941	1,204	35.8	364	38.7
1964	3,655	1,640	1,317	36.0	462	28.2
1965	3,963	1,550	1,374	34.7	463	30.0
1966	4,405	1,960	1,608	36.5	611	31.2
1967	4,595	2,870	1,557	33.9	659	22.9
1968	5,045	2,649	1,585	31.4	724	27.3
1969	5,700	2,481	1,964	34.5	861	34.7
1970	5,716	3,305	1,910	33.4	829	25.1
1971	5,138	3,280	1,699	33.1	654	19.9
1972	5,010	1,714	1,994	39.8	682	39.8

Source: Bureau of Labor Statistics.

surrounding strikes and the issues involved. Most strikes take place at the time a new contract is negotiated, but as many as one-third take place during the course of an agreement. (It should be noted that such strikes do not necessarily violate the agreement, which may not include a no-strike clause.) Any increase in this type of strike could reflect worker resentment at job conditions and an unwillingness to wait for contract renewal time to show dissatisfaction. However, there has been relatively little change in the proportion of strikes occurring while an agreement has been in effect (table 5). Although the number of these strikes increased during the 1960s, it dropped off in 1970 and 1971. During the 1961–71 decade, it fluctuated between 30 to 36 percent of all strikes; for 1971 the figure was 33 percent. Most of these strikes were brief, with at least half of them settled within three days. The result is that although such strikes constitute about one-third of the total in any one year, their proportion of total strike idleness is quite small, declining from 10–12 percent during the early 1960s to only 4.4 percent in 1971. One reason for this decline may be the special efforts made by management and unions in the construction industry, where many of these strikes occur, to eliminate or limit interunion jurisdictional disputes.

Examination of the issues in all strikes may also reveal changes in sources of worker discontent. Traditionally the major reported cause of strikes is general changes in wages and related fringe benefits. This formed the main issue for about half the strikes in the late 1960s and early 1970s, somewhat higher than the early 1960s (table 6). Increases have also taken place in the proportion of strikes concerned with plant administration and various working conditions (physical facilities, safety measures, supervision, discharge and discipline, work assignments, work loads, and various work rules). This group of issues, which includes many of the factors affecting the work environment, has been the chief cause of about 20 percent of strikes in recent years, up from about 15 percent ten years ago. Since this increase encompasses such a wide variety of issues, it is difficult to conclude that it specifically reflects any basic change in work attitudes. Nonetheless, the increase in the proportion of strikes related to working conditions may be an indicator of a shift in worker interests.

CONTRACT REJECTIONS

Another way the individual worker can express his dissatisfaction is to vote down a proposed dispute settlement recommended by his union leadership. This question came into considerable prominence several years ago when the Federal Mediation and Conciliation Service re-

TABLE 6. DISTRIBUTION OF TOTAL WORK STOPPAGES BY MAJOR ISSUE
(PERCENT OF TOTAL)

Year	General Wage Changes	Supplementary Benefits	Wage Adjustments	Hours of Work	Other Contractual Matters	Union Organization	Job Security	Plant Administration	Other Working Conditions	Inter Union Issues
1961	40.3	4.3	4.6	.2	.8	15.4	7.2	13.7	1.4	10.8
1962	42.3	3.0	5.0	.2	.9	16.1	6.1	14.3	1.2	9.7
1963	39.3	2.3	4.9	.3	1.0	15.8	6.2	16.3	1.7	11.3
1964	38.8	2.8	4.6	.3	1.7	15.2	5.8	16.3	1.4	12.4
1965	40.3	2.9	5.0	.4	1.5	15.0	5.1	14.9	1.7	12.0
1966	43.4	1.6	6.2	.1	.9	13.6	4.1	15.5	2.2	11.7
1967	46.1	1.3	5.4	.2	1.0	12.8	5.0	15.3	2.3	10.2
1968	50.4	1.8	4.9	.1	1.8	10.2	3.6	14.4	2.8	9.4
1969	49.6	1.2	5.1	.0	1.5	10.4	1.6	15.5	4.0	8.8
1970	49.9	1.0	3.8	.1	1.9	10.3	3.0	16.1	3.1	9.9
1971	50.6	.8	3.1	.1	2.3	9.4	4.1	17.6	3.0	8.1
1972	40.3	1.8	5.0	.1	1.9	10.2	4.6	23.4	4.3	7.9

Source: Bureau of Labor Statistics.

ported a sharp increase in such rejections in situations handled by FMCS mediators. In 1967 contract rejections reached a total of 14 percent of all cases recorded as going to the "joint meeting" stage (both parties present at a joint meeting rather than simply meeting separately with a mediator). Since then, this percentage gradually declined until it reached 10 percent in 1971 and 1972 (table 7). The decline may

TABLE 7. CONTRACT REJECTIONS RECORDED BY THE
FEDERAL MEDIATION AND CONCILIATION
SERVICE (1964–1972)

Fiscal Year	Joint Meeting	Number of Rejections	Rejection Percentage
1964	7,221	629	8.7
1965	7,445	746	10.0
1966	7,836	918	11.7
1967	7,193	1,019	14.2
1968	7,485	893	11.9
1969	8,028	991	12.3
1970	7,509	843	11.2
1971	7,991	795	9.9
1972	7,215	732	10.1

Source: Annual Reports, Federal Mediation and Conciliation Service.

indicate that union leaders have either sharpened their judgment regarding the needs of their members, or perhaps they are simply doing a better selling job. At any rate, the data on contract rejections do not indicate any increased disaffection with the present structure of labor-management relations.

GRIEVANCES AND ARBITRATION

One aspect of worker complaints not subject to measurement is the number of grievances filed. What is available are incomplete data regarding arbitration cases, the final step in the grievance process. Both the Federal Mediation and Conciliation Service and the American Arbitration Association report continuing increases in their work load. However, this trend is difficult to evaluate since the number of union-management agreements has also been increasing steadily. Data on the number of agreements are not sufficiently precise to judge whether there has been an increase in arbitrations per collective bargaining agreement. One source of the increase in arbitrations is the public sector, where grievance procedure, including arbitration, is increasingly utilized instead of the traditional federal or state civil service appeals system. The increase in arbitrations may also reflect an increased interest by unions or management in taking grievance cases to arbitration (or greater financial resources to do so).

CHANGES IN UNION LEADERSHIP

While the degree of democracy within some unions is still subject to debate, there appears to be a greater consensus that an aspiring candidate for union office can, under the legislative protections of the Landrum-Griffin Act, be assured a fair and honest election. In fact, the past decade has seen an increasing number of incumbent presidents defeated for reelection in such national unions as the Mineworkers, Steelworkers, International Union of Electrical Workers, and State, County and Municipal Workers. Strong opposition was a factor in a president's retiring or failing to stand for reelection in several other unions.

All this has contributed to a higher rate of turnover and shorter tenure in office among presidents of major unions. Between five successive two-year periods, 1961–71, the number of national unions changing presidents reached between 20–30 percent of the total. For the period 1969–71, 49 unions or 28 percent changed union presidents. At the end of that time, the presidents of 94 unions (54 percent) had been in office less than five years. Another 37 (21 percent) had been in office five to ten years. At the other extreme 16 union presidents (9 percent) had served more than twenty years.

While these shifts are reassuring from the standpoint of union democracy, they may not reflect any widespread dissatisfaction among the rank and file. Most changes in the 1969–71 period in national union officers were attributable to death, retirement, resignation, or failure to seek reelection. In only three cases was an incumbent president defeated, though in a number of other situations opposition to the incumbent probably helped him decide to resign or not to seek reelection.

In the more prominent contested elections for national union office, the issues seem to have been the traditional ones focusing on which candidate could best serve the interests of the membership. None of the candidates for office made a special point of the boredom or monotony of the particular type of job over which the union has jurisdiction. However, a number of candidates did stress related issues such as health and safety conditions on the job (a major issue in the Mineworkers election). In several prominent cases the incumbent president was vulnerable because he had been spending union funds for personal pleasures or had appointed relatives and personal friends to union positions.

Any widespread disaffection with union representation or with the labor relations system in general would be more evident in contests for local union offices. Unfortunately, very few studies have been undertaken to measure this turnover, and none is available which provides comparable data over an extended period of time. One such study covering a specific locality indicated relatively high turnover; during 1963–66, more than half the local unions in the Milwaukee area changed presidents and 17 percent had two or more changes.

DECERTIFICATION ELECTIONS

When workers feel, for whatever reasons, that the union that they have chosen has not been giving them adequate representation, they have the right to file a petition with the National Labor Relations Board asking that their union be decertified. If the petition meets certain board requirements, it leads to a board-conducted election in which the employees in the bargaining unit decide whether or not to continue their union representation. To some extent, such petitions represent an indicator of worker satisfaction with their union representation and the labor relations system in general.

Such cases have never been very numerous but they have increased in recent years. For fiscal year 1972, 1,080 petitions were filed, up from a level of about 600–700 ten years ago (table 8). This represents about 9 percent of the petitions which unions filed in 1972 seeking to represent workers in new bargaining units. Ten years ago, decertification petitions were only 7 percent of union requests for representation.

In 1972 these petitions led to 451 elections, about double the number of the early 1960s. The bargaining unit in such cases is typically small, averaging about 40–50 employees. Unions won about 30 percent of these 1972 elections including roughly half the eligible workers; such proportions have remained relatively stable over the past decade. Thus, although workers have shown some increased interest in terminating their union representation, the relatively small number and size of the decertification cases, together with unions' success in winning one-third of these elections, has meant that in 1972 only 10,000 workers terminated their union representation through the National Labor Relations Board, a small proportion of the 19 million union members in the United States.

TABLE 8.   PETITIONS TO NLRB FOR DECERTIFICATION OF COLLECTIVE
BARGAINING REPRESENTATIVE
(1960–1972)

Fiscal Year	Cases Received	Number of Elections	Won by Unions	Percent Won	Employees in Elections Won by Unions		
					Employees Eligible to Vote	Number	Percent of Total Eligible
1960	607	237	74	31.2	17,421	8,726	50.1
1961	593	241	80	33.2	18,364	7,757	42.2
1962	698	285	99	34.7	19,253	12,323	64.0
1963	679	225	60	26.7	13,256	5,223	39.4
1964	679	220	67	30.5	13,732	8,333	60.7
1965	593	200	72	36.0	12,565	7,847	62.4
1966	651	221	64	29.0	10,510	4,449	42.3
1967	624	234	69	29.5	12,705	7,708	60.7
1968	767	239	83	34.7	15,554	10,750	69.1
1969	769	293	99	33.8	21,771	12,422	57.1
1970	766	301	91	30.2	20,344	11,786	57.9
1971	942	401	122	30.4	20,726	9,953	48.0
1972	1,080	451	134	29.7	20,790	10,762	51.8

Source: Annual Reports of National Labor Relations Board.

Evaluating the Evidence

The evidence just reviewed is composed of many fragments which do not form a simple, easily recognizable pattern. Some evidence provides modest support to the proposition that there is increasing disenchantment with work, including, for example, the decline in labor force participation by middle-aged and older men, the increase in the rate of unscheduled absences over the past five years, the increasing proportion of strikes over working conditions, and the continuing increase in decertification petitions filed with the NLRB.

On the other hand, each of these points has to be qualified. The decline in labor force participation by middle-aged and older men is more than offset numerically by the sharp growth in the rate at which women have been entering the labor force and the absence of any decline among younger people. The significance of the increased rate of unscheduled absences is not clear; to some extent, it may simply reflect individuals taking advantage of newly won paid-leave privileges. The increasing proportion of strikes over working conditions covers so many issues that the implications in terms of attitudes toward work are uncertain. Finally, the increase in decertification petitions must be put in proper perspective; the number of workers voting to oust their union representatives is but 5–10 percent of the total voting to install union representation.

Other indicators give little or no support to any decline in the work ethic: the absence of any long-term trend in the quit rate, the rebound in the rate of productivity improvement, and the relative stability of labor relations activity even in such an active collective bargaining year as 1973.

In summary, Americans may be more unhappy at work, but there is very little evidence to show that this has affected their economic performance. An individual's job may be the most important aspect of his life, but his contribution to the economy may not diminish simply because he has problems with his supervisor, is disgusted with his working conditions, or feels that his job is too rigidly defined. On the other hand, the absence of any clear-cut economic data pointing to disaffection with work raises the possibility that people may be more satisfied with their jobs than many writers have suggested. If so, the force of two underlying developments may have been overlooked:

1. A number of industrial and economic changes over the past two decades have had the effect of making many jobs more satisfying.

2. With respect to the less satisfying elements, some progress has been made and avenues to improve these aspects of the job remain open.

Each of these points is worth some elaboration.

IMPROVING THE WORK ENVIRONMENT

The avalanche of news stories and surveys pointing up job dissatisfaction has tended to obscure a number of longer-range developments operating to create a more favorable working environment. Consider for example the following:

1. Changes in the occupational structure have emphasized the rise of professional, technical, and other white-collar jobs at the expense of the blue-collar occupations. Many routine low-paying jobs remain, especially in manufacturing and service industries, but the effect of technological change has been to eliminate many burdensome, backbreaking laboring jobs. Many of the newer type jobs (computer operations, waitresses, clerical positions) may have elements of monotony and may not require much training, but they are not as physically burdensome as the ditchdigging type jobs that have been phased out.

2. There have been major improvements in the work environment. For one thing, most jobs are no longer jammed into the middle of the urban centers. Gradually work has spread out into the more pleasant surrounding areas, and small manufacturing plants outside the metropolitan centers have tended to replace the older, ugly sprawling plants in the cities. In the period 1958–1967, the proportion of employees in manufacturing working in the central city declined from 45 to 40 percent of the total in metropolitan areas. For wholesale and retail trade, the decline was even more pronounced. In the older cities of the East and Midwest, the shift in manufacturing employment is even more striking. From 1947–1967, production-worker employment in manufacturing declined 32 percent in the central city of Boston. In Cleveland, the decline was 37 percent, in Detroit, 48 percent, New York, 19 percent and Pittsburgh, 38 percent.

Moreover, improved lighting, ventilation, temperature, noise control, sanitation and other amenities have been built into the newer industrial facilities. Perhaps the ultimate ideal factory has not been achieved, but working conditions have certainly improved. As a result of the extensive capital expenditures during the past two decades, an increasing proportion of the work force now has more modern facilities.

3. The increasing emphasis on education, leisure, and retirement has given a new look to the role of work in American life. There are three components to this new look: a longer preparatory period of education before working, a revolution in paid leisure time during the work career, and a longer period of income-supported retirement. Currently, paid vacation time for all but the newest employee is a minimum of two weeks, and vacations of as long as six weeks are not uncommon for seniority employees. Paid holidays range between eight to twelve days a year under various bargaining agreements. The shift in holiday observance to Mondays, creating additional three-day weekends, has helped to make available additional blocks of leisure time. All these developments allowing more time away from work open up a wider range of opportunities for creating a full and satisfying life.

4. Important changes have been taking place in the schedules for working hours. Most significant is the growth in part-time jobs, which have particular appeal to women and young people. The part-time labor force grew over 50 percent during the 1962–72 period while the full-time labor force was increasing by only 20 percent.

5. Finally, what about the increase in levels of pay? Working on a General Motors assembly line may provide little satisfaction for the inner man, but the pay of $4.60 an hour (plus health insurance, pen-

sions, paid vacations, holidays, and other fringe benefits) with $9,000 annual earnings (more with overtime) may cover up most of the pain.

These points do not erase any cause for job dissatisfaction, but they may have the effect of making work more tolerable economically than in the past.

LABOR RELATIONS ADAPTABILITY

Another element helping to defuse the issue of job dissatisfaction concerns the adaptability of the nation's basic labor relations institutions. Business management and union representation sometimes act as tradition-bound institutions oblivious to change, but the interaction of the two, plus the independent prodding of the employees, generally operates more effectively than may be obvious. Even a glance at any major bargaining agreement will reveal extensive provisions dealing with numerous working conditions, health and safety, rest periods, job classification, work assignment, procedure for filling vacancies, and a host of other issues.

Recently collective bargaining negotiators seem to be giving somewhat less attention to wage issues in order to spend more time on working conditions. As one example, the long-neglected question of industrial health and safety moved to the center of the bargaining arena with the passage of the 1970 Occupational Safety and Health Act. A lengthy strike against a major oil refinery centered around this specific question. Other industries are also in negotiations on this question, and industry seems willing to spend considerable extra funds for safeguards to protect employees' health and safety.

The speed of the assembly line has always been a contentious issue, and in 1972 two major strikes in auto assembly plants were fought over this and related issues. A strike at the Lordstown, Ohio, Chevrolet plant caught the attention of the nation's journalists because the work force was so young. However, a similar strike at the Norwood, Ohio, plant, whose work force was not so young, made an even greater impact on union-management relations as the longest General Motors strike on record. Eventually in both cases, labor and management were able to work out an accommodation aimed at satisfying (at least) the minimum worker demands while preserving management's requirements for production.

Another issue coming to the fore is the concept of voluntary overtime. Traditionally workers have fought for the privilege of overtime work at premium rates, but more recently in industries such as autos, where overtime has been chronic, workers are demanding the option to refuse overtime assignments. This was an important issue in the 1973 auto negotiations, but here again the final agreement on this question represented an accommodation between the views of management and the workers.

In other situations, management initiatives have been coming to the fore. Of special mention are experiments with new work schedules, including the four-day week and flexible starting and quitting times to ease the discipline of the time clock. More and more managements, aware that their job structures may have become over specialized, are trying techniques of job enlargement and job enrichment.

The present system has a number of built-in advantages. Individuals have a wide variety of occupational and job choices. Few impediments are placed on quitting or changing jobs. Employees are free as individuals and through their representatives to press for change in management's way of doing business. Unions have proved to be forceful spokesmen for change by organizing employee requirements into meaningful channels. Collective bargaining procedures have provided basic guidelines in the employment process as well as a mechanism for modifying rules to meet changing economic conditions.

Up to now, there is only limited evidence that dissaffection with work has interfered with the performance of the national economy. This may be in the process of changing as the bond that ties individuals to their work tends to loosen in a world of higher incomes, greater leisure, and more competitors for an individual's time. In such a world, if work is to retain its traditional attraction, management and labor may have to change some attitudes and techniques, perhaps even their basic approach to the work environment. However, the demonstrated adaptability of the nation's labor relations institutions provides some confidence that any such changes can be successfully adopted.

Richard E. Walton

6

Innovative Restructuring of Work

In today's climate of worker malaise, many work organizations are exploring the idea of a basic restructuring of work to meet both the changing expectations of employees and to improve performance. It is increasingly apparent that employee alienation is not a "passing phenomenon," and that it is at the root of such critical workplace problems as high turnover, low productivity, poor morale, and sometimes even sabotage.

Recognizing that the costs of alienation are borne by both the workers and their employing organizations, a limited number of companies launched, in the 1960s, experimental work systems that were designed to attack both sides of the problem. These innovative systems strove to achieve a total, "systemic" restructuring of the way work is done.

This chapter assumes that parties wishing to take similar initiatives can benefit from the experiences of the early innovators. The first section argues that employee alienation is a basic, long-term, and mounting problem and hence warrants solutions of comparable form. The second, third, and fourth sections treat various aspects of a class of pilot efforts to solve the problem, analyzing their common features, how they were introduced, their results, their long-term viability, and their diffusion. These sections are based on a preliminary review of twelve pilot experiments in eleven different companies. Observations

RICHARD E. WALTON *is Edsel Bryant Ford professor of business at Harvard and director of the Division of Research there. A consultant to many industrial firms and government agencies in the field of applied behavioral science, Dr. Walton is the author of three major books and dozens of articles on current social problems.*

are based partly on field research in many of these firms under my supervision and partly on accounts developed by others as listed in a note at the end of this chapter.[1]

Experimental projects were included in the sample only if (a) they involved a relatively comprehensive restructuring and included operator-level personnel, (b) had existed more than two years, (c) were judged by their originators to have been initially effective, and (d) some satisfactory account of the project was available to me.

The sample includes most of the experiments which have received substantial publicity in recent years, although it does omit some notable firms which have innovated in this field. Of the eleven firms, four are in the United States, two in Canada, one in Great Britain, three in Norway, and one in Sweden.

Diagnosis of the Problem

As I mentioned earlier, the costs of alienation are borne both by workers themselves and by their employing organizations. Employee alienation *affects* productivity and *reflects* the social costs incurred in the workplace.

Increasingly, blue- and white-collar employees and, to some extent, middle managers tend to dislike their jobs, resent their bosses, and rebel against union leaders. They are becoming less concerned about the quality of the product of their labor and more angered about the quality of the context in which they labor.

In some cases, alienation is expressed by passive withdrawal—tardiness, absenteeism and turnover, and inattention on the job. In other cases, it is expressed by active attacks—pilferage, sabotage, deliberate waste, assaults, bomb threats, and other disruption of work routines.

EVOLVING EMPLOYEE EXPECTATIONS

Both passive and active worker reactions are overt manifestations of a conflict between changing employee attitudes and organizational inertia. Increasingly, what employees expect from their jobs is different from what organizations are prepared to offer them. These evolving expectations of workers conflict with the demands, conditions, and rewards of employing organizations in at least six important ways:

1. Employees want challenge and personal growth, but work tends to be simplified and specialties tend to be used repeatedly in work as-

[1] I have a current, albeit in some cases incomplete, understanding of the majority of situations. However, in a few cases the written accounts on which I must rely were prepared in the late 1960s or early 1970s.

signments. This pattern exploits the narrow skills of a worker, while limiting his or her opportunities to broaden or develop.

2. Employees want to be included in patterns of mutual influence; they want egalitarian treatment. But organizations are characterized by tall hierarchies, status differentials, and chains of command.

3. Employee commitment to an organization is increasingly influenced by the intrinsic interest of the work itself, the human dignity afforded by management, and the social responsibility reflected in the organization's products. Yet organization practices still emphasize material rewards and employment security, while neglecting other employee concerns.

4. What employees want from careers, they are apt to want *right now*. But when organizations design job hierarchies and career paths, they continue to assume that today's workers are as willing to postpone gratifications as were yesterday's workers.

5. Employees want more attention to the emotional aspects of organization life, such as individual self-esteem, openness between people, and expressions of warmth. Yet organizations emphasize rationality and seldom legitimize the emotional part of the organizational experience.

6. Employees are becoming less driven by competitive urges, less likely to identify competition as the "American way." Nevertheless, managers continue to plan career patterns, organize work, and design reward systems as if employees valued competition as highly as they used to.

PERVASIVE SOCIAL FORCES

The foregoing needs and desires that employees bring to their work are but a local reflection of more basic, and not readily reversible, trends in United States society. These trends are fueled by family and social experiences as well as by social institutions, especially schools. Among the most significant are:

The Rising Level of Education—Employees bring to the workplace more abilities and, correspondingly, higher expectations than in the past.

The Rising Level of Wealth and Security—Vast segments of today's society never have wanted for the tangible essentials of life; thus they are decreasingly motivated by pay and security, which are taken for granted.

The Decreased Emphasis Given by Churches, Schools, and Families to Obedience to Authority—These socialization agencies have promoted individual initiative, self-responsibility and control, the relativity of values, and other social patterns that make subordinacy in traditional organizations an increasingly bitter pill to swallow for each successive wave of entrants to the United States work force.

The Decline in Achievement Motivation—For example, whereas the books my parents read in primary school taught them the virtues of hard work and competition, my children's books emphasize self-expression and actualizing one's potential. The workplace has not yet fully recognized this change in employee values.

The Shifting Emphasis from Individualism to Social Commitment—This shift is driven in part by a need for the direct gratification of human connectedness (for example, as provided by commune living experiments). It also results from a growing appreciation of our interdependence, and it renders obsolete many traditional workplace concepts regarding the division of labor and work incentives.

These basic societal forces underlie, and contribute to, the problem of alienation. Actually, I believe that protests in the workplace will mount even more rapidly than is indicated by the contributing trends postulated here. The latent dissatisfaction of workers will be activated as (a) the issues receive public attention and (b) some examples of attempted solutions serve to raise expectations (just as the blacks' expressions of dissatisfaction with social and economic inequities were triggered in the 1950s and women's discontent expanded late in the 1960s).

INADEQUACY OF PIECEMEAL REFORMS

Over the past two decades we have witnessed a parade of organization development, personnel, and labor relations programs that promised to revitalize organizations:

Job enrichment would provide more varied and challenging content in the work.

Participative decision-making would enable the information, judgments, and concerns of subordinates to influence the decisions that affect them.

Management by objectives would enable subordinates to understand and shape the objectives toward which they strive and against which they are evaluated.

Sensitivity training or *encounter groups* would enable people to relate to each other as human beings with feelings and psychological needs.

Productivity bargaining would revise work rules and increase management's flexibility, with a quid pro quo whereby the union ensures that workers share in the fruits of the resulting productivity increases.

Each of the preceeding programs *by itself* is an inadequate reform of the workplace and has typically failed in its more limited objectives. Each approach is only a partial remedy; therefore, the organizational system soon returns to an earlier equilibrium.

The lesson we must learn in the area of work reform is similar to one we have learned in another area of national concern—the social services. It is now recognized that a health program, a welfare program, a housing program, or an employment program alone is unable to make a lasting impact on the urban-poor syndrome. Poor health, unemployment, and other interdependent aspects of poverty must be attacked in a coordinated or systemic way.

So it is with meaningful reform of the workplace: we must think "systemically" when approaching the problem.

Comprehensive Reform

Systemic redesign of work systems involves the way tasks are packaged into jobs, the way workers relate to each other, the way performance is measured and rewards are made available, the way positions of authority and status symbols are structured, the way career paths are conceived. Moreover, because these types of changes in work organizations imply new employee skills and different organizational cultures, transitional programs must be established.

Before describing these features in some detail, let me provide some additional background regarding the sample on which my analysis is based. As I mentioned earlier, it includes twelve experiments in eleven different companies.

The United States Companies—An early innovator, Non Linear Systems, Inc., instituted changes in the early 1960s affecting the entire workforce of this small instrument firm. It is one of a few in the sample that explicitly abandoned the experiment and returned to conventional organization.

Donnelly Mirrors, Inc., is another early innovator that introduced incremental changes throughout the 1960s.

An experiment at Corning Glass was initiated in an assembly plant in Medfield, Massachusetts, in 1965. In the fourth United States firm, General Foods Corporation, detailed planning for change began in 1968; the experiment was initiated in a new pet food plant in Topeka, Kansas, in January, 1971.

The Canadian Companies—These are Alcan (aluminum) and Advanced Devices Center, a division of Northern Electric Company (subsequently renamed Microsystems International, Ltd. In 1964, a group of Alcan managers concentrated their innovative efforts on one of the fabrication plants in the works at Kingston, Ontario. At about the same time, Northern Electric was designing a radically different organization for a new facility which was occupied in January, 1966.

The European Companies—These form the remainder of the sample. Shell U.K. introduced change in several locations in the mid-1960s, including two of the plants in this sample—an established wax plant in 1966 and a new refinery at Teesport which came on stream in 1968.

Three projects were carried out in different industries under the Industrial Democracy Project, an action research program sponsored jointly by the Norwegian Federation of Employers and the Trades Union Council of Norway. Social scientists associated with the Work Research Institutes in Oslo also participated. The projects involved a department for assembling electrical panels at the Nobo-Hommelvik firm in Trondheim, a fertilizer plant at Norsk Hydro in Porsgrunn, and a department in the Hunsfos pulp and paper mill near Kristiansand. All three experiments were initiated in the mid-1960s.

A Swedish experiment in the truck assembly plant in Volvo is the final entry in the sample. This effort began in 1969.

All of the experimental units were manufacturing plants in the private sector. The manufacturing processes were continuous in slightly more than a third of the sample, assembly in another third; the rest were mixed, including batch processing.

More than half of the experimental units (plants or departments) employed between 100 and 500 employees; the other units had fewer than 100 employees. Their locations were about evenly divided between urban and rural small towns. More than half were unionized, but none of the plants in the United States sample involved unions.

Although all reports covered more than two years of operating experience, the actual periods varied from two years to over a decade. A third of the sample covered two or three years, a third involved periods from four to seven years, and the rest were eight or more years. In total they represented about 70 years of experience.

Finally, although each unit in the sample has a unique identity, as well as many differentiating characteristics, all units nevertheless have many features in common, not the least of which is the commitment to comprehensive workplace reform. In the remainder of this section, I shall discuss these features under three headings: (1) primary features, (2) secondary features, and (3) tertiary features.

PRIMARY FEATURES: DIVISION OF LABOR

Central to all of the organization innovations considered here is the division of labor. In this regard, three design tendencies can be observed: work teams, whole tasks, and flexible assignment patterns. Let us examine each in turn.

Self-Managing Work Teams—These de-emphasize the idea of one-man/one-job in favor of groups that take collective responsibility for performing a set of tasks, as well as for some self-management.

The size of the team depends upon the nature of technological and and social requirements. For example, many of the preassembly teams in Volvo were comprised of three to six workers. Typically, however, the teams contain from seven to fifteen operators, a size range large enough to include a natural set of interdependent tasks, yet small enough to allow face-to-face meetings for decision-making and coordination.

The reliance upon groups in these experiments is based partly on the belief in the power of face-to-face contact. This provides group members with social satisfaction and individual identification and develops goals, norms, and other capacities for self-management. Groups are also consistent with the idea of whole tasks and flexibility.

Whole Tasks—According to this concept, work that has been fractionated into simple operations is organized into more meaningful wholes that require more operator knowledge and skill. This may mean, for example, that the individual worker assembles whole units rather than merely adding one small part to the unit as it moves quickly through a work station. In continuous process departments, it could involve comprehension of and attention to a major segment of the process.

More significantly, tasks are made "whole" by incorporating functions that previously were performed by other service or control units. In every experiment the work teams took on substantially more inspection and quality control testing for their own work, often eliminating separate inspection departments or positions. The large majority of cases allowed operators to perform increasingly more of the maintenance on their own equipment. In batch processing departments, such as those in one plant in Alcan, operators set up their own machines.

Custodial work—housekeeping the teams' own work area—is frequently included, especially where contamination of products is a critical problem.

In all cases, operators' work was designed to include planning as well as implementation, although the amount of planning responsibility varied widely. Scheduling of product runs and plant shutdowns for maintenance are examples of planning activities previously performed by supervisors or staff specialists that were assumed by work teams.

In the Nobo assembly department brief planning-reporting meetings involving all 30 employees were held each morning. Rotating coordinators took special responsibility for planning. Before the experiment, the planning concerns of workers were limited to their own individual activity on a daily basis. After six months, the workers' planning now effectively embraced the total group of 30 persons and covered a one-week time span. A year later, the planning was still on the group level but covered four weeks. After three years, worker planning had progressed to the point where it embraced five groups (the original experimental unit plus four others now brought into the system) and covered a three-month time span.

Members of teams often have additional enriching responsibilities. For example, the Volvo project included workers on consultation teams. Team members in the General Food, Alcan, Shell, and other experimental units served in roles normally reserved for staff personnel or supervisors. These involved heading the plant safety committee, dealing with outside vendors, exchanging documentation with ship officers, and traveling to investigate or troubleshoot a customer's problem.

Whole tasks are consistent with various social-psychological ideas. For example, by integrating support functions into line groups, one eliminates many of the interfaces which tend to create intergroup friction. Also, the greater challenge in the resulting work is both motivating and confirming of self-worth.

Flexibility in Work Assignments—Flexibility is manifested in a variety of ways: (a) temporary reassignment from one position to another to cover for absences, (b) temporary redivision of work in order to handle a cluster of tasks at different manning levels, (c) progressive movement from one set of tasks to the next in order to master an increasingly larger segment of all work in a team and then in the larger experimental unit, (d) systematic rotation through a set of positions.

Flexibility has the obvious advantage of allowing effective use of available manpower, and it promotes individual skill development.

The mutual learning helps reinforce coordination and teamwide planning activities. And the work team can usually decide how its members rotate through or learn a larger set of tasks.

Thus, the above three design tendencies constitute an internally consistent scheme for the division of labor. Teams make it possible to put together whole tasks. Identification with the team's "whole task" provides a rationale for learning all of the interrelated jobs. The flexibility options, in turn, provide an immediate decision function for cohesive, self-managing teams. Moreover, the personnel movement is more likely to produce psychological gains (e.g., variety, learning) that outweigh the costs (e.g., uncertainty) when it is self-managed by a group rather than controlled by a separate authority.

SECONDARY FEATURES

The effectiveness of a division of labor with the above features depends upon the nature of the supervision and the design of the information and reward systems. The former should provide greater autonomy and enhance a worker's self-esteem and commitment to the work system. The latter should provide workers with the necessary tools to effectively assume greater responsibility and the appropriate rewards to achieve equity.

Supervision—Self-managing of teams requires that supervisors delegate many of their traditional functions of motivating, planning, and controlling. For example, in the pet food plant, the scope of decision-making delegated to the work team included: (a) coping with manufacturing problems that occur within or between the teams' areas, (b) temporarily redistributing tasks to cover absentees, (c) selecting members for plantwide task forces, (d) screening and selecting employees to replace departing operators, (e) counseling operators who did not meet team standards.

To effectively delegate such functions, supervisors must attend more to facilitating the processes and development of groups, longer-range planning, and external relations of the unit for which they are responsible. Sometimes they may do work previously done by their superiors or by staff units.

These changes imply basic shifts in the distribution of influence and expertise above the operator level. In the cases studied, the participative pattern of supervision was facilitated in two ways:

First, at least half of the cases involved significant trimming of supervision and staff. For example, several experiments omitted the first-line foreman and work groups reported directly to a general foreman. In one large works which included an experimental plant, the levels of supervision were reduced from seven to four.

Second, invariably supervisors were trained and coached to become more participative. Most managements reported career casualties among the supervisors who were expected to change—some could provide this type of leadership effectively, but others could not and lost their supervisory positions or were transferred.

Information System—While factory workers may be capable of assuming far more decision-making authority, they do not *automatically* have either the analytical tools necessary to plan and control or the economic information needed to decide on the matters which fall within their enlarged sphere of influence.

Thus, the more sophisticated operations studied provided employees with economic and technical information typically given only to higher levels of supervision. In some cases, innovators discovered the necessity for new measurement procedures and operating feedback loops. The point is illustrated by the following conclusion reached during the design stage of the Hunsfos chemical pulp experiment:

> Firstly, considering the qualitative aspect of pulp production, we found that, among the output criteria most relevant to process control, only degree of digestion, brightness and tearing strength were measured systematically by the laboratory technicians. Cleanliness was judged subjectively from special test sheets, but factors such as pitch and homogeneity were too expensive or difficult for regular measuring. While there were no measurements on the quality of the input chips, information about pH value and percentage of sulphur dioxide in the acid were rarely based on statistical calculations. Because of the great variances observed in some of the quality measurements of individual batches, it was difficult to reveal long-term trends in the process control. The lack of feedback on this level reduced possibilities for continuous learning and control (Englestad).

Those who were restructuring the work in this pulp unit proceeded to clarify and define measurements of the quality and quantity of incoming and outgoing materials as well as quality control limits for each performance criterion. Gradually the measurements were instituted.

The experimentors used two general methods for exchanging current information: (1) regular meetings of operating teams or their representatives, supervision, and sometimes engineering personnel; and (2) an "information center" that posted all information about the state of the system.

Space factors also played an important role. Work team meetings and larger assemblies require space which can accommodate the right number of people and is free of noise and other interferences. The design of the Northern Electric system gave special attention to this aspect, probably because it focused heavily on professional and managerial personnel and a large variety of communication patterns was envisioned.

Reward System—The greatest diversity among the innovative systems studied was in the nature of the compensation system.

All of these systems involved an increase in worker duties and responsibilities. The worker used more of his faculties and accepted more responsibility for the performance of some unit of the organization. In such a situation, what is the quid pro quo for his extra investment? He is rewarded intrinsically through satisfaction from the work itself and the pride associated with higher status. He is also rewarded extrinsically—e.g., through increased pay and economic security. This subsection is primarily concerned with the latter. There are four important aspects of extrinsic rewards:

1. The form of payment. Most pay schemes in the systems studied involved a move from hourly wages to salary and made pay treatment for plant workers parallel to that previously afforded clericals, professionals, and other nonexempt office workers. Among other effects, this move tended to assure stable earnings over longer periods of time.

2. The assurance of employment. Because employment insecurity can undermine worker efficiency and commitment, many managements took steps to assure workers they would not be laid off for lack of work.

3. The levels of individual compensation. How these are determined is a critical issue. The following plan was employed in two of the experiments—the General Foods pet food and Norsk fertilizer plants—where employees manned a continuous processing technology.

Individual pay increases were geared to an employee mastering an increasing proportion of jobs, first in the team and then in the total plant. Increases also could be obtained on the basis of technical skill—e.g., electric maintenance in the General Foods plant—or increased theoretical knowledge—e.g., chemistry or measurement technique in the Norsk plant. Team members were, in effect, paid for learning more and more aspects of the total manufacturing system. Further, because there were no limits on the number of operators who could qualify for higher pay brackets, employees were encouraged to teach each other.

This plan, of course, contrasts with the traditional wage schemes which feature large numbers of differentiated jobs and numerous job classifications, with pay increases based on progress up the job hierarchy. Who, then, decides when an employee has qualified for a higher pay bracket? In the General Foods plant, these decisions were made by the first-line supervisor, usually after consultation with team members. In the Norsk unit, the general foreman and shop steward made joint judgments.

On the one hand, this form of pay progression in the absence of a job hierarchy reinforces the personnel development required by a flexible division of labor. It also provides an incentive for one of the more meaningful forms of interpersonal cooperation, namely, teaching and learning.

On the other hand, the plan is not easy to administer. The evaluative implications of awarding different rates of pay can stir strong emotions in people who work so closely with each other. Are the judgments about job mastery appropriate? Does everyone have an equal opportunity to learn other jobs? Do judges depart from job mastery and other specified criteria and include additional considerations in making "promotions"? Such questions naturally arise.

Another consequence of this plan can be a rapid rate of pay increases, relative to rates of progression in conventional work systems. In the General Foods plant, for example, many employees were able to learn nearly all of the operations in the plant in two and a half years. They progressed from starting rate to near top rate in that time period—thereby earning a very substantial pay increase. While the obvious effect of such rapid progression is an increase in the overall level of worker compensation, many employees in the General Foods plant still did not perceive the plan as an adequate quid pro quo for the level of involvement and contributions they were making. In mid-1973, they were exploring group bonus schemes as vehicles for additional awards.

In the Corning plant, management's response to the "escalating climate of work involvement" was to change "toward a pay process more clearly based on merit (including appraisals for hourly and weekly salaried clerical and technical employees as well as for managerial and professional personnel)" (Beer and Huse). I do not know whether this scheme resulted in substantially higher average compensation levels or merely a distribution of pay more closely linked to differential performance.

4. The level of overall compensation. This probably becomes the most significant issue over the long term. (I emphasize "over the long term" for reasons to be treated later.) The quid pro quo involving higher compensation levels is related to various aspects of the work system itself.

The simplest relationship is illustrated by Non Linear Systems. In this experiment, management simply pegged wage rates higher to generally compensate for extra worker involvement. But other relationships are more complex:

Time in lieu of pay: "Compensation" may have to be taken in forms other than money. For example, wage rates for pre-assemblers and manning tables for certain pre-assembly units in the Volvo truck division were fixed in the union contract; therefore, employees were not able to earn additional compensation, but could consume the fruits of increased efficiency via the length and convenient timing of work breaks.

Higher pay for flexibility: The Shell, U.K. experiments were initiated while productivity bargaining between management and the union was being conducted. Management was seeking to exchange pay increases in return for a relaxation of restrictive work rules, and the types of flexible work patterns involved in the experiments were radical examples of what management was trying to negotiate with the union. Thus, the experiments not only provided both union and management with experience related to the bargaining but also were conducted in a context in which it was clear that the innovations would involve increased rates. And they eventually did.

Cost reduction formula: Compensation levels were linked to credible promises of future performance in one case. At Donnelly Mirrors, management related the size of the annual increase in base pay to (a) collective judgment about the feasible magnitude of cost reductions over the next year and (b) collective commitment to achieve the cost reductions that would pay for the increase. This innovative system also provided for group bonuses.

Cost and quality bonuses: Compensation levels were often linked to the work systems' actual results. In three Norwegian experiments, as with Donnelly Mirrors, group bonuses were a central feature. Two of these involved somewhat complex formulas incorporating significant factors which workers could influence. The fertilizer-factory bonus was based on production volume of acceptable quality, loss of nitrogen, total man-hours for production and service workers, and certain other cost factors. The chemical-pulp department bonus was paid on cleanliness, tearing strength, and degree of digestion and brightness.

The foregoing diversity in the provision for rewards reflects, I believe, a lack of consensus among the designers of the various work-system experiments. Many managers and psychologists tend to play down the matter of extrinsic rewards. Indeed, in the *short run* extra pay in the form of higher individual rates or group bonuses may not be necessary to elicit involvement. Short run, the intrinsic rewards involved in change, challenge, and personal development are sufficient. In the longer run, however, a sense of equity and sustained effort by workers requires a sharing of the extra fruits of productivity.

TERTIARY FEATURES

Another set of factors that help create appropriate attitudes and skills for systemic redesign of work involve symbols of status and trust and methods of training and recruitment.

Symbols of Status and Trust—Almost every experiment had features expressly designed to enhance the status of operators and to communicate trust in their exercise of self-control. Typically, there were no time clocks and workers were placed on salary and given the normal privileges of salaried employees.

Other devices were employed to minimize status differentials. For example, the General Foods pet food plant had an open parking lot, a single entrance for both office and plant, and a common decor throughout the reception area, offices, locker rooms, and cafeteria.

Training and Recruitment—The innovative systems studied also required greater technical and social skills than conventional systems. These were acquired by a combination of formal training, on-the-job learning, and recruitment.

During the period when the systems were being established, management provided considerable amounts of formal training. In a few cases, however, longer-term manning levels allowed 15 to 25 percent of employee time in continuing training activities.

Where the external labor market is favorable, a firm can tailor the work force to the innovative system, in terms of both a capacity for development of multiple skills and a receptivity to cooperative social patterns. Some companies in the sample did attempt to recruit workers with skills and interests that were consistent with the new system's requirements. In several cases, where new facilities were being manned, management selected from an unusually large pool and also provided applicants with information which encouraged appropriate self-selection. The General Foods pet food plant screened over 600 people to select about 70. And the Shell, U.K. refinery had 3000 men apply for the 156 jobs available. A recruiting advertisement for the Norsk experiment is illustrative of the ads used by General Foods and Shell:

We need workers to take care of process and maintenance in the new fertilizer factory (process-workers, maintenance-workers, pipers, eventually instrument makers). The company is going to try to develop new kinds of cooperation to the benefit of employees as well as the company itself. Therefore we want to get into contact with employees who are interested to

a) learn and develop themselves further through the work
b) take responsibility
c) become active members of a work-group
d) participate in the training of others
e) participate in developing jobs and ways of cooperation which create conditions for personal development through the work.

It may be necessary to alter many of the usual norms within the organization, such as formal organization and contents of the different jobs. At the moment, it is considered probable that work-groups with optimal competence within maintenance and process-control will have to be formed (Bregard, et al.).

Although the Norsk innovators decided against getting "an elite group of men into the factory, but rather to find persons with qualifications close to the average in the company" (Bregard, et al.), the advertisement and the screening procedure probably did produce an above-average group, at least in terms of receptivity to the innovation.

Except for the foregoing three cases, there were relatively few attempts to preselect a work force with skills and attitudes especially appropriate for the innovative system. And at Northern Electric, where the new system subsequently gave way and returned to more conventional modes, the originators place part of the blame on their failure to give more attention to selecting employees for "fit."

THE NEED FOR CONSISTENCY

As indicated in the foregoing discussion, there is a strong need for consistency between primary features and support systems in the work environment. A change that is intended to embrace the major aspects of the work situation may in fact turn out *not* to be sufficiently comprehensive. In short, unless all aspects of an organization send similar signals, workers will sense the "ambivalence" and become frustrated in their attempts to respond to the innovation. The following inconsistencies are illustrative:

The appropriate leadership may not be ensured. The autonomy and self-regulatory aspects of work teams must be reinforced by the supervisory leadership pattern. This may take time, however, because supervisors with authoritarian personality traits will likely find it difficult to meet new role requirements.

The information system may be inadequate for the goal-setting and decision-making roles of work teams. Team members must understand business criteria, have competence in analytical techniques, and receive timely information about other units. The latitude to make decisions without the relevant skills and information creates an inconsistency that weakens the organization.

The reward system may not provide reinforcement for the behavior prescribed by other aspects of the innovative organization. For example, the work system may require a lot of mutual assistance among team members yet reward personal development rather than group performance. Another example is where greater skills and responsibilities enable workers to increase productivity but the reward system does not give them a share of the increased productivity.

To avoid these and other errors of inconsistency in innovative work systems, the primary, secondary, and tertiary features must be mutually supportive. Thus it is crucial to understand their interrelationships. The target of the innovation, of course, is enhanced quality of work life for employees and improved effectiveness for the organization.

Introduction of the Innovation

The impetus for the experiments took a variety of forms. In over half the cases, there was a philosophical commitment, albeit often tentative, to create more humane and effective work systems. In several instances, the experiment was fostered by a key manager's strong interest in the behavioral sciences. In many cases, persistent, sometimes chronic problems of turnover, productivity, and morale prompted innovation. Frequently, the impetus came from a combination of the above sources.

METHOD

A general pattern did emerge, however, in the way companies pursued organizational change. Typically, a limited experiment was conducted in a unit of the corporation. The experiment was conceived as a pilot project from which the larger organization could learn. (Two exceptions to this pattern were the relatively small, owner-managed firms—Non Linear Systems and Donnelly Mirrors.)

At Alcan and Volvo the experiments were introduced into particular units of a large existing complex. Subsequent changes were instituted incrementally over many years. Similarly, one project at Shell, U.K. involved an established unit.

Just as often, however, new concepts were introduced as part of a new unit at a new site. Cases in point are the Corning instrument plant, the General Foods pet food plant, one of the Norsk plants, and the Shell refinery. A slight variation on this pattern occurred at the Northern Electric project, where the introduction of the innovative system coincided with a move from Montreal to Ottawa and a doubling of the work force.

Before discussing the early results of these pilot programs, I should note that a number of conditions are especially favorable to their successful implementation. Based on the case studies, I have isolated seven conditions which seem especially important. These are listed immediately below:

Seven Conditions Favorable to Pilot Project Implementation

1. Typically, small towns provide a community context and a work force that is more amenable to the innovation. Half of the experiments were implemented in this type location.
2. Smaller work forces make individual recognition and identification easier. Half of the initial experiments involved fewer than one hundred employees.
3. It is easier to change employees' deeply ingrained expectations about work and management in a new plant culture. About half of the experiments were in situations of substantial "newness."
4. Geographic separation of the experimental unit from other parts of the firm facilitates the development of a unique plant culture. Advantageous geographic separation appeared to be a factor for the pet food plant, the refinery, and the assembly plants of Nobo and Corning.
5. The use of outside consultants as change agents provides objectivity and know-how to the experiments. The majority of the firms had a pattern of using outside consultation in organization development, knew how to use this type of assistance, and were not subject to criticism.
6. The long lead times that are implicit in start-ups allow large blocks of time for training and acculturation. This was a significant factor in several cases.
7. Where there is no union, or where union-management relations are positive, it is much easier to introduce the type of work systems studied. The unionized seven plants had positive union-management relations when the experiment was undertaken. Here, the parties typically agreed to a "sheltered" experiment, in which the normal contract provisions and practices were relaxed for a limited time period, and the changes would not set precedents for other units and that the experimental unit would return to its earlier pattern in absence of mutual consent.

EARLY RESULTS

By design the sample included only experiments which yielded at least initially positive results. In this section, I shall review the types of results claimed for these experiments, even though, with one exception, I cannot vouch for the validity of the claims made by the participants or researchers. The exception is the General Foods pet food plant where I was closely involved as a consultant.

Two cases—Nobo and General Foods—illustrate a middle ground between the more modest and more ambitious claims of early results:

1. After one year, a follow-up study at Nobo showed that (a) the group system had been transferred from the original group of 30 to four additional groups totaling over 100 employees; (b) productivity went up 20 percent; (c) quality control and other service activities were satisfactorily decentralized to the groups; (d) the time perspective of workers increased from three hours to three months; and (e) only a small minority preferred the old system to the new group system, where respondents were referred specifically to variation in work role, job learning, participation in decisions, relations with work mates, relations to company, and breadth of responsibility.

2. The pet food plant had a manning level of fewer than 70 people, rather than the 110 estimate based on industrial engineering standards. This difference resulted from the team concept and the integration of support activities into team responsibilities. Further, after 18 months, the new plant's fixed overhead rate was 33 percent lower than in the old plant. Reductions in variable manufacturing costs (e.g., 92 percent fewer quality rejects and an absenteeism rate 9 percent below the industry norm) resulted in annual savings of $600,000. The safety record was one of the best in the company and the turnover was far below average. While new equipment was responsible for some of these results, more than one half of them derived from the innovative human organization. Operators, team leaders, and managers alike had become more involved in their work and also had derived high satisfaction from it. For example, when asked what work was like in the plant and how it differed from other places they had worked, employees typically replied: "I never get bored." "I can make my own decisions." "People will help you; even the operations manager will pitch in to help you clean up a mess—he doesn't act like he is better than you are."

Quality of Work Life—All experiments reported early improvements in the quality of work life, although the degree of positive employee responses in the early period was quite varied, as were the pat-

terns of these responses over subsequent time periods. Individuals differ in their preferences for variety versus routinization and stability of
job-related duties. These differences have been found in survey studies
and have been reported in some of the innovations reviewed here.

One administrator in the Northern Electric Company tried to summarize the difficulties inherent in implementing the new approach:

> A lot of people felt it would be automatic, just by changing the structure.
> The weakness was the assumption that people would be highly motivated
> in this kind of environment and they're not. There's a threshold value of
> personal maturity or outlook, and below it people are more effective in a
> hierarchical, not an open system. The . . . system doesn't take into con-
> sideration the differences in basic behavior of people. Some will accept the
> freedom and thrive in team organizations. But others are just not respon-
> sible or self-disciplined enough to make this work. These differences are
> not divided according to discipline or education. It's a function of per-
> sonality and it's in all areas. I'd say that there are about 25% who truly
> respond properly in the participative sense. The other 75% don't (Gabarro
> and Lorsch).

These individual differences raise the question: How many persons
do gain significantly from the changes involved in the innovative organization? The answer obviously varies from one group of employees
to the next and therefore must be assessed on a case-by-case basis.

For example, in sharp contrast to the above Northern Electric estimate of a 25-percent positive response, I judge that approximately 80
percent of the General Foods workers experienced relatively large
gains in the quality of their working life relative to their work histories. The balance of the experiments in the sample would fall some-
where between the Northern Electric and General Foods statistics during their initial periods.

Organizational Performance—Early gains in organizational performance were almost uniformly reported. For example:

1. Higher production efficiencies were reported in at least six cases;
these were derived from less wastage of materials, less down-time, or
more efficient methods.

2. Quality improvements were significant in five cases.

3. A reduction in overhead was common—for example, due to a
leaner supervisory and staff structure and less paperwork.

4. In several cases, the more rapid development of skills produced
promotables at a more rapid rate, increasing the number of operators
who were promoted to foremen outside their assigned department.

5. Turnover and absentee rates were usually reduced.

An excerpt from a report on the Shell, U.K. wax department helps to illustrate the interdependence of worker satisfaction and organizational performance when the innovative work system is applied to continuous processing technology:

> The finishing unit capacity was increased by 40% over the 1965 figure again primarily due to technical improvements—some of which were suggested at the Department Meetings.
>
> . . . the understanding and knowledge which the operators had of the changes made played an important part in maximizing the gains made possible by the changes.
>
> The most important increase in output was in the second and third units. . . . Important because this is the limiting section of the plant and output was increased 100%—but most important because it is largely manually controlled. This part of the plant is extremely demanding because it has sixteen operating variables which must be closely controlled. Of course controls themselves are instrumented but the inter-action of the controls cannot be because of the nature of the process. To optimize such a process required knowledge of the operation, manual skill and constant attention to the job. As the output increases so does the demand for attention to detail with the need for frequent minute adjustments to the plant. This is the type of job which can only be successfully accomplished by highly motivated operators—and the output increase indicated is a measure of the success achieved. There is no doubt that provision of laboratory testing facilities on the plant helped motivation—because the operators were able to get immediate feedback on the results (which) is satisfying psychologically. This point was made to me many times by the operators concerned— but they felt they knew how well they were doing, and this encouraged them to go on. The whole unit appeared to be under their control—and that is just what we were aiming for (Burden).

Problems of Survival and Growth

Thus far, we have been exploring *initial* design features, *introduction* of the innovation, and *early* results. What has happened over a longer time frame? As I pointed out earlier most of these experiments were pilot projects in particular units of larger organizations. Originators of a project expect that if it is initially successful, the innovation will continue to evolve toward its original ideals, and be emulated elsewhere. Thus we distinguish three aspects of the development of organizational innovations: (1) origination, (2) continuation, and (3) diffusion.

The rationale for continued viability and evolution is that the original change will develop a plant culture with the values which underlie the innovative organization. Further, it is expected that the results will reinforce both the participants' involvement and their superiors' support.

Diffusion is projected because it is assumed that an organization pattern which works better than its predecessor will be recommended by superiors and emulated by peers. In practice these two projected tendencies of continuation and diffusion are often complicated or nullified by a host of other dynamics. Although I have not completed the process of establishing measures of whether, and to what extent, the innovations in my sample have reverted to more traditional patterns after an initial period of successful change, the evidence permits some rough summary observations.

At least three plants have returned to conventional patterns. Serious efforts are being made to revive one of these. Many others have regressed somewhat after a few years of successful evolution toward the ideals underlying the innovation. The work situations still remain, however, significantly unconventional. Several other innovative plants, as of this writing, are still successful and evolving in the direction that they were launched.

What has tended to undermine those innovations which have terminated or regressed? In the cases of continued success, what factors and dynamics, if any, have threatened the system? What can be done to minimize these threats?

LACK OF HIERARCHICAL SUPPORT

In many of the cases studied, a higher official had in effect "held an umbrella over the experimental unit," protecting it from premature evaluation and absorbing some of the risks involved in the venture. When the higher executive was replaced by one who was not sympathetic, the personnel in the unit felt increased career risks.

In some cases, innovation raised expectations of employees, who were subsequently disappointed because management failed to follow through. The Norsk case is illustrative:

The Norsk experiment after four years revealed mixed results. Productivity had gradually increased and down-time was cut by more than half. Worker satisfaction was still relatively high. The majority of workers had mastered all blue-collar skills in the factory. Yet, despite the increase in worker competence, management had been unwilling to reduce supervision and materially increase the workers' influence in critical decisions. According to Gulowson, the failure to delegate more supervisory tasks to workers, together with a decline in the incentive of learning new operator tasks (as mastery levels climbed), had made monotony a problem once again. Gulowson concluded:

> The experiment has demonstrated the conservatism of large organizations. To the extent that the experimental area has been dependent upon changes in the environment, these changes have only seldom been made. In terms of total system behavior, the environment has forced the experimental system almost back to where it started.

Thus, to promote the viability of the innovation, higher management must sustain philosophical support over a number of years and must be prepared to make further organization changes as they are indicated.

LOSS IN INTERNAL LEADERSHIP AND SKILLS

Turnover in leadership within a unit has created problems. The top position in one experimental unit was refilled four times in six years, during which the innovative system almost died out. Subsequent leaders did not take decisive actions to recreate a more conventional form, but acted in ways inconsistent with the spirit of the innovation, and the result was the same.

In several instances, where the experiment was introduced during a plant start-up, training of operators was begun well in advance, and learning through errors was tolerated during the early phases of the start-up. Thus, the bank of necessary skills was built.

But the requisite bank of skills cannot be maintained if the turnover rate exceeds a certain threshold level. This threshold rate appeared to be less than 10 percent in one case. After the Teesport experiment was underway, management found it necessary to reduce the range of work flexibility among team members and put back a level of supervision. Hill's account of this partial retreat in the design mentioned the relatively high turnover of 10 percent along with technical difficulties and additional tasks. Hill attributes the 10 percent rate to the existence of unusual opportunities for overseas assignments.

The loss of skills through turnover not only can promote a scaling down of an innovative project but also can arrest the development of an overall change program, such as that launched by Shell, U.K. in 1965.

During 1967–68, many changes in job assignments occurred, reducing the skilled resources available to facilitate the changes initiated. For example, of the eleven senior managers who participated in the original planning conference, only six remained. Also, two principal consultants departed for overseas. Although some changes were unavoidable retirements, others resulted from career changes.

Hill concluded that this severe dispersal of resources "undoubtedly hindered a fuller realization of the potential developments at that time."

I believe that such turnover among the leadership of innovative units, the expert staff, and the consulting resources is a natural tendency. For example, I would expect the leaders of organizational innovations to be relatively able and secure as persons. Thus, if the experiment should show signs of success, these leaders would become even more visible, and new career opportunities would present themselves.

These innovative organizations appear to require greater stability of personnel than the conventional organizations they replace. Under normal circumstances the attractive aspects of the work system will tend to produce low turnover rates among workers, thereby ensuring this particular condition for its own success. If higher turnover rates are nevertheless encouraged by exogenous factors, management must take extra steps to stabilize the work force. The problem of turnover of key managers, staff personnel, and consultants is a different matter —where success undermines itself. *Therefore, it is desirable to secure longer-term commitments from key personnel at the outset.*

STRESS AND CRISES

New demands may also tax the system's ability to perform and survive, producing a return to more conventional patterns. The cases illustrate two types of demands: technical problems and competitive pressures.

Technical Problems—As I mentioned above, the necessity to put back a level of supervision and reduce the range of job flexibility in the Teesport refinery was attributed not only to the turnover but also to (a) the expansion of the work performed in the refinery and (b) technical problems. According to Hill, the technical problems "tended to prevent the establishment of steady state operation . . . and induced a certain amount of unexpected stress in the social system." The social stress placed a premium on more predictability; and certainty was sought through less movement of personnel, more specialization among workers, and closer supervision.

Competitive Pressures and the Survival Syndrome—"Survival" patterns developed in several firms sometime after innovative work systems were launched.

Two of these companies came under new, severe, and long-term competitive pressures that resulted in new initiatives and influence patterns emanating from the top. Higher management began emphasizing cost reduction and near-term results, insisting upon discipline and compliance with their programs, and in general providing an inhospital environment for the innovative work system.

Authoritarian decisions and "do it" commands tended to erase the premise that a subordinate could freely challenge superiors in unguarded dialogue. Politically based influence techniques undermined the premise that a person's influence would be a function of his expertise and information. And, as cliques formed to exercise influence, interpersonal relationships were corrupted, trust was eroded, and the sense of "community" began to deteriorate.

In a third case, Non Linear Systems, the organization returned to a conventional form when revenues dropped rapidly in 1970 and 1971 —from $6 million in 1965 to $3.5 million in 1971. Significantly, this slump was a part of a general downturn in the aerospace and many related high-technology industries. There are differences of opinion about which, if any, of the innovations instituted many years earlier contributed to NLS' downturn and which ameliorated the decline. The president, Andrew Kay, blames the experiments for the fact that he delegated so thoroughly and lost touch with the operational aspects of the business. Yet rebuttals of some former executives and consultants indicate that certain developing realities in the business were brought to Kay's attention and that he made a personal choice to believe what he wanted to believe, namely his "dream."

Fortunately, for the present analysis, one need not determine whether the Non Linear Systems innovations were a hindrance or a help in coping with the economic downturn. Rather, one is satisfied to conclude that the business crisis contributed to the decision to abandon the experiment. (This is not to deny that other factors, including the personality of the president, undoubtedly must be considered in explaining both the origination and the subsequent termination of the innovation.)

Participants in an innovative system and higher management must be alert to the regressive tendencies that accompany stress and crises. If, for example, the situation appropriately requires more direction from the top and extra measures to avoid mistakes, these needs can be discussed at all levels and the demoralizing effect of the changes can be minimized, thereby preserving the widespread commitment to return to precrisis patterns after the crisis subsides.

TENSIONS IN EXTERNAL RELATIONS

Parties external to the experimental unit often become increasingly concerned about how the unit functions, apart from how well it performs. These parties include superiors, peer departments, staff departments, labor unions, customers, and vendors. Their impact ranges from the capability to declare an end to the experiment to the ability to force demoralizing compromises. Nevertheless, their preoccupations are similar: "How much may the innovative unit be allowed to deviate from general practices?" Thus the dilemma for an innovative system is between maintaining internal integrity and external consistencies.

Equity Issues—Unresolved equity questions can result in damaging pressures from outside parties. Consider, for example, the Teesport refinery. In establishing the refinery experiment in 1966, management persuaded the union to negotiate a local contract that was separate and completely different from the existing national contract. Although both parties recognized that changes might be needed in the future, the contract allowed the freedom necessary to conduct the experiment. With this latitude, the parties agreed to higher pay and other favorable terms to match the additional skills developed by employees and the extra work flexibility and responsibility.

Later (1968–70), management and the union engaged in productivity bargaining at other work sites. The bargaining in other refineries

> tended to bring their terms and conditions of employment—such as annual salary and staff status—closer to those of Teesport without, however, approaching the level of job flexibility and responsibility achieved at Teesport. The effect of this partial closing of the gap has been to create pressure to close it further *by moving the Teesport job structuring back towards the conventional norm* (Hill; emphasis mine).

Consider the implications of the last statement in the preceding paragraph. It suggests that the equity concept is so strong that even though employees may be intrinsically rewarded by taking on high responsibility and making high contributions, their extrinsic reward must also be in line with their relatively high work inputs. If this is not the case, their sense of injustice will cause them to scale down their level of involvement.

Pressures for Uniformity—In almost every case, the experimental unit came under strong pressure from peer and staff units to conform to company policies and conventional norms. The pressure often mounted after an initial period of grace, when it appeared that the innovations were not failing of their own weight and might become permanent.

These strong conformity pressures are probably inevitable, but I have observed a particular tendency on the part of members of some experimental units which exacerbates the problem. It is sometimes referred to as an "evangelical syndrome"—a "holier than thou" stance toward outsiders who are as yet still "conventional" in their approach to work organization. This "superiority complex" causes bosses and staff units to pressure the unit back into line and peer units to reject similar change for themselves.

Collective Bargaining Dynamics—In one case, union relations contributed to the "undoing" of the innovation. Many features of the new work system had been introduced during a period when, according to management, the union leadership had been stable and politically secure. The philosophy of the earlier leaders was illustrated by their pride in the absence of formal grievances. Later, however, the union became more legalistic—and tended to write up all complaints. Management believed that the union officials became too insecure to sort out legitimate grievances from those where an employee was simply trying to take advantage of a loophole or the informal understandings which had developed on the work floor. There were signs of a vicious cycle:

A foreman feels exploited if he observes an employee abuse the informality (of no time clock, for example) by coming late and then making a claim for a short period of overtime on the other end of the shift. If the worker gets away with the claim, then more co-workers will say, "O.K., if that's the name of the game, I'll do it too." If the foreman cracks down, as he did sometimes, then a hard-nosed management is seen as turning away from the norm of informal problem-solving which characterized the innovative plant society.

Some of the above tensions in the external relations are avoidable. For example, the sponsors can avoid an "evangelical" effort to sell the innovative work system to sister units. However, to some extent these tensions are inevitable. Therefore, the sponsors must negotiate resolutely to preserve the integrity of the system.

COSTS VERSUS BENEFITS FOR INDIVIDUAL PARTICIPANTS

A premise of the new work systems is that participants will gain when they accept greater responsibility and more complicated human interdependencies on the one hand and exercise more influence, receive social support, and enjoy personal growth on the other hand. The former typically have psychological "costs" associated with them; the latter typically yield psychological "benefits." Thus, one can speak of a more or less favorable or unfavorable ratio of (psychological) costs and benefits associated with the work organization.

Earlier, in the discussion of "results," I acknowledged that individual workers differed in their preferences for these potential benefits and costs associated with innovation. Moreover, the viability of several systems was threatened by such individual differences.

Designers of innovative work systems face a dilemma. If an innovative system does not accommodate those who prefer much less task responsibility, variety, and human interdependence than is idealized, and if these persons are selected out, then there is a tendency for the others to regard the system as a special case; this will limit its diffusion, confine its constituency, and isolate it. If, however, there is a tendency to press toward the least common denominator in terms of employee skills and readiness to accept responsibilities, then job design will tend back toward a conventional organization.

My recommendations would be (a) launch innovative work systems where the work force is generally favorable, (b) provide candidates with information which allows some appropriate self-selection, and then (c) cope with the minority who do not immediately "buy-in" by providing some diversity in work demands.

The problem associated with psychological costs and benefits may be even more complicated than this. The ratio may shift over time—with critical implications for the viability of the new unit.

I assume that the levels of human energy available for the organizational effort are related to a favorable exchange of psychological costs and benefits, and that the terms of these exchanges are altered as an innovation progresses. The following scenario presents some hypotheses consistent with my preliminary observations.

How is the human energy elicited for the initial experimental stages? The extra effort required for the learning, planning, and persuasion activities probably derive from the desire to create; prove it can be done; collaborate with others; get recognition; and learn and develop new skills. But this investment of energy does not pay off immediately. There is an early period of deferred gratification, while some suffer set-backs and others are taking a wait-and-see stance.

Assuming the innovation begins to "take" and produces encouraging results, there follows a period during which participants are highly interested in exercising more influence and accepting the responsibility that goes with it. During this period, participants are more ready to rise to the challenges of tasks which fully tax their capabilities, the demands of personal growth, and the trials of living with the uncertainties involved. They spontaneously devote the high level of energies all of this requires. There is also a keen sense of enjoyment in the personal flexibility allowed by fluid relations and low structure.

Participation in this type of innovation frequently is a vehicle for a major episode of personal development, creating the *commitment* source of energy. Yet, while desire for personal growth never ends, high levels of commitment to the growth process cannot be sustained indefinitely. Thus I suspect that the intense period of growth for the individual is of a shorter duration than the period over which the *organizational* energy requirements remain high.

Let's explore further the idea of a temporary period of high psychological benefit for participants in the innovation. I believe it is marked by a high visibility and attention from others because of its newness and novelty, a high stimulation from behavioral science consultants, and a high rate of demonstration of new competencies and mastery. If so, there must be a letdown when outside attention declines and the consultants leave, when one has learned about the related tasks, and when one is sharpening existing skills rather than acquiring new ones. Furthermore, during the period of high involvement, participants often limit some other life relationship—family, friends, hobbies, recreations. At some point, they want to rebalance their on-the-job and off-the-job commitments. And this desire is likely to sap the personal energy source.

Still another tendency can be hypothesized: at some point, the desire of the originators to promote the diffusion of the innovation may begin to compete with their desire to focus on further evolution of the original innovation. The diffusion task offers them the opportunities to develop new skills and to gain additional professional visibility.

The dynamics just hypothesized, if valid, involve subtle management issues. *It is desirable to take advantage of the extra energy elicited by the newness experienced by individual participants. Thought should be given also to ways of ensuring that a high level of energy will be sustained until the viability of the work system is secure, perhaps by infusing new participants.*

ISOLATION—FAILURE TO DIFFUSE

Failure to diffuse changes made in the innovative unit to other parts of the organization can hurt the original effort. Without diffusion, the managers and supervisors in the new unit will have developed skills and experience that are perceived by others and by themselves to have only local relevance. Moreover, their desires for upward mobility in the company will conflict with their commitment to the ideals of the innovative unit. In short, either their enthusiasm will flag or their tendency to isolate the innovative system will increase.

In about half the cases studied, there *was* diffusion of the innovation from the pilot project to other units in the same firm. The significance of innovations in these "cousin" units has not yet been ascertained. Nevertheless, I can offer a few ideas about how this diffusion tends to occur and what tends to inhibit it:

Transfer of key personnel from the original innovation can promote diffusion. In several cases, a series of moves placed the leaders of an earlier experiment in high positions where they promoted diffusion into a number of additional units.

Visits by other interested groups to an experimental unit often result in the diffusion of innovative ideas. All of the experiments studied were visited, visited, and revisited.

Evangelism may be self-defeating and hierarchical support may decline, undermining diffusion efforts.

Rivalry may exist among organizational peers. In a number of cases, personnel involved in the experiment noted the very many visitors from outside the company and the few, if any, from other units within their own company. Unfortunately, rivalry is sometimes acute even among innovators in different units of the same firm. They share a common philosophy but work hard to differentiate their approaches. In several large firms this rivalry frustrated the development of an internal collegial network which could serve as a forum for exchanging ideas, identifying barriers to innovation, and exercising collective influence.

An innovation, successfully established in a plant unit, must be diffused or it may die.

Conclusion

SUMMARY

Analysis of changing expectations of employees shows why we need major reform and innovation in the workplace. Employees increasingly want their work to be characterized by challenge, mutual influence patterns, dignity, positive social relevance, balanced attention to emotionality and rationality, and cooperative social patterns. In order to substantially increase these ingredients, the work situation must undergo comprehensive change. Piecemeal reforms, such as job enrichment, management by objectives, and sensitivity training are inadequate.

The organization redesign should be systemic. First, redesign must focus on the division of labor, involving, for example, the formation of self-managing work teams, recreation of whole tasks by reversing the trend toward fractionation of work, and an increase in the flexibility in work assignments by a variety of means.

Second, the redesign must embrace supporting elements, such as a trimming of supervision and more delegation of authority. Also, the information and reward schemes must be tailored to facilitate the delegation of decision making and to reinforce team work.

Third, other elements in the work situation must enhance the status of workers and communicate trust in their exercise of self-control— e.g., salaried payroll and no time clock. Similarly, recruitment and/or training are required to ensure the necessary skills.

Obviously, the revisions in these many elements must be coordinated and must result in a new, internally consistent whole.

The impetus for work restructuring experiments of this kind comes from prior philosophical commitment, an interest in the behavioral sciences, and compelling personnel or productivity problems.

A number of conditions are favorable to the introduction of such experiments: new plants with small, nonunionized work forces, located in rural communities geographically separate from other parts of the firm. None of these are necessary conditions, but each facilitates the rapid introduction of the innovative work system.

By design of my sample, the experiments reviewed in this study reportedly produced positive results in the first year or two of their existence—in terms of both quality of work life and productivity indexes.

However, several of the experimental units suffered set-backs after an initially successful introduction. A number of factors can threaten termination or create regression in these innovations: a lack of internal consistency in the original design; loss of hierarchical support; loss in internal leadership and skills; heightened stress and crisis; tensions with various parties external to the unit; an unfavorable ratio of psychological costs to benefits for individual participants; and isolation resulting from a failure to diffuse. With foreplanning, sponsors and leaders of innovative work systems can minimize the potential threats listed above.

NEEDED: ADDITIONAL EXPERIENCE AND KNOWLEDGE

Managers, union officials, and workers themselves should be encouraged to join in efforts to redesign work organizations. In this effort, four factors require special attention.

First, we have relatively little experience with comprehensive work restructuring in unionized situations in the United States. Unions have tended to be, for a variety of reasons, suspicious of these schemes. They tend to see them as a threat to union existence. I do not. There are two core functions of collective bargaining that are not in any way eliminated by systemic redesign of work: (1) providing appeal mechanisms that ensure due process and (2) bargaining over factor shares. Hopefully, a number of United States unions will enter into "sheltered" experiments in the next few years so that they—and all of us—can further judge how innovation serves employee interests and affects labor as an institution.

Second, compensation is the least understood element of these new work systems. To what extent and in what form can workers be provided with a quid pro quo for the qualitatively different and greater contributions they make? How can one acknowledge individual differences and reinforce group level cooperation? Effective linkage of economic rewards with new work schemes reinforces the results.

Third, we do not know how to handle the fact of individual differences in designing new work schemes. Should entire plants have a uniformly challenging culture and the appropriate self-selection made at the plant level? Should smaller work units within a plant be varied, so a worker can find a unit with demands that fit his personal preferences? Or should each work group contain assignments that represent the full range of challenge, allowing for diversity within work teams? These issues deserve more attention.

Fourth, my preliminary research has confirmed what I suspected when I began my field investigation several months ago—namely, that even after successful introduction and early signs of effectiveness, a host of factors threaten the continued viability of the redesigned units and frustrate efforts to extend innovation to other units.

NOTE: *The author acknowledges the research assistance of Richard Harmer and the support of a grant from The Ford Foundation; that the first section of this chapter reiterates an analysis in his article,* "How to Counter Alienation in the Plant," Harvard Business Review *(November–December, 1972), which also contains a detailed analysis of one of the plants mentioned here; and that other observations were based on the following accounts developed by others describing experiments in several companies reviewed in this chapter:*

Bregard, A., Gulowson, O. Haug, Hangen, F., Solstad, E., Thorsrud, E., and Tysland, T., "Norsk Hydro: Experiment in the Fertilizer Factories" (Unpublished report, Oslo, Norway, January 1968, 23 pp.); Beer, Michael, and Huse, Edgar F., "A Systems Approach to Organiza-

tion Development," The Journal of Applied Behavioral Science *(1972, 8 [1], pp. 79–101)—Corning Glass; Burden, Derek W. E., "A Participative Approach to Management: Shell, U.K. Ltd.—Microwax Department" (Unpublished report, April, 1970, 17 pp.);* Business Week, *"Where Being Nice to Workers Didn't Work" (January 20, 1973, pp. 99–100)—Non Linear Systems, Inc.; Engelstad, Per H., "Socio-Technical Approach to Problems of Process Control,"* in Design of Jobs, *Louis E. Davis and James C. Taylor, eds. (Middlesex, England: Penguin Books Ltd., 1972)—Hunfos; Faux, Victor, and Greiner, Larry, "Donnelly Mirrors, Inc." (Copyrighted by the President and Fellows of Harvard College, 1973, 32 pp.); Gabarro, John, and Lorsch, Jay W., "Northern Electric Company (A), (B), (C), (D), and (E)," (Intercollegiate Case Clearing House, Harvard Business School, 1968, 14 pp.); Gulowson, Jon, "Norsk Hydro" (Unpublished report issued in April, 1972, by Work Research Institutes, Oslo, Norway); Hill, Paul,* Towards a New Philosophy of Management *(Tonbridge, Kent, England: Tonbridge Printers Ltd., 1971)—Shell, U.K.-Teesport; Thorsrud, Einar, "Democratization of Work Organizations; Some Concrete Ways of Restructuring the Work Place" (Working paper, Work Research Institutes, Oslo, Norway, June, 1972, pp. 6–12)—Nobo–Hommelvik.*

Sam Zagoria

7

Policy Implications and Future Agenda

A reader, having come this far in the book, may wonder what steps are necessary—and desirable—to bring the fruits of research and experimentation in job satisfaction into the lives of more American working men and women. The answer is not simple nor can it be brief.

The long view of developments in civil rights, student rights, or women's rights recognizes that change has come about gradually but persistently, mostly peacefully, by legislation, by court decisions, and by educating and arousing public opinion to alter public policy. And so it will be, I would predict, in reforming the workplace.

The Status Quo

THE WORKER

The principal consideration in the pace and path of change is the worker himself. If massive numbers of workers really wanted job enrichment, work teams, job rotation, even participation in decision-making, many of the obstacles standing in the way would be swiftly shoved aside. Unions would be energized, unionized and unorganized employers would be besieged, public policy would be pummeled, and change would emerge.

SAM ZAGORIA *is director of the Labor-Management Relations Service of the National League of Cities, U.S. Conference of Mayors, and National Association of Counties. He is a former member of the National Labor Relations Board and was previously administrative assistant to U.S. Senator Clifford P. Case and reporter for* The Washington Post.

This is not happening and I think the reason is obvious. All workers are not alike; they are not cast from the same mold. They come in assorted shapes, sizes, education and experience, attitudes and ambitions. Some work for a living; for others working is living. Some think of work as their central purpose in life; others consider work as a way of providing the necessities and look to the time away from work as the real joy of living. The net of this is that while many workers look on their jobs as unexciting, boring, repetitive exercises that require only part of their potential capability, others enjoy the regularity, repetition, and steadiness of a job. They are delighted to leave to a management all the headaches and heartaches of a competitive, high risk economy. Truly, one man's straitjacket may be another's security blanket.

• A five-and-one-half-month experiment in participative management involving six field crews in the Ohio State Department of Highways resulted in little improvement in morale, none in productivity. The conclusion was that "some workers are simply not prepared to accept responsibility and prefer to perform in an atmosphere of authoritarian leadership. This is particularly true if the worker feels easy about this dependency."

• Professor Milton Derber of the University of Illinois has commented that some workers' reluctance to participate is because it "requires affirmative action beyond the ordinary job requirements, such as thinking about improvements in work methods, attending meetings, getting into arguments, making recommendations and possibly helping to make decisions." Some workers prefer to leave the driving to management.

But in a society where institutions—private and public—are constantly growing larger and larger, there are bound to be many workers who resent the captivity of the unending assembly line or the confinement of the clerical paper factory.

• A conference of the United Auto Workers union heard "a collective judgment" that workers' unhappiness stems not from job boredom but from "a plant management system the workers see as brutal and oppressive, and union contract procedures they regard as inadequate in winning them relief from management's excesses."

• "The most deadly feeling I know is to go to a typical key-punch center with 100 people crammed together punching tapes," said Arthur N. Brown of the General Mills Corp., according to *U.S. News & World Report.*

• An added grievance cited by Irving Bluestone, UAW vice president, is that the industrial world is governed by an "Alice in Wonder-land" system of justice—verdict first, trial second. He argues:

> In a democracy, the rules of society are fashioned with the consent of those who must live by them, and the individual is guaranteed a fair trial on the basis of the principle 'innocent until proven guilty.' In the workplace, management decides the rules to be lived by and arbitrarily imposes its will by exercising its authority to impose disciplinary sanctions in case of individual transgression.

Then a worker may file a grievance and seek a hearing.

Auto manufacturers have recognized a problem, too. Malcolm Denise, vice president of the Ford Motor Company, reported: "There is also, again especially among the younger employees, a growing reluctance to accept a strict authoritarian shop discipline. This is not just a shop phenomenon, rather it is a manifestation in our shops of a trend we see all about us among today's youth."

Up until the arrival of job enrichment, worker complaints about their job in life were met with varied efforts to give them more time away from it—shorter hours, holidays, sick leave, rest periods, coffee breaks, wash-up time, vacations, sabbaticals, conference attendance, and earlier retirement. "Thirty and out" is still a union battle cry in many an industrial plant—thirty years of service should entitle a worker to a full pension, regardless of age, is the argument.

In sum, workers vary in their job objectives. For most, whether by conscious choice or unconscious acceptance of life as they find it, a job which provides a living is enough. For others, and in increasing numbers I suspect, taking home a paycheck is not enough—they want a chance for self-fulfillment in the many years they spend in the workplace.

THE UNION

Managements and unions have tried to make jobs more acceptable by making them better lighted, weather-conditioned, healthier, safer, and better paid. The pay has made it possible for many workers to live better, to drive their own cars to work, or to travel farther away on vacation.

Such improvements have helped the union achieve the objectives of individual members and also to enhance its institutional situation. The higher the ratio of free-time to work-time, the more likelihood of more workers being hired—and the more workers, the more union members, the more dues income, the more prestige in labor circles and the more union clout at the bargaining table.

A program of job enrichment, on the other hand, may drive a wedge between the desires of an individual worker and the union as an organization representing workers collectively. In simple terms, if job designers are right, and satisfied and motivated workers produce more and/or better goods and services, the union becomes concerned. First, that new work standards may be set with fewer workers required. Second, that the less capable may be unable to meet the standards. Third, that the company may have found a way to squeeze more production out of workers without adding to their material rewards. Thus, while an individual worker may heartily approve of a change in the content of his job, the union may feel it necessary to object and resist such change in the interest of protecting the wage rate, size of the work force, and its particular union jurisdiction. The result: a barrier and conceivably, if enough union members take a liking to the job redesign, they may decide they do not want a union.

This scenario, while still far from today's American industrial and commercial life, has been a real concern abroad. A report of an Austrian thrust toward "humanization" noted frankly that some union spokesmen were concerned "that job satisfaction could be manipulated to the point where workers would find their unions dispensable."

This concern may undergird the cool, if not downright hostile, reaction to job enrichment in most union circles.

• Thomas R. Brooks in the October 1972 AFL-CIO *American Federationist* complains that

> management talks of job enrichment and the sociologists of participatory democracy in the workplace. Both tend to overlook the unions . . . Job enrichment programs have cut jobs just as effectively as automation . . . Collective bargaining gives working men and women some say about the condition of their employment. No other technique of job enrichment has done as much.

• William Gomberg in a subsequent issue, the June 1973 AFL-CIO *American Federationist,* notes suspiciously that one enrichment expert advertised his wares as providing a strategy and tactics to avoid a union and simultaneously to gain union-management cooperation if you have a union—"a little something for everybody."

As one examines the list of firms and plants working on job redesign, it is clear that for the most part they are occurring in nonunion places. Where unions are on the scene, they have not been involved. It is also clear, in examining the experiments, that in almost all cases they originated with management and are continuing that way. Therefore it is understandable that union leadership looks on the change-

over with apprehension. The reaction is not diminished by company responses that this is none of the union's business.

Some union leaders would agree. They tacitly accept the nature of the job in the industrial system and concentrate their energies on making it as well-paying and comfortable as possible.

One union reaction has been to pooh-pooh the whole process. Machinists union Vice President William W. Winpisinger tells firms bluntly, "If you want to enrich the job, enrich the pay check . . . If you want to enrich the job, begin to decrease the number of hours a worker has to labor . . . If you want to enrich the job, do something about the nerve-shattering noise, the heat and the fumes."

Another union official, Anthony Connole of UAW, takes a different approach. He urges, "The unions should get hep. We believe that experiments with jobs must be joint programs or, in the long run, they are bound to fail . . . We want to be partners, not reactors." His colleague, Irving Bluestone, UAW vice president, in testimony before a Senate committee, was even plainer: "Unless management and the union mutually and cooperatively attack this problem in a sensible, rational way, there is going to be the damnedest explosion you have ever seen in these plants down the road."

Bluestone has proposed:

> There is every reason why democratizing the work place should be undertaken as a joint cooperative, constructive non-adversary effort by management and the union. The initial key to achieving this goal may well be open, frank and enlightened discussion between the parties, recognizing that democratizing the work place and humanizing the job need not be matters of confrontation but of mutual concern for the worker, the enterprise and the welfare of society.

At the moment this is a somewhat academic issue since union members are not pushing their leaders toward the bargaining table in search of job satisfaction. If they did, there would be a problem for the union leadership because of the law and tradition regarding managerial prerogatives. The law holds that managements may be required to bargain, where a majority desire for a union has been proven, about certain items in the broad categories of wages, hours, and conditions of employment—these are mandatory. In addition there are permissive items on which parties may bargain by mutual agreement, but a party —union or firm—may not be required to do so if it does not want to.

Currently, such matters as job content and job assignment have been considered essential to the power to run the business and part of managerial prerogatives. Bargaining about them has been possible only to the extent that management has been willing to discuss them. If a union should insist on bargaining about job content and a company says "No," in the present state of the law it is not clear that the firm would be ordered to bargain. On the other hand, strong unions have managed to wield their strength strategically so that firms eager to resolve "mandatory" issues have ultimately found it desirable to discuss "permissive" issues. The matter of job enrichment is still somewhat in a legal no-man's land. Most industrial contracts leave to management alone the responsibility to decide on how to produce its goods or services.

Another approach to the matter of job content is the grievance route—the union could raise an issue about a particular job enrichment. The "Catch 22" here is that the grievance has to zero in on a provision of the contract and if such a provision has not been bargained and adopted, the grievance may fail to find a home. Indeed today most contracts between sophisticated employers and unions spell out very carefully what is grievable, and all else is pegged for the wastebasket.

Since workers are interested essentially in the same job objectives as members of the management team—variety, challenge, and recognition—there is a growing feeling of dissatisfaction on the job with the "double standard." Union leaders are referring increasingly to the differences between hourly workers (who get paid only when they work) and salaried officials (who get paid regardless); special parking lot accommodations, dining facilities and flexibility in working hours.

• Precision Castparts Corporation, Portland, Oregon, after a series of "pitch-a-bitch" sessions, liberalized working hours for hourly personnel, consistent with team needs, permitting them to schedule their own eight-hour day by modifying their arrival, departure, break and lunch times. The flextime concept, popular in Western Europe, is receiving growing attention here.

Union opposition, anticipated rather than realized, is probably acting as a deterrent to job enrichment pilot projects. A recent survey completed by the University of Dayton among manufacturing firms in the area showed 53 percent expected a negative reaction from the unions. Thirty percent forecast a positive reaction and another 15 percent a neutral reaction. Yet union attitudes reflect more interest with 30 percent positive.

In looking for ways to give unions a substantial role, Professor Walton has suggested that management "enter into a dialogue with the union about the changing expectations of workers, the need for change, and the nature and intent of the changes contemplated. Out of such dialogue can come an agreement between management and union representatives on principles for sharing the fruits of any productivity increases."

Another possibility would be a two-stage operation, commencing with the usual consultation between management representatives and the individual workers involved, with the union representative, perhaps the shop steward, informed of the project and its progress. This could be a joint effort, too, as assuring plant safety is in some plants. The second stage, after the changes were worked out and ready to be activated, would involve negotiations over job reclassification and a formula for sharing the gains. This recognizes the role of the union as the chosen representative of the individual workers and retains its traditional role in working out the economic package.

Union leadership will be steadily nudged in the direction of finding "a handle" on job satisfaction because of the growing interest and concern in the subject. Workers are not oblivious to the outpouring of conferences, reports, studies, articles, and books on the subject. Each contributes to a growing awareness. Sometimes people do not know they have a problem until they stop and think about their situation. Then they want action!

Unions historically have concentrated on bread and butter improvements for their members. The concept of job satisfaction is one for which there is as yet little demand from dues-payers; it is hard to define in the customary terms of labor contracts, and other routes are not yet developed. The danger, of course, is that it may develop into an exclusive management tool, and when members start seeking aid they will find the barn door shut and union leadership belatedly fumbling for a key.

THE EMPLOYER

The constraints on management initiatives in job enrichment are largely self-imposed. They arise from the very real difficulties involved in restructuring any organization and carrying a new message through layers of management. Also more vague apprehensions are involved regarding where such employer-employee initiatives may eventually lead.

There are other reasons, too. The 1973 *Work in America* report cited several in explaining why there has been no employer "stampede" to the job enrichment gate:

1. The disappointing experiences of employers with other catchy personnel theories have left them cold to a new one.

2. Some employers do not know how to get started; they do not know where to turn for help.

3. Employers, looking over the pioneering projects, fail to find one in their own industry or business and decide to wait until somebody tries first.

4. Some lack capital for transitional costs such as training and cannot afford to wait out long-term benefits in quality and production.

5. They fear opposition from trade unions.

David Sirota and Alan D. Wolfson, behavioral science consultants, have accumulated eleven inhibitors, including several on the *Work in America* list. Some of the notable additions:

1. An Ideological Block—"The belief that job fragmentation and rigid controls over workers are necessary for productive efficiency still prevails in most companies, not just among industrial engineers, but among line managers as well."

2. Managerial Turnover—"The shorter the time a manager expects to be in a job, the less interest he has in projects oriented toward the future. Also job enrichment projects are begun and then discontinued as new managers, not involved from the beginning, take over." (One authority estimates the life expectancy of the average plant manager at fourteen months.)

3. Management Pride—"Change often represents an implicit admission that past behavior has been in error; for many managers, it is akin to eating crow . . . As long as a manager continues to do things the way they have always been done, he is safer when something goes wrong."

Another problem, inherent in the process, is that job enrichment is not a standard formula that can be learned and implemented en masse. Rather, it requires a great deal of study of individual tasks and individual capabilities and the design developed may apply only in one unit of one department of one plant of one company. This, too, makes managements project-shy.

Middle management is another problem. Roy W. Walters, a management consultant, reminds, "At middle manager levels today there are many, many comfortable people who have achieved all the marks of success working at half of their capacities. They tend to resist any dislodgement from their comfortable daily operations . . ." Also, as our editor, Jerome Rosow, has earlier observed, many supervisors are hostile to the upgrading involved in job enrichment because they have a low opinion of worker capability and their potential for growth.

Middle management itself has its job dissatisfaction "blues." A recent American Management Association survey shows more than half find their work "at best, dissatisfying" and 18 percent would join a union immediately and another 17 percent would consider doing so. "Economic and social insecurity is at the heart of the managers' discontent and the leaders of American business will be treading on thin ice if they ignore or deny the possibility of a revolt in the ranks of supervisory and middle management," the report concluded.

Robert N. Ford of American Telephone and Telegraph Company, a pioneer in the field, warns that projects require consistent topside management support. He counsels, "First, get the management, then go to the people."

But even assuming executive suite approval, management faces an immediate problem in "how" to introduce the new project. If the emphasis is placed on improving job satisfaction, the program takes on a goody-goody tone which is likely to be anathema to directors and stockholders; if it is launched amidst the traditional oratorical waves of improving productivity and ultimately profits, it may be greeted by the employees as just another way to introduce speedup of work and shortchanging of pay envelopes.

This sort of dilemma leads to a certain amount of soft-shoe dancing. Witness this comment from one of Mr. Ford's constituents:

> The purpose of "Work Itself" is not to increase productivity. The purpose is to give a man or woman more responsibility according to individual ability and willingness to take on greater responsibility. If "Work Itself" is properly applied, the result will be decreased turnover because of greater job satisfaction. A by-product can be increased productivity.

Put another way by management consultant Walters, "Job enrichment is not designed to make workers feel better. It is not a 'sweetness and light' program. It is, rather, a hard, cold, money-making approach to human utilization. And yet, employees do feel better and happier when given more meaningful work to perform."

It is this mixed motivation that seems to have contributed to the secrecy syndrome. Ted Mills, director of the Quality of Work Program of the National Commission on Productivity, reports that many managers involved in the process

> have expressed serious concern to me about full disclosure of what they are doing in the field, even to the union involved. Infinitely more activity in Quality of Work innovation is going on in this country than any one knows about. The reasons for secrecy include fear of union participation, a desire to prevent the competition from knowing what's been achieved and fear that publicity could destroy a beginning effort.

Mills is involved in an effort to launch some pilot projects and arrange
for the diffusion of know-how to employers, employees, and unions
in industry, commerce, and government.

There are dangers of overselling the potentials of job enrichment
to employees and employers; there are dangers of mismatching, at-
tempting to make job enrichment paper over such basic inadequacies
as low pay or employment insecurity. But with these and all the other
inhibitions recounted here it is heartening to come across the words
of a leading industrialist, William F. May, chairman of American Can
Company and director of the National Association of Manufacturers:

> It is time for business and union leadership to devise incentive systems—
> not expediencies—by which labor at all levels shares both the rewards of a
> system that produces satisfaction and the penalties when it doesn't. Obvi-
> ously, this involves full labor participation in the planning function.

Job satisfaction efforts are still in the experimental stage in this
country, counted in the hundreds, rather than the thousands. Managements, not yet convinced about their dollar and cents advantages, apprehensive about change and its effect on middle management and
labor-management relations, are reluctant to join the ranks of the pio-
neers. Let others go forth is the reigning view.

International Developments

Americans, undoubtedly, are among the most generous residents
on earth, but when it comes to holding onto power, they yield it be-
grudgingly and in the smallest amounts possible. This attribute under-
lies a good deal of the unspoken hesitation about embarking on any
basic change in the worker-employer status. Many employers are still
resisting collective bargaining because it brings them in confrontation
with their employees in a process which they feel steadily shifts power
from one side of the table to the other. One is reminded of the comment of UAW Vice President Douglas Fraser that "the only prerogatives management has left are the ones we haven't gotten round to taking away from them yet."

Job enrichment, to many employers, involves worker participation
in an area which has usually been management's exclusive preserve.
They are apprehensive that if such realignment of relationships takes
place, others will be sought and may follow. They recite experiences
abroad as scare stories of where it all may lead—workers owning and
operating major cooperatives in Israel, worker representatives on corporate boards in Norway and Sweden, workers sitting in powerful

posts in the nationalized industries of England, France and Austria, sharing in the co-determination of the policies of the coal and steel industries of West Germany, and running the industries of Yugoslavia completely through elected self-management.

If job enrichment is the seedbed of such developments, most management of American industry would prefer to let it stay abroad.

Actually, the comparison is a little like trying to compare oranges and tangerines side by side. As Professor Everett Kassalow of the University of Wisconsin, a veteran observer of the European labor scene, has pointed out,

> In Western Europe the percentage of union organization is generally much higher than it is in the United States. If a little less than one third of the wage and salary force in the United States is organized, typically in Europe it would be over 40, even 50 percent. In Great Britain it is over 40 percent, in the Netherlands it is 50 to 60 percent, in Belgium 60 to 70 percent, in Austria nearly 70 percent, in Sweden close to 80 percent. So the degree of organization is generally much higher; giving union labor numerical power in the society.

Another big difference is the pervasiveness of unionization abroad. Military officers, the diplomatic corps, doctors, judges and, in some cases, even members of the clergy are in the unions.

One impact of such numerical and strategic strength is that unions influence and often dominate political parties to a degree unknown in this country. Professor Kassalow notes,

> The political parties with and through whom the trade unions work in most European countries, usually the Socialist party or the Labor party, have been in government and close to being the government constantly throughout the post World War II period. There is almost no country in Europe that I can think of, in Western Europe, which has not had a Socialist government or Socialists participating in almost every government or every other government. This has immeasurably strengthened the position of trade unionism in the society, helped ensure its bargaining successes, enhanced its general social and political power.

It may be worthwhile to take a look at these developments, recognizing that they have emerged in a union-political climate much different than our own.

YUGLOSLAVIA

Perhaps the most far out, from an American point of view, is the Yugoslavian system. In 1950, a full-fledged system of worker self-management was adopted based on the proposition that all are workers *and* managers. In each plant all workers became part of a workers' assembly, which in turn selected a workers' council, made up of worker representatives. The council elected a management board and permanent committees entrusted with making various decisions. The director of the enterprises was appointed by the workers' council after the post had been publicly advertised and candidates invited. He serves for four years and stands for reelection by the council.

The effort was aimed at removing "the alienating characteristics of the management-labor confrontation" in the words of Ichak Adizes in his book *Industrial Democracy: Yugoslav Style*. Bureaucracy was also to be averted by the policy of rotation of elected officials—"every elected person should go back to his previous job. . . . In self-management everyone should have the opportunity to manage and become involved." There is much opportunity for there is provision that the director and other executives may not act until specific authority is tendered them by the action of committees, meetings, and referendums.

Adizes found mixed results in striving toward the objectives. In his study of two major companies he found among workers a feeling of gaining influence on the system. However, the young college graduate executives felt powerless since they could not discipline or fire workers. A change in the 1960s put emphasis on maximizing production, resulting from economic pressure to enter into competitive world markets, and this elevated the status of the "technocrats"—those with special education and knowledge—at the expense of the professional political leaders. Another effect of the higher status of those with professional competence was that participative meetings were reduced to meaningless formalities.

Another observer, Josip Obradovic, found mixed responses from participants and nonparticipants in management in regard to their satisfaction with wages, physical working conditions and the like, but unexpectedly found that participants from the technological groups were more alienated than nonparticipants because of frustrations encountered with workers' councils. The author concluded that participation in self-management should not be overemphasized as a source of satisfaction.

AUSTRIA

In Austria, about 70 percent of industry is nationalized, yet, reports Professor Joseph Mire of American University, "these organizations are not in the forefront of experimentation to improve workers' participation in management."

WEST GERMANY

In West Germany, where workers are often placed on management boards, Professor Mire found that while democracy at the workplace had been a matter of intense discussion for several years, such interest had now "largely evaporated" partly because "unions have become alarmed at the manner in which forces of the extreme left have tried to seize upon the demand for direct workers' democracy as a means of undermining both capitalism and 'trade union bureaucracy.' " The unions continued to press for equal representation on boards of directors, which they have already achieved in steel and coal mining companies, but one observer has cautioned, "any sharing of decisions with workers would raise the fundamental problem of liability and responsibility. . . . A trade union which is directly involved in management decisions would no longer be in a position to effectively defend the interests of the workers."

UNITED KINGDOM

In England, where nationalization of certain industries had led to experiments in collective management, the participation of union representatives in management bodies was expected to mean they would take on management functions in addition to representing labor interests. Experience has proved otherwise. One observer said that when trade union representatives joined the English boards, they abandoned all trade union functions and the result was that unions did not receive "a share in power as such." In short, the workers were co-opted.

A different kind of British experiment in industrial democracy was the subject of a major study. It parallels American interest in the Scanlon Plan where labor and management share in production planning and in profit-sharing. The study describes the John Lewis Partnership, an eight-store enterprise commonly owned by its employees, where each is rewarded according to his contribution to the common good. Managers—high and low—are accountable for their decisions to the managed and surveys show "most workers like their jobs."

NORWAY

In Norway, the union movement first pressed for equal or partial representation on the boards of directors of several firms but, as Professor Kassalow has reported, "found no very spectacular results. . . . They discovered when a workers' representative got up to the board he had to act like a regular member of the board of directors or he'd be ineffective. . . . He might be a little more humane . . . but no great change seemed to result, as far as the ordinary worker was concerned, in his day-to-day work life."

Instead of pressing for directorships, a new and imaginative effort has been launched under the title "The Industrial Democracy Project," with plans for long-term research sponsored jointly by the Confederation of Employers and the Trades Union Council. In a few enterprises suffering from monotony, assembly-line work, and high turnover, action committees, consisting of an equal number of company and worker representatives, were appointed to undertake experiments. They examine production processes and pay procedures and then work on developing job redesign, rotation, and semi-autonomous groups. This is followed by sensitivity training for foremen and programs for upgrading workers on a continuing basis.

In this initiative, as well as in others in Norway, an important resource has been the Work Research Institute in Oslo, headed by Dr. Einar Thorsrud, one of the world's leading practitioners in job satisfaction and experimentation. The Institute is supported by government, union, and industrial funds. While others were pushing membership on the boards of directors of firms as the route to improving the quality of working life, Dr. Thorsrud was arguing that the really effective way to improve the worker's lot was to involve the worker directly in a system that would permit him to develop himself through his work and take on increasing responsibility. One offshoot of the industrial experimentation is that the Norwegian Department of Labor has appointed a special committee to review the results with a view toward adopting some of the private sector experiences in the public sector.

SWEDEN

In Sweden, the reservoir of expertise is the Development Council for Collaborative Questions. This is a creature of the Swedish Employers Confederation, and functions in cooperation with the country's major unions. The Council now has ten experiments underway in various industries.

In 1970, the Swedish prime minister indicated the importance he attached to the problem by noting that while the country had made great progress in improving standards of housing, nutrition and education, work was as dissatisfying as it had always been. He declared the "task of the seventies must be to give the worker a better surrounding and more say over his work at the workplace."

Management was interested because it was suffering from serious labor shortages, high absentee rates, and obvious job dissatisfaction. One firm that stepped forward was the Scamia Automotive Plant where the Saab cars are made. The employer had been beset by high turnover, much sick leave, repeated and costly halts in the assembly line. In 1968, the firm, working closely with the workers' council, launched a job design experiment in new plants under construction.

In the process, a development committee (with representation from company and workers) discussed all tool and machine designs before construction began. Quality control was made the responsibility of each worker for the first time. Care and maintenance of machines were also turned over to the workers and they were encouraged to learn several jobs. The usual plant assembly line was broken down into several assembly groups placed along an automatic conveyor belt.

Now Saab takes full-page ads to emphasize that its products are made by interested (not bored), experienced (since there is less turnover), and caring workers (since they are responsible for a whole process rather than one nut on a bolt). "It's a slower, more costly system for us, but we know it builds better cars," declaims the company.

Another experiment in a tobacco factory at Arvika, Sweden, was initiated in 1969–70 by the Swedish Delegation for Industrial Democracy, a section of the Swedish Department of Industry. The conclusion: job revamping resulted in workers perceiving increased opportunity to take part in decisions related to their tasks and their department, more varied work with increased opportunities to learn, increased willingness to help workmates, greater interest in production, better planning, and better relations with the foreman. Who could ask for more?

While the Scandinavian efforts are proving themselves out, some observers looking at the string of strikes in Western Europe in the 1969–71 period are warning that individual workers are restless. They are moving along the strike route, without union headquarters approval, to seek new gains or to redress grievances. This does not mean that they are hostile to their unions, but rather that they look beyond them to solve problems at the local level.

This seems to fit in with the recent recommendations of the European Economic Community Commission in Brussels, which noted that

> too often present work systems, particularly assembly-line operations, waste human capability, especially intellectual capacity, and deny to the worker adequate freedom and responsibility in the organization of his work. . . . Action must be taken at the community level to redress the tendency to dehumanize work organization and methods.

Change

SOME POLICY CONSIDERATIONS FOR THE EMPLOYER

The changing composition and character of America's work force suggest some philosophical questions. For example, *does an employer share the responsibility to assist an employee to realize his fullest capability?*

If the question had been posed in terms "sole" or "major responsibility" the answer would be difficult. Unless we view employment as simply a hire, use, and discard relationship with the employer buying workers' services on a purely market basis, it is clear there is a social obligation to treat workers as humans, rather than as inanimate machines. This question passes over any economic advantages which such self-fulfillment would bring the employer, but we will look at this later.

In exploring how employers can move in the direction of sharing the responsibility for enlarging job lives, it may be useful to look at where we are now in hopes of developing some future guidelines.

In bringing up our young people we accept the proposition that there is a duty to help each achieve education to the maximum of his ability. We provide scholarships, loans, and other subsidies to help a qualified youngster climb the educational ladder if he cannot afford the means himself. Yet once he leaves school, he is literally and figuratively on his own so far as continuing his intellectual growth. There are community colleges, libraries, and the like financed with public funds, but for the most part preparing for promotions, new careers, or leisure-time interests must be self-initiated and largely self-financed.

Much of this policy is premised on the good old days when son followed father and signs over establishments frequently read "John Smith and Sons"; when workers ran their entire work course in one employ and wound up with the gold watch and a 30-year history in the same place on the same job. Now there are new days when fathers encourage sons to do other things; when fathers themselves think of second acts in their work lives and read John W. Gardner's *Self-Renewal* with personal interest; when job applicants want to know not only about the starting job but what the chances are for mounting the career ladder and where it goes; when one family in five moves at least across county lines each year and the usual reason is a new job.

• The United States Labor Department warns, "No longer can a boy or girl expect just one occupation to cover a lifetime of work. Even today, a 20-year-old man could be expected to change jobs six or seven times during his worklife expectancy of 43 years."

There are other changes, too. Sixty-two percent of the workers in America in 1970 were engaged in furnishing services and only 38 percent in producing goods. By 1980, it will be more like 70 to 30. Managerial-technical types already outnumber skilled craftsmen and the tilt continues. Less than 2 percent of all workers are involved in assembly-line work. On the other hand employees of government represent one in every six in the work force and by 1980 the ratio is expected to rise to one in every five. We are becoming a nation whose people are largely engaged in providing services. Since labor is a much larger component of delivery of services than in producing goods, labor's needs and desires influence quality and quantity even more than in a nation of producers.

The achievement of job motivation, challenge, variety, and individual recognition by those furnishing the services thus becomes even more important. A recent newspaper report told of a columnist's experience in renting a car from a firm that spent tens of millions of dollars improving its customer relations, but blew it all forever when this customer was met by sullenness and disinterest. As he said, "It is often the lowest paid employee who has the face-to-face contact with the customer, and who 'represents' the company to the public."

Employers brought up in the Frederick Winslow Taylor scientific management school of the early 1900s learned how Taylor taught steel workers to shovel 47 tons of pig iron a day instead of 12.5 tons. According to Professor Daniel Bell, Taylor specified every detail of the man's job—the size of the shovel, the bite into the pile, the weight of the scoop, the distance to walk, the arc of the swing, and the rest periods that steelworker Schmidt should take. By systematically varying each factor, Taylor got the optimum amount moved.

Taylor also knew "what sort of man could fit into this strait jacket—'one of the very first requirements for a man who is fit to handle pig iron as a regular occupation is that he shall be so stupid and so phlegmatic that he more nearly resembles an ox than any other type,' " Professor Bell recounted. Well, darned few oxen are applying for jobs these days, but lots of well-educated, well-traveled, independent, and ambitious young men and women are.

Employer self-interest assumed that employees were best served by establishing pension plans which put a high premium on staying with the same firm. This theory is undergoing some second thoughts. In all too many enterprises there now exist executives and rank and file employees who, in the words of Robert Ford, have left the firm mentally, but haven't gone yet physically. They are competent but unhappy people with enough unhappiness to slop over on all who come in contact with them—customers, executives, subordinates, and peers. If they could take their pension credits and move on, they would be happier and, most likely, so would customers, executives, subordinates, and peers.

Large-scale employers are also recognizing that in the dynamic economy there is frequent reason to shift bases of operations as supplies and markets change, to reduce or close operations for the same reasons, to merge or sell units. Employees and the communities affected would accept these changes better if appropriate shares of the earned pensions were credited and permitted to lubricate the local economy. A portable pension plan would accommodate to employee desire for mobility and changed careers and to the employer's need for manpower flexibility.

On the surface, the objectives of increasing job satisfaction and expediting job mobility may seem in conflict, but many authorities consider them complementary. The first seeks to maximize the interest of the worker in his present job, the second accepts the view that limits will be reached in one location and the best thing that can be done for the worker and the firm is to make it easier to continue his career elsewhere or perhaps to undertake a new career.

Another aspect of employee freedom lies in such matters as work-time scheduling. The Western European concept of flextime gives employees some leeway in scheduling their work day. This has many potential benefits: freedom for employees to take care of errands, carry out social or recreational pursuits, and finish tasks rather than quit at an arbitrary time; reduction in traffic congestion and air pollution as reporting times are spread; reduction in absenteeism and disciplining for tardiness; and, occasionally, stretched hours of service to customers, when employers can open earlier and close later.

Query: *Does an employer have a responsibility to achieve a job-satisfied work force even if the economic advantages of such change are unproven?*

There is a tendency in a free enterprise society to load responsibility upon employers. They have resources; they are accorded leadership homage in the community; they—despite the inroads of collective bargaining—still retain a good deal of the father image where employee needs are concerned. But corporate employers are changing away from personalized, physically present, and accessible managers into professional, impersonal, and often distant executives. Communities recognize that employers cannot be asked (too often) to commit corporate assets to accommodate to local or employee needs not directly related to the production of goods and services. They are profit-making enterprises and not eleemosynary institutions. They vary widely, too, in their view of corporate social responsibility and their financial ability or willingness to consider extra costs.

Thus, when we talk about helping an employee realize his fullest capability, the employer is especially interested if this will also help him achieve some corporate economic gain—less turnover, less sick leave, less absenteeism, or less product rejects. If he believes job enrichment will do this, and if he can overcome the many inhibitions and obstacles earlier cited, he may try. But if this is not the case, he is hardly tempted.

Here are some thoughts on the subject:

—Sidney Harman, president of the Jervis Corporation, said, "Work satisfaction—which is to say the attainment of a sense of purposefulness in his or her work, the achievement of a sense of personal worth and dignity—should be seen as a fundamental right of employees, and therefore a fundamental obligation of employers."

—A Chrysler Corporation official declared, "Any system we originate has to have a favorable cost-benefit ratio. Our motivation for the career ladders' experiment is self-serving. We care about community good will, but if we can't measure the results of changes through money saved, then a program such as this does us little good."

—C. Jackson Grayson, former chairman of the Price Commission, said, "The answer to the decline in the traditional work ethic is to create a new work ethic for the 70s—one that does not merely demand blind and unquestioning dedication to authority or tradition, but one that celebrates and rewards autonomy and individuality."

Now a tougher question: *Does an employer have a responsibility to the community to design jobs in such a way as to minimize job-related social costs (care of alcoholics, narcotics addicts, the mentally upset)?*

Many employers will accept such a responsibility without outside pressure. Others may not recognize the human damage inflicted by their work processes and still others may shift this problem to the community. Perhaps the philosophy undergirding the national environmental control policy has application here—that none should be permitted to pollute air, water, or other resources for their own advantage. In order to deter such conduct there is provision for federal directives and fines.

How to identify and isolate such costs would be an immediate problem. Another big problem would occur where one company dominates the local economy. We have already seen some pollution control mandates unify employers and job-concerned employees in their opposition.

But if our public understanding of job woes and their effects on individuals continues to expand, such an approach, whether local or federal, may evolve.

SOME POLICY CONSIDERATIONS FOR THE UNIONS

Let us begin with the question: Does a union have the right—and does it have a responsibility—to bargain for job enrichment?

For the 75 percent of the work force which has not chosen to be represented by unions there is little concern with this question. For the remaining 25 percent this is clearly a significant consideration. Union initiatives can make things happen; union disapproval can discourage attempts or slow things down if they are tried. The legal obstacles, as I have suggested, are not insuperable—conditions of employment have already been stretched wide. Here, I believe, more depends on the voices of the worker-members, as well as the foresightedness of union leadership, than on changes in public policy. Some union leaders already are moving, anticipating needs before the members do and out of concern, too, that if they do not act this will become an exclusively management tool.

Job enrichment is a difficult thing to structure into a contract, even if employers are willing to do so. It does not deal with classes of workers, nor with fixed conditions, but rather represents a great deal of interaction with individual workers, both in the process of job enrichment and in the achievement. It also requires a substantial amount of fluidity often trespassing on job classifications or union jurisdictions. Think of the Swedish auto worker who is charged with and held accountable for not only assembly work, but now also for maintenance and quality control. An American union would have to accommodate to a great deal of flexibility in contract interpretation to make such job broadening possible. As long as members are content to focus their union activity on improving wages, benefits and working conditions, there is little incentive for union leadership to become involved in the uncertain, complicated, and potentially volatile issues which are likely to arise in job enrichment.

• Senator Charles H. Percy (R-Ill), a former industrialist himself, told a National Conference on the Changing Work Ethic that much job dissatisfaction arises from

> an entrenched, authoritarian industrial system that has taken decades and decades to build. . . . There is a strong feeling that managerial and labor

institutions have sometimes grown too rigid. Too often they have become blind to the broader needs of our society.

SOME POLICY CONSIDERATIONS FOR GOVERNMENT

Is there a community responsibility to help the employee—even as it assisted him or her to achieve a proper education?

Federal Agency—At the federal level this can be done by creating an agency or public corporation to assist firms by providing relevant case histories, advice, and a roster of qualified consultants and generally establishing a clearing house for research, experience, and experiments. This has been proposed by the *Work in America* task force almost as a public health expenditure because it should provide savings in governmental spending for rehabilitation of job-unhappy workers suffering from alcoholism, drugs, or mental problems.

A bipartisan group of eighteen senators, led by Senator Edward M. Kennedy (D-Mass), sponsored legislation in 1973—the Worker Alienation Research and Technical Assistance Act—which would attack the problem as a matter of continuing public policy and energize resources in the Department of Health, Education and Welfare and the Department of Labor to conduct research on the extent of job discontent and its costs to industry and society generally, to provide technical assistance for those seeking to experiment in ways to meet alienation, and to launch some pilot demonstration projects.

Representative William A. Steiger (R-Wis) likes the idea of tax incentives. "We seem to have little problem in giving tax breaks for capital investment and machine depreciation, but meet great resistance at suggestions of tax incentives for employee training and job upgrading. It is, however, an option which should be explored." If we can assist an employer in getting new equipment, we should be willing to assist a worker begin a new work life—that seems to be the argument.

Education—Our view of education needs the most drastic overhaul of all. The idea of packing all the training into one block at the outset of a person's life is almost a surefire way of stunting further intellectual growth and cutting off tremendous potential for individual development during working years. Depriving people of continuing ties to education contributes to the barrenness of the steadily lengthening retirement years. This is not to overlook the many existing resources for adult education, self-education, in-house job training, and other forms of mind-stretching. Yet as we consider how most people spend their free-time during the job years and the pension years, we must admit that the available training and effective encouragement to make use of it falls short.

Dr. Herbert E. Striner, former dean of continuing education at American University, after looking at several major European programs, has argued that worker retraining should be looked upon as a "national capital investment" which brings substantial returns to the nation in the form of productivity and taxes and in the avoidance of labor shortages or the costs of unemployment compensation. Dr. Striner advocates a broad program of subsidized education throughout life, financed by dormant unemployment insurance funds, which would make education "the key to unlocking a continuously interesting life experience."

Here are some possibilities for revision in the United States: provision for interrupted high school and college training so that work could be mixed in; sabbaticals for the middle-aged workers, perhaps charged against their ultimate pension rights or delaying actual retirement an equal amount; greater availability and reliance on equivalency tests so that work-educated employees could achieve their "credentials"; revised basic training so that, rather than teaching preparation for one skill and one work career, courses impart a foundation for learning several skills and taking on training almost without end; employment incentives to increase education such as employer subsidies, career development loans (as we now do with public school teachers), or union scholarships with pay improvements as courses are completed; adult education offerings on work premises to encourage greater ease and use; weekend retreats centered on particular topics or on generally understanding self and others; release-time from work for job-related training; educational counseling by employers and unions; reservation of a channel on municipally controlled cable television system for community-oriented training.

Fifty-five percent of those enrolled in the television "Open University" programs have been full-time workers.

Minimum Requirements—Assume that employers and unions, for reasons of their own, are reluctant to venture down the yet uncharted route to job satisfaction. Can and should government in the interests of the general welfare of the nation, as well as in harnessing unused capability for the gross national product, take a leaf out of the Fair Labor Standards Act or the Occupational Safety and Health Act and establish some minimum requirements in job satisfaction?

The argument for such an initiative is that if Congress has seen the need to take these steps to protect the wages and working conditions of employees, why not take a related step? This, too, seems ahead of today's reality because there still is doubt about the lasting efficacy of much of job enrichment, its applicability to many—if not most—workers, and, perhaps most important of all, in terms of individual freedoms, whether workers would want such directives from Uncle Sam. At the moment, the workers' wishes are subdued.

Government at all levels can exercise another role, that of the model employer, by introducing job satisfaction concepts into its own operations—no tiny part of the nation's jobs. There have been some beginnings—in local government, largely in the innovative West, there are experiments underway in participatory management, job rotation, team efforts, erection of job ladders backed by special educational efforts, and some beginnings of job redesign. The Wisconsin state government and the Nassau County, New York, government have each begun productivity programs with emphasis on job enrichment. The Social Security Administration is negotiating a pilot program in its West Coast office for the same objective. Significant experiments worth watching.

Agenda for the Seventies

I shrink from the omniscience implied in laying out such a program, but a volume of this kind seems to indicate a "what to do about it" prescription. The following is presented as a starting point for clinical consultation:

GOVERNMENT

1. Should establish a national policy objective, in the model of the Full Employment Act of 1946, stating that achievement of a minimum level of job satisfaction for all workers is necessary to improve standards of living, protect mental and physical health and welfare, and advance individual fulfillment.

2. Should develop an active national manpower policy which recognizes the dynamics of our economy as well as the pressures for growth, variety, and individual freedom in human development. This would aim at fullest possible utilization of resources through implementation of job mobility—both vertical, in the form of promotions and rotation, and horizontal in removing blocks to job and career change and improving facilities for movement, such as expanded Employment Service capability and relocation assistance.

3. Should establish a national agency or nonprofit institute on the order of the National Science Foundation to centralize and mobilize

resources and interests in attaining the national policy objective. Among its duties would be the conduct of surveys identifying the causes of job dissatisfaction, the extent in industry, commerce and government, and analysis of how it could be remedied. The agency would: encourage creation of joint labor-management committees to experiment with various remedial techniques; convene conferences; distribute literature on experiences; stimulate and perhaps subsidize business schools, trade associations, and unions to develop case history reports; assemble a roster of qualified experts to assist parties; fund and monitor demonstration grants in fields where employers and others were slow to take the initiative. As in the case of Upward Mobility programs, funds could go to firms, unions or associations, whichever had the idea, the initiative, and the capability.

4. Should appoint a commission to review current educational practices from the perspective of the changing needs of people in order to make education a lifelong experience. The report of the commission, which would affect many matters besides job satisfaction, could be the starting point for a national dialogue on the objectives and practices of education.

5. Should act as a model employer in initiating projects to improve the quality of work life. This would apply to federal, state, county and city levels with provision for adequate reporting and dissemination of results.

EMPLOYERS

1. Should review the potential of job enrichment as a means of improving production as well as enhancing worker satisfaction, attempt pilot projects and give them an adequate chance to mature and weather. In the process a proper role for workers and their union representatives should be developed and incorporated.

2. Should analyze and review present managerial practices which set double standards—uncertain hourly pay versus fixed weekly salaries; scavenging for parking spaces versus reserved spots near work; half-hour lunch periods versus unlimited luncheon hours; austere cafeterias versus plush dining rooms and the like. Where the differences are really status symbols rather than job-justified, employers should consider changes to increase management-rank and file consultation and interaction.

3. Consider experiments in flextime work scheduling. This concept, giving employees some leeway in scheduling their work day, accepts the premise that employers should set standards—whether in personnel testing or in scheduling—that have a realistic connection with the

demands of the job. If it is only traditional to require attendance on fixed hours, the employer gains nothing. Yet he is denying an employee flexibility, which may mean a great deal in terms of convenience and independence, and creating a double standard with those in higher supervisory ranks who accord themselves such flexibility. A similar approach could be taken to employer dress and grooming codes—applying a standard that what is job-required is necessary, the rest could be flexdress—giving workers the chance to exercise style and whim.

UNIONS

1. Should accept a responsibility for achieving minimum standards of quality of working life through the processes of collective bargaining, legislative enactment and administrative procedures.

2. Should join with employers in encouraging promising pilot projects, in building joint bodies to assist and monitor their development and disseminate results. This may involve some substantial concessions on union jurisdiction and issuance of union travel or transfer cards.

3. Should (those representing government workers) press for experiments in the white-collar paper mills so pervasive in public service, spreading the examples of job rotation, team efforts, job ladders, and job redesign throughout departments and agencies.

4. Should seek to enlarge the grievance process so as to encompass issues of job design and job content. The grievance process, with its emphasis on settlement at the level closest to the worker, lends itself particularly to these individualized issues.

In summary, as John W. Gardner has said in his excellent essay on *Self-Renewal,* "We must discover how to design organizations and technological systems in such a way that individual talents are used to the maximum and human satisfaction and dignity are preserved. We must learn to make technology serve man not only in the end product but in the doing."

The need for this is clear in the observation of Professor Alva F. Kindall of the Harvard Business School that industry frequently uses only 30 to 40 percent of the average worker's capabilities—what a waste of the other two-thirds.

Sometimes one must wonder if we are not paying too much attention to the whole subject, but then we learn that in a comprehensive fifteen-year study of the aged, the strongest factor in predicting longevity was work satisfaction. He who enjoyed his work lived longest.

Index

Abel, I. W., 109
Absenteeism, 7, 14, 73, 75, 77–78, 86, 100, 114–116, 122–125, 130, 140, 146
Adizes, Ichak, 188
Adjustments of workers, 10, 11, 78–90, 96–97; apathy as form of, 84–87; job as primary source of satisfaction, 82–84; to nonchallenging work, 87–90; personality vs. organization hypothesis, 79–82
Advanced Devices Center, 150
Advancement, dreams of, 90
Agriculture, 50–51, 52
Alcan Aluminum Corporation, 150–152, 160
Alcohol, 129–130
Alcoholics Anonymous, 130
Alienation, 42, 145–148
Alienation and Freedom (Blauner), 87
Allport, Gordon, 32
American Arbitration Association, 137
American Federation of Labor, 101
American Federation of State, County and Muncipal Employees of the AFL-CIO, 116, 138
American Indians, 70
American Management Association, 185
American Telegraph and Telephone Company, 115
Apathy, 11, 84–87

Aquinas, St. Thomas, 21
Arbitration, 15, 137–138
Argyris, Chris, 11, 79, 85, 88, 89
Attitudes of workers, 2–3, 10, 74–78; changes in, 77–78; extent of dissatisfaction, 74–75; routine work, impact of, 75–77
Austria, 187, 188
Automation, 104–105
Automobile Workers and the American Dream (Chinoy), 90

Beer, Michael, 156
Bell, Daniel, 31, 193
Birth rate, 64–65
Blacks, 9, 34, 51, 57, 60–62, 70, 148
Blauner, Robert, 87, 90
Blood, Milton, 81
Blue-collar workers, 2, 5, 53–54, 85, 92
Bluestone, Irving, 108, 178–179, 181
Bregard, A., 159
Brooks, Thomas R., 101, 180
Brown, Arthur N., 178
Burden, Derek W. E., 164

Calvinism, 21
Career development program, 116
Carnegie Commission on Higher Education, 69
Child-rearing practices, 80
Chinoy, Ely, 90
Chrysler Corporation, 114–115
Civil Rights Act of 1964, 61

Civil rights movement, 30
Collective bargaining, 10, 12, 13, 69, 103–104, 110–111, 114–117, 124, 143, 144, 170, 175, 186, 201
College youth, 36–41
Communes, 26, 148
Communication Workers Union, 115
Communications industry, 52, 126
Confederation of Employers (Norway), 190
Congress of Industrial Organizations (CIO), 102
Connole, Anthony, 181
Construction industry, 50–51, 52, 135
Consumer movement, 14, 30, 31, 128
Contract rejections, 15, 135, 137
Corning Glass Works, 149, 161
Corporations, 52–53
Counter-culture, 83
Couzens, James, 101
Crozier, Michael, 97
Cultural trends, 8, 20, 23–47; college youth and, 36–41; economic security, 8, 27–28, 38; efficiency, cult of, 31–33, 35, 43; entitlement, psychology of, 30–31, 34, 36, 38–39, 44; impact of, 36–47; noncollege youth and, 41–43, 46; success, definitions of, 23–26, 47; women and, 28–29, 43–45
"Culture of Poverty" (Lewis), 78

Decertification elections, 15, 139–141
Decision-making, participatory, 148, 177
Denise, Malcolm, 179
Derber, Milton, 178
Development Council for Collaborative Questions, 190
Disability compensation, 104
Discipline, 108–109, 113, 115, 179
Discrimination, 61–64, 69–70
Donnelly Mirrors, Inc., 149, 157, 160
Drugs, 129–131
Dubin, Robert, 82

Ecology movement, 30
Economic effects of worker dissatisfaction, 13, 119–144; labor input, 120–126; labor relations, 132–140, 143–144; performance on job, 127–131; productivity, 131–132
Economic security, 8, 27–28, 34–35, 38, 147
Economy, changing contours of, 9, 49–56; entrepreneurial and organizational structure, 51–53; industrial composition, 50–51; occupational distribution, 53–54
Education, 60–62, 67, 69, 70, 95, 142, 147, 197–198, 200
Efficiency, cult of, 8, 31–33, 35, 43, 105–108
Emery, Fred E., 6
Encounter groups, 148
Entitlement, psychology of, 8, 30–31, 34, 36, 38–39, 44
European Economic Community Commission, 191
Expectations of workers, 3–4, 59, 146–147

Fair Labor Standards Act, 198
Family life, 19, 28–29, 44–45
Farm workers, 53–54
Federal Mediation and Conciliation Service, 135, 137
Federationist, 101, 116, 180
Finance industry, 52, 124
Fine, Sidney, 103
Fisher, Benjamin, 100
Flexibility in work assignments, 152–153
Flextime, concept of, 194, 200–201
Flint strike, 102–103
Ford, Henry, 12, 101, 102
Ford, Robert N., 115, 185, 194
France, 187
Fraser, Douglas, 105, 186
Full Employment Act of 1946, 199

Gabarro, John, 163
Gallup Poll, 34, 74, 85
Gardner, John W., 192, 201
Gay liberation movement, 30
General Foods Corporation, 149, 152, 155–156, 158, 161–163
General Motors Corporation, 12, 100–101, 103–108, 143
Gifford, Charles, 113
Ginzberg, Eli, 8–10, 49–70
Godfrey, Joseph E., 107
Goldfinger, Nat, 109
Goldthorpe, John H., 83
Gomberg, William, 180
Grayson, C. Jackson, 195
Great Britain, 187, 189
Greening of America, The (Reich), 78
Grievance procedure, 7, 15, 109, 112, 114, 115, 133, 137–138, 179, 182, 201
Guest, Robert H., 6
Gulowson, 165–166

Hackman, J. Richard, 81
Harman, Sidney, 195
Health, Education, and Welfare, Department of, 2, 197
Health and safety, 91, 104, 111, 113, 114–115, 143
Henle, Peter, 13–15, 119–144
Herman, Judith, 87
Herzberg, Fredrick, 85, 86, 89, 95
Hiestand, Professor, 51
Hill, Paul, 166–167, 169
Hulin, Charles L., 81
Human Meaning of Social Change, The (Kahn), 43
Hunsfos pulp and paper mill, 150, 154
Huse, Edgar F., 156

Incentives, 5, 35
Industrial Democracy: Yugoslav Style (Adizes), 188
Industrial Democracy Project, 150, 190

Industrial Jobs and the Worker (Turner and Lawrence), 81
Industrial Workers of the World, 101–102
Information system, 154–155, 160
Innovative work systems, 15–17, 145–175; comprehensive reform, 149–160; early results, 162–164; employee alienation, 145–148; information system, 154–155, 160; introduction of, 160–164; labor, division of, 151–153; reward system, 155–158, 160; status and trust symbols, 158; supervision, 153–154; survival and growth of, 164–175; training and recruitment, 158–159
International Union of Electrical Workers, 138
Israel, 186

Job enrichment programs, 100–101, 113, 115–116, 144, 148, 177, 180–187, 195–201
Job rotation, 83, 101, 112, 177
John Lewis Partnership, 189
Jones, Lee, 112

Kahn, Robert, 43
Kay, Andrew, 168
Kennedy, Edward M., 197
Kerr, Clark, 83
Kindall, Alva F., 201
Kohn, Melvin L., 93

Labor, Department of, 192
Labor, division of, 8, 151–153
Labor force, changing characteristics of, 9, 56–59; blacks, 60–62; 1920, 56–58; 1970, 58–59; participation rates, 120–122, 140; women, 62–64; youth, 64–66
Labor unions, 15, 68, 70, 74, 90, 99–117, 132–140, 143–144, 170, 175, 179–183, 201; collective bargaining, 10, 12, 13, 69, 103–104, 110–

Labor unions *(Cont.)*
  111, 114–117, 124, 143, 144, 170,
  175, 186, 201; contract rejections,
  15, 135, 137; decertification elections, 15, 139–141; early, 101–102;
  efficiency, struggles over, 105–108;
  leadership, changes in, 138–139;
  in 1930's, 102–103; policy considerations for, 196–197; post-war
  priorities, 104–105; rank and file,
  challenges by, 108–113; UAW
  negotiations (1973), 114–115; in
  Western Europe, 187, 189; *See
  also* Strikes
Landrum-Griffin Act, 138
Lawler, Edward E., 81
Lawrence, Paul, 81
Legend of Henry Ford, The (Sword),
  102
Leisure, 4, 6, 83–84, 113–114, 142
Lewis, Oscar, 78
Life values, 22–23, 33–36
Lordstown strike, 12, 73, 77, 105–107,
  143
Lorsch, Jay W., 163
Luther, Martin, 21

McClelland, David, 11, 80, 88
McGregor, Douglas, 11, 79
Maier, Norman, 11, 79
"Man on the Assembly Line, The—A
  Generation Later" (Guest), 6
Manpower Report of the President
  (1968), 74
Manufacturing, 50–53, 124, 126, 141
Maslow, Abraham, 11, 79–80, 88
May, William F., 186
Mental health, 74, 75, 91–92
Microsystems International Ltd., 150
Mills, Ted, 185–186
Minimum wage, 4, 66
Mining, 50–51, 52, 126, 138
Morality, 22–23
Morgan, John, 115
Morris, George, Jr., 110–111
Morse, Nancy, 84

Nader, Ralph, 31
National Commission on Produc-
  tivity, 2
National Council on Alcoholism, 130
National Labor Relations Act of
  1935, 102, 103
National Labor Relations Board, 139,
  140
National Science Foundation, 199
Nationalization, 188, 189
New York State Narcotics Addiction
  Control Commission, 130
Nixon, Richard M., 20
Nobo-Hommelvik firm, 150, 152, 161–
  162
Non Linear Systems, Inc., 149, 157,
  160, 168
Noncollege youth, 41–43, 46
Norsk Hydro, 155–156, 158–159, 161,
  165–166
Northern Electric Company, 150, 155,
  159, 161, 163
Norway, 186, 189–190
Norwegian Department of Labor, 190
Norwegian Federation of Employers,
  150
Norwood strike, 12, 106, 143

Obradovic, Josip, 188
Occupational distribution, 53–54, 62–
  63
Occupational Health & Safety Act of
  1970, 2, 111, 143, 198
Ohio State Department of Highways,
  178
Opinion polls, 34, 74, 85
Opinion Research Company, 24
Overtime, 68, 69, 110, 113, 114, 116,
  143–144

Participatory decision-making, 148,
  177
Partnerships, 52
Part-time jobs, 142
Pensions, 3–5, 104, 110, 193–194
Percy, Charles H., 196

Performance on the job, 14, 127–131
Personality, 11, 92–93
Personality vs. organization hypothesis, 79–82, 85
Pluralistic Economy, The (Ginzberg et al.), 51
Politics, 93
Precision Castparts Corporation, 182
Product quality, 7, 127–129
Productivity, 2, 7, 14–15, 43, 77, 86, 131–132, 145
Productivity bargaining, 148–149
Proprietorships, 52
Protestantism, 21, 22
Psychic needs, 5–6
Psychological benefits, 35–36

Quality of workmanship, 127–129
Quit rates, 14, 77, 125–126

Racial discrimination, 61–62, 69–70
Rationalization, 31–33, 43
Reich, Charles, 78
Retirement, 4, 116, 120, 122, 142
Reuther, Walter, 13, 104, 105, 113
Reward system, 155–158, 160
Roosevelt, Franklin D., 102
Rosow, Jerome M., 1–18, 184
Routine work, impact of, 75–77
Rural workers, 11, 81–82

Sabotage, 107, 127, 145, 146
Salpukas, Agis, 12–13, 99–117
Scamia Automotive Plant, 191
Scanlon Plan, 189
Schooler, Carmi, 93
Self-actualization, 11, 79–80, 148
Self-fulfillment, 25–26, 29, 35–36, 38, 41, 47
Self-Renewal (Gardner), 192, 201
Sensitivity training, 148
Service sector, 51, 53–54, 67, 124, 141
Sex discrimination, 62–64, 69–70
Shell, U.K., 150, 152, 157, 158, 160, 161, 164, 166, 169
Sirota, David, 184

Smith, Patricia, 92–93
Social rights, concept of, 30–31
Social Security Administration, 199
Steelworkers union, 109, 113, 138
Steiger, William A., 197
Strauss, George, 10–11, 34, 73–98
Strikes, 7, 12, 15, 73, 75, 77, 102–103, 105–107, 114, 116, 133–136, 140–141, 143, 191
Striner, Herbert E., 198
Student movement, 30
Success, definitions of, 8, 23–26, 47
Supervision, 153–154, 159, 184
Susman, Gerald I., 81
Sweden, 186, 190–191
Swedish Delegation for Industrial Democracy, 191
Swedish Employers Confederation, 190
Sward, Keith, 102

Taylor, Frederick Winslow, 101, 107, 193
Thievery, 127, 128
Thoreau, Henry David, 19
Thorsrud, Einar, 6, 190
Tilgher, Adriano, 20
Trade unions, *see* Labor unions
Trades Union Council of Norway, 150, 190
Transportation industry, 52, 124
Truman, Harry S., 103
Turner, Arthur, 81
Turnover rates, 7, 73, 75, 112, 115, 116, 125–126, 130, 145, 146, 166–167
Tyler, Charles, 108

Unemployment, 27, 34, 57, 59, 65
Unions, *see* Labor unions
United Auto Workers (UAW), 12, 105–108, 111, 113–115, 127, 178
University of Dayton, 182
University of Michigan's Survey Research Center, 74, 78

Upward Mobility programs, 200
Urban workers, 11, 81–82

Volvo, 150, 151, 152, 160
Vroom, Victor, 80

Wage and price controls, 111
Wages, 4–5, 104, 110, 142–143
Wallace, George, 74
Wallace, Mike, 113
Walters, Roy W., 184, 185
Walton, Richard E., 15–17, 145–175
Weber, Max, 31–33
Weiss, Robert, 84
West Germany, 187
White-collar workers, 53–54, 67
Whole tasks, concept of, 151–152
Wilensky, Harold, 83
Wilson, Charles E., 104
Winpisinger, William W., 116, 181
Wolfson, Alan D., 184
Women, 9, 19, 23, 28–31, 43–46, 57–
    58, 62–64, 67, 70, 122, 148
Woodcock, Leonard, 13, 100, 108, 117

Work in America (HEW), 2, 183, 184,
    197
Work ethic, 2, 8, 19–47, 81; contempo-
    rary meaning of, 22–23; religious
    origins, 20–22
Work rate, 106, 127
Work Research Institute, Oslo, 150,
    190
Work systems, innovative, *see* Inno-
    vative work systems
Work teams, 151, 159, 177
Work values, 8, 20, 36–40
Worker Alienation Research and
    Technical Assistance Act, 197
Worker self-management, system of,
    187–188
Working hours, 68, 69, 194
Wurf, Jerry, 116

Yankelovich, Daniel, 8, 19–47
Youth, 9, 32, 34–43, 46, 64–66, 94–95,
    121, 122, 179
Yugoslavia, 187–188

Zagoria, Sam, 17–18, 177–201

About The American Assembly

The American Assembly was established by Dwight D. Eisenhower at Columbia University in 1950. It holds nonpartisan meetings and publishes authoritative books to illuminate issues of United States policy.

An affiliate of Columbia, with offices in the Graduate School of Business, the Assembly is a national educational institution incorporated in the State of New York.

The Assembly seeks to provide information, stimulate discussion, and evoke independent conclusions in matters of vital public interest.

AMERICAN ASSEMBLY SESSIONS

At least two national programs are initiated each year. Authorities are retained to write background papers presenting essential data and defining the main issues in each subject.

About sixty men and women representing a broad range of experience, competence, and American leadership meet for several days to discuss the Assembly topic and consider alternatives for national policy.

All Assemblies follow the same procedure. The background papers are sent to participants in advance of the Assembly. The Assembly meets in small groups for four or five lengthy periods. All groups use the same agenda. At the close of these informal sessions, participants adopt in plenary session a final report of findings and recommendations.

Regional, state, and local Assemblies are held following the national session at Arden House. Assemblies have also been in England, Switzerland, Malaysia, Canada, the Caribbean, South America, Central America, the Philippines, and Japan. Over one hundred institutions have co-sponsored one or more Assemblies.

ARDEN HOUSE

Home of The American Assembly and scene of the national sessions is Arden House, which was given to Columbia University in 1950 by W. Averell Harriman. E. Roland Harriman joined his brother in contributing toward adaptation of the property for conference purposes. The buildings and surrounding land, known as the Harriman Campus of Columbia University, are fifty miles north of New York City.

Arden House is a distinguished conference center. It is self-supporting and operates throughout the year for use by organizations with educational objectives.

The background papers for each Assembly program are published in cloth and paperbound editions for use by individuals, libraries, businesses, public agencies, nongovernmental organizations, educational institutions, discussion and service groups. In this way the deliberations of Assembly sessions are continued and extended.

The subjects of Assembly programs to date are:

1951——United States–Western Europe Relationships
1952——Inflation
1953——Economic Security for Americans
1954——The United States' Stake in the United Nations
——The Federal Government Service
1955——United States Agriculture
——The Forty-Eight States
1956——The Representation of the United States Abroad
——The United States and the Far East
1957——International Stability and Progress
——Atoms for Power
1958——The United States and Africa
——United States Monetary Policy
1959——Wages, Prices, Profits, and Productivity
——The United States and Latin America
1960——The Federal Government and Higher Education
——The Secretary of State
——Goals for Americans
1961——Arms Control: Issues for the Public
——Outer Space: Prospects for Man and Society
1962——Automation and Technological Change
——Cultural Affairs and Foreign Relations
1963——The Population Dilemma
——The United States and the Middle East
1964——The United States and Canada
——The Congress and America's Future
1965——The Courts, the Public, and the Law Explosion
——The United States and Japan
1966——State Legislatures in American Politics
——A World of Nuclear Powers?
——The United States and the Philippines
——Challenges to Collective Bargaining
1967——The United States and Eastern Europe
——Ombudsmen for American Government?
1968——Uses of the Seas

———Law in a Changing America
———Overcoming World Hunger
1969———Black Economic Development
———The States and the Urban Crisis
1970———The Health of Americans
———The United States and the Caribbean
1971———The Future of American Transportation
———Public Workers and Public Unions
1972———The Future of Foundations
———Prisoners in America
1973———The Worker and the Job
———Choosing the President
1974———Land Use
———The Future of Museums
———The Multinational Corporation

Second Editions, Revised:

1962———The United States and the Far East
1963———The United States and Latin America
———The United States and Africa
1964———United States Monetary Policy
1965———The Federal Government Service
———The Representation of the United States Abroad
1968———Cultural Affairs and Foreign Relations
———Outer Space: Prospects for Man and Society
1969———The Population Dilemma
1972———The Congress and America's Future